FEDERALISM

CONTRIBUTORS

George Carey

Karl Cerny

Valerie Earle

Harry Kantor

William Livingston

Alpheus Mason

Henry Teune

FEDERALISM

INFINITE VARIETY
IN THEORY
AND PRACTICE

EDITED BY

VALERIE EARLE

Georgetown University

F. E. PEACOCK PUBLISHERS, INC.

ITASCA · ILLINOIS

T HE INSPIRATION FOR THIS COLLECTION of essays on federalism was initially derived from the observance of Georgetown University's one hundred and seventy fifth anniversary. The University was founded in 1789, the year of inauguration of the American federal constitution. On being invited to propose a topic for scholarly discussion during the anniversary year, the Department of Government concluded that an examination of federalism and of federal systems was both appropriate and relevant.

Though the diversity in form and practice so clearly shown in the following essays does not surprise, the varying purposes which federalism may serve demonstrate its adaptability, and challenge the ingenuity of men engaged with contemporary problems of government. Conventional treatment of American federalism, from which have flowed many frequently cited studies of federalism, emphasizes the theme of unity without uniformity, that is, the use of federalism in uniting states more effectively and in more disciplined fashion than does a confederacy, at the same time leaving to the member states a broad, imprecisely defined area of authority. Until very recently, almost without variation, those who updated the study of American federalism emphasized the degree and complexity of arrangements of cooperation among governments and strongly inferred that the initiative in cooperation rested with the national government, not simply because of its superior financial resources but also because national action more accurately reflected the realities of social and economic conditions as well as citizen attitudes and needs.

Contemporary inquiries seek to determine whether federalism may be helpful in effecting socialization, in creating a state where only the legal fiction exists. Contemporary emphasis in nation states where federalism is a going concern is upon devolving responsibility for solution to exceedingly stubborn problems, for the compelling reason that no single government can generate the ideas, or recruit the talents and enegies required in sufficient quantity.

"Creative federalism" is no new conception. It is simply the "new federalism" or "cooperative federalism," with an urgent insistence upon the involvement of governments at all levels, in creative fashion, which may bring nearer solutions to the problems of the cities, of poverty, of citizen rights.

I wish to express my warm appreciation to the authors of the essays in the collection. They have selected interesting and relevant topics, and treated them thoughtfully. They have also been patient with my editorial suggestions and with the delays in bringing the collection into print.

Georgetown University has been generous in financial support, and in providing time for completion of the manuscript.

It was Professor Gerard F. Yates, S.J., of the Georgetown Department of Government, who first suggested the appropriateness of a discussion of federalism. I give him sincere thanks, for a good idea, perhaps imperfectly carried out.

Valerie Earle
Spring, 1968

Georgetown University

I CONTENTS

PART I

AMERICAN FEDERALISM

INTRODUCTORY ESSAY

T HE THREE ESSAYS TREATING the origin and contemporary aspects of American federalism underscore the infinite variety in perceptions of federalism and in its practice.

Professors Mason and Carey have examined historical events and constitutional arguments in late eighteenth-century America to gain insight into the nature of American union and the intrinsic characteristics of the American polity. Doubtless in agreement about the events leading to dissolution of the tie with Britain, but more importantly, certainly in agreement about the constitutional dilemma posed for Britain by the colonists' demand for near-autonomy in major areas of policy (although not in all), they differ in their judgment of the solution found at Philadelphia in 1787. Professor Mason asserts that a "middle way" was found, which permits the existence of two governmental authorities, Federal and State, in the same territory, having jurisdiction over the same people. Professor Carey denies that any middle way *could* be found, that sovereignty *could* be divided, or that any of the members of the Convention in fact believed that such a vertical division of power had been accomplished.

That no clear line was drawn to demarcate the powers of the national government and the States, either in the original docu-

ment or in the Bill of Rights, is proof positive for Professor
Mason that a division was intended, and the division was to be
meaningful in the sense that both governments were to have
significant powers. Had a clear, sharp line been drawn, he believes this would have redounded to the strong, perhaps fatally
strong, advantage of the States. There would have been a recur-
rence of the defect of the Articles of Confederation—and indeed
of the irreconcilable contentions between Colonies and Parliament.

Quoting Madison, that the States were to be retained insofar as
they could be "subordinately useful," Mason declares that the
Convention proposed a national government of indefinite powers,
supreme within its constitutional sphere of action. The States
were to play an important part in the functioning of the national
government.

Plainly the Constitution may be interpreted in diverse ways
respecting the roles of the Federal and State governments, as
Madison himself demonstrated in moving from a strongly nationalist view at the time of the Convention and in the first years of
the new government to a position of dual federalism by the late
1790's. Professor Mason believes that it is a great strength in the
American polity that such diversity of interpretation is possible.

That the diversity is continuing is witnessed by the present Mr.
Justice Harlan's advocacy of judicial restraint in dealing with
such issues as procedures for guaranteeing the rights of criminal
defendants, legislative reapportionment and standards for determining obscenity which have historically been left to the States.
For Mr. Justice Harlan the division of powers which is of the
essence of a federal system is essential for the protection of
freedom; judges should be reluctant to break down that division,
irrespective of claims made in the name of individual rights.

On this point Professor Mason takes exception to Justice Harlan, noting that Jefferson, before the calling of the Convention,
had observed in regard to his State of Virginia that legislative
power must be restrained, that he had pressed this view upon
Madison in a letter from Paris during the struggle for ratifica-

tion, and that Madison, by the time of drafting the amendments which were to become the Bill of Rights, had come to accept the necessity for a check in the judiciary.

Thus Professor Mason makes explicit that for him the essential elements of the American constitutional system are both a division of powers—not precise, therefore shifting, certainly always debatable—and a judicial check upon legislative and executive authority, both Federal and State, through application of a Bill of Rights—the meaning of which is not entirely precise, therefore in degree shifting, and always being debated. To restate a familiar theme: The political checks upon arbitrary power, although they are infinitely multiplied in a Federal system, are not, even so, sufficient. There must also be the check of law.

Professor Carey argues that no one of the men at Philadelphia was so deficient in his understanding of power as to believe that a "middle ground" could be discovered, that is to say, a true division of power establishing two sovereign governments in the same territory, operating upon the same citizens. He emphasizes that the Framers used the word "federal" as a form of "confederate" or "confederal." For Madison, he believes, what emerged from the Convention was a composite of unitary and confederate, the precise character of which could not be described. Madison believed it better than what had been provided in the Articles of Confederation and therefore more strongly national. But no man at the Convention or later in the Ratification debate could either prescribe a means of resolving conflict between the national government and the States or indicate what the mechanism might be, for no man believed that a governmental system could divide sovereignty and be viable. In conflict one would have to give way.

By political circumstance, rather than by constitutional arrangement, there did indeed develop a division of functions between the nation and the localities. Although political circumstance is not always strongly infused with the philosopher's logic or rationality, it is generally reflective of what the people want, however imperfect their perceptions of what they can have or ought to want. The political process is flexible and pragmatic and therefore infinitely preferable to principled argument in a constitutional context.

Professor Carey's prescription is that we should retain our flexibility—we should avoid recourse to constitutional principle —we should avoid a "mind set" in which the law, as expounded by judges, is accorded a sacrosanct position beyond the reach of legislative and executive decisions. His conviction that reliance upon the political process is the proper course has not been altered by the reapportionment or desegregation cases, although these appear to be instances where political remedies were not available.

Professor Mason's final counsel is that both parties, the Federal government and the States, should seek to avoid a constitutional confrontation. He appears, then, not so far removed from Professor Carey's view. Or are Professor Mason's views of the Bill of Rights and the judicial check a removal, not in degree, but in kind?

The third essay suggests that by far the larger meaning of American federalism has been supplied, not by constitutional principle or confrontation, but by cooperation, a partnership between governments in which each is usually little concerned about legal rights and authority but rather about getting a job done.

There can be little argument that the domestic problem of first magnitude presently is the problem of the city, of the decaying center whose inhabitants cannot break out of their ghettoes because they are uneducated, unemployable, physically sick and spiritually deranged, and who now so conduct themselves as increasingly to threaten the very existence of the urban complex.

This problem is in reality a complex of problems, all very difficult, all very costly, all appearing to be time bombs set to go off very shortly.

If the explosion is to be avoided, diverse talents and multiple energies must become involved in a working relationship at all levels of government, a working partnership of a magnitude of effectiveness not previously attained.

The chaos of structure and functions so well described by Morton Grodzins seems to inhere in magnified form in public programs to make war on poverty and to restructure the American city. Yet as Professor Grodzins wrote, "The system of American government . . . works, it works—and sometimes with beauty."[1]

---

[1] Morton Grodzins, *The American System—A New View of Government in the United States,* ed. Daniel Elazar (Chicago: Rand, McNally & Co., 1966), p. 7.

ALPHEUS THOMAS MASON
Princeton University

FEDERALISM:
HISTORIC QUESTIONS AND
CONTEMPORARY MEANINGS
THE ROLE OF THE COURT

F EDERAL-STATE RELATIONS are again, as often before in our history, in the headlines. The picture widely broadcast on June 12, 1963, of Governor George C. Wallace of Alabama standing at the entrance of the State university determined to prevent the admission of two Negroes acting under Federal court orders dramatically highlights the issue. The conflict is broad gauged. Against judicial assertion of enlarged national responsibility for human rights and human needs, extreme remedies are proposed.

Seared by Supreme Court decisions upholding Federal intervention into fields long considered immune—education, voting, representation and the administration of criminal justice—the States, speaking through the Council of State Governments in 1962, proposed three far-reaching amendments.[1] One would undo

SOURCE: At a Conference on Federalism, held as part of the observance of Georgetown University's 175th anniversary, Professor Mason delivered a paper on American federalism in 1787 and in the immediate post-Convention decades. This essay is an enlargement of the conference paper. Parts of it appeared in the July, 1966, issue of the *Texas Law Review*.

[1] For the full text of the proposed amendments, see *State Government*, XXXVI (1963), 10–15.

the reapportionment decisions which struck at the rotten-borough scandal in various State legislatures. Another would permit State legislatures to amend the Federal Constitution without consideration or discussion in any national forum.[2] The third would set up a super Supreme Court—a "Court of the Union"—consisting of the chief justices of the fifty States, empowered to overrule Supreme Court decisions in cases involving Federal-State relations. This triple threat to federalism, endorsed in whole or in part by twelve States, now seems doomed.[3] But yet another version of Senator Everett Dirksen's drastic proposal upsetting the Supreme Court's decision requiring election of both houses of the State legislatures on the basis of population is still pending.[4]

[2] The second proposal was anticipated as early as 1787 in the Virginia Plan submitted to the Federal Convention at Philadelphia by Edmund Randolph. Resolution Thirteen declared that "the assent of the National Legislature ought not to be required" in the amending process. Farrand, *The Records of the Federal Convention of 1787* (Rev. ed., 1937), II, 22. For reasons current States-righters might find ironical, Elbridge Gerry opposed the provision of Article V directing Congress to call a convention upon application of two-thirds of the States. Gerry suggested that "two thirds of the States may obtain a Convention, a majority of which can bind the Union to innovations that may subvert the State-Constitutions altogether." Hamilton feared the opposite result. "He did not object to the consequences stated by Mr. Gerry." Pointing to the very situation that today threatens national supremacy, Hamilton warned that "the State Legislatures will not apply for alterations but with a view to increase their own powers." *Ibid.*, pp. 557–58. George Mason was apparently not satisfied with Article V, even with the provision allowing the States to initiate amendments. He insisted that "by this Article Congress only have the Power of proposing Amendments at any future time to this Constitution, & shou'd it prove ever so oppressive, the whole people of America can't make, or even propose Alterations to it; a Doctrine utterly subversive of the fundamental Principles of the Rights & Liberties of the people." *Ibid.*, IV, 61.

[3] See Briggs, "Three-Pronged Movement to Weaken Powers of Supreme Court Quietly Gains Ground," *Louisville Courier-Journal*, 1963, reprinted in *Trenton Evening Times*, May 8, 1963, p. 40, col. 1. See also *Congressional Quarterly Weekly Report*, XXI (1963), 662–63. For a probing analysis of various attacks and plans to undermine national authority, see Swindler, "The Current Challenge to Federalism: The Confederating Proposals," *Georgia Law Journal*, LII (1963), 1.

[4] See "Legislative Apportionment: The Latest Proposal Analyzed," Extension of Remarks of Senator Joseph D. Tydings, *Congressional Record*, CXI (daily ed., Nov. 2, 1965), A6215; Millstone, "Dirksen Hires Publicity Firm to Promote His Amendment," *St. Louis Post-Dispatch*, Feb. 6, 1966, Sec. A, p. 15, col. 3. On April 20, 1966, Senator Dirksen's attempt failed for the third time when his revised proposal was defeated in the Senate by seven

Feeding the flame of controversy are the justices themselves. Justice Harlan, dissenter in recent controversial cases, accuses his colleagues of violating basic constitutional principles—federalism and separation of powers—which "lie at the root of our constitutional system." [5]

"We are accustomed," Harlan observes, "to speak of the Bill of Rights and the Fourteenth Amendment as the principal guarantees of personal liberty. Yet it would surely be shallow not to recognize that the structure of our political system accounts no less for the free society we have. Indeed," he continues, "it was upon the structure of government that the founders primarily focused in writing the Constitution." [6]

Justice Harlan holds that the Founding Fathers "staked their faith that liberty would prosper in the new nation not primarily upon declarations of individual rights but upon the kind of government the Union was to have. . . . It is manifest that no view of the Bill of Rights or interpretation of any of its provisions which fails to take due account of [federalism and separation of powers] . . . can be considered constitutionally sound." [7] Justice Harlan's target is of course the Warren Court's conviction that the Bill of Rights, now largely incorporated into the Fourteenth Amendment, is "the heart of any Constitution." [8]

Current cleavages echo earlier Federal-State conflicts. Underscored is the continuing States-rights strain in our culture. Outraged by the Alien and Sedition Acts, Jefferson formulated the

votes. *New York Times*, April 21, 1966, p. 1, col. 3. In 1967, Congress received petitions in a variety of forms for the calling of a convention to consider removing the issue of apportionment of State legislatures from Federal jurisdiction. Article V of the United States Constitution leaves unanswered a number of significant questions regarding the calling of a constitutional convention by Congress on petition of two-thirds of the States, including whether Congress "may" or "must" issue the call, how delegates shall be selected, whether the work of the convention is to be limited to the matter proposed in State petitions.

[5] Harlan, "The Bill of Rights and the Constitution," *American Bar Association Journal*, L (1964), 920.

[6] Harlan, "Thoughts at a Dedication: Keeping the Judicial Function in Balance," *American Bar Association Journal*, XLIX (1963), 943–44.

[7] Harlan, "The Bill of Rights and the Constitution," *loc. cit.*

[8] *The Public Papers of Chief Justice Warren* (Christman ed., 1959), vol. VII.

Kentucky resolutions declaring that if the Federal government assumed powers not delegated, State nullification was the proper remedy.[9] The Union was again imperiled in 1814, when certain New England States adopted the so-called Hartford Convention resolutions, urging the States to protect their citizens against unconstitutional Federal militia and draft legislation.[10] When Congress in 1828 enacted the "Tariff of Abominations,"[11] the protesting South Carolina Exposition declared that a sovereign State has the right to determine whether an act of Congress constitutes such a danger as to "justify the interposition of the State to protect its rights."[12] It was not, however, until 1861 that certain southern States,[13] using States rights to keep a subject race in bondage, committed the "gross heresy" Hamilton deplored.[14] Proclaiming State sovereignty in the most extreme form, the South then went on to Harper's Ferry, Shiloh and Appomattox.

It remained for this generation, after a united nation had fought and won two world wars and at a time when our security is gravely tested, to witness the most defiant assertion of State sovereignty since Appomattox. Calling for a "great national debate" on the proposed States-rights amendments, Chief Justice Warren commented, "If proposals of this magnitude had been made in the early days of the Republic, the great debate would be resounding in every legislative hall and in every place where lawyers, scholars, and statesmen gather."[15] The debate which the Chief Justice invites is again in full swing.

I

The Declaration of Independence and the Constitution embody the negative and positive aspects of the greatest of eighteenth-

[9] Kelly and Harbison, *The American Constitution: Its Origin and Development* (3rd ed., 1963), pp. 208–9.

[10] *Ibid.*, p. 246.

[11] *Ibid.*, p. 305.

[12] *Ibid.*

[13] *Ibid.*

[14] *The Federalist* No. 22 (Wright ed., 1961), p. 199. (All citations are to this edition.)

[15] *New York Times,* May 23, 1963, p. 23, col. 3.

century political achievements: assertion of the right of revolution against a tyrannical mother country and establishment of a government resting on reason and consent rather than on coercion and force. The affirmation was bold enough; action based on it was required to be even more so.

Colonial experience had developed a schizophrenic desire for union, resulting in large part from displeasure with British policy, and resistance to union, grounded in an almost instinctive distaste for all centralized authority, reinforced by Great Britain's arbitrary rule. Tension manifested itself even before independence. In the First Continental Congress of 1774 James Duane, John Dickinson and Robert Morris had urged the creation of a central government. James Galloway, submitting his Plan of Union to the First Continental Congress, doubted whether the empire could "hold together without it." Congress rejected the Galloway Plan, and America thus inherited the puzzle Britain and the colonies had proved powerless to solve. Independence had been achieved, but not union.

America's first attempt at constitution making, the Articles of Confederation, was an aberration. Resting on the sovereignty of organized power and avowing the independence of disunited States, the Articles departed from the principles of popular sovereignty and the right of revolution enunciated in the Declaration of Independence.

In affirming the "sovereignty, freedom and independence" of the States, the Articles of Confederation made inevitable the chaos that had worked such havoc in British-colonial relations. Although the idea of federation had been frequently broached as a solution of their differences, Britain and the Colonies proved unable to convert it into a mutually agreeable plan of government. "There is no possible medium," loyalist Daniel Leonard had observed fatalistically, "between absolute independence [of the colonies] . . . and subjection to Parliament."[16] Repudiation of parliamentary sovereignty would mean that the provincial

---

[16] Leonard, *Letters Addressed to the Inhabitants of the Province of Massachusetts Bay,* Jan. 16, 1775, in *Novanglus and Massachusetts* (1819), p. 174.

legislatures alone would be sovereign, the result being *imperium in imperio,* the height of political folly. "If we should succeed in depriving Great Britain of the power of regulating our trade," loyalist Samuel Seabury predicted, "the colonies will probably be soon at variance with each other. Their commercial interests will interfere; and there will be no supreme power to interpose. . . ." [17]

The Revolutionary fathers deplored *imperium in imperio,* pronouncing it a political monster subversive of all government. Yet the War of Independence had scarcely been won before the new nation found itself plagued by several supreme and independent authorities attempting to govern in the same community. Americans were to realize again, as did John Adams in 1775,[18] that it is as impossible for two supreme and independent authorities to exist in the same state as for two supreme beings to rule the universe. Needed was an over-all common power—perhaps a "medium" between absolute State independence and absolute subjection to a central authority. Could America find the "middle ground" which the colonists and Britain alike had come to consider a hopeless search?

II

Mounting demands for a more energetic central authority obscured the gradual development of elements later identified with nationalist doctrine. A most significant development within the new States was judicial review, putting courts against the dominant legislative power. Jefferson had early lamented legislative invasion of property and contract rights. In his own State of Virginia he had seen that "one hundred and seventy-three despots would surely be as oppressive as one." In his draft of the 1776 Virginia Constitution he had included individual rights in the article on the Judiciary. On May 25, 1784, Jefferson urged the calling of a convention to revise Virginia's Constitution, making it supreme so that acts contrary to it could be adjudged void. A basic tenet in Chief Justice Marshall's argument in support of

---

[17] Seabury, *A View of the Controversy Between Great Britain and Her Colonies,* in *Letters of a Westchester Farmer (1774–1775)* (Vance ed., 1930), p. 127.

[18] A. T. Mason, *Free Government in the Making* (3rd ed., 1965).

judicial review had thus been anticipated by nearly twenty years.

Jefferson concurred in the views of ardent nationalists such as Alexander Hamilton, John Jay, and James Wilson that even under the Articles of Confederation the united States were in many respects one undivided, independent nation, with "all the rights, and powers, and properties, by the law of nations incident to such." The Articles of Confederation constituted a kind of higher law, Jefferson declared, not to be altered by State legislatures. Yet Jefferson shared the prevailing sense of urgency deriving from the perilous weakness of the nation. In 1783 he had written Edmund Randolph, expressing his fear that unless "the band of our confederacy" were strengthened, "the States will go to war with each other in defiance of Congress."

James Madison explored current difficulties in depth. The multiplicity, mutability and injustice of State laws had betrayed a defect so glaring as to bring "into question the fundamental principle of republican Government, that the majority who rule in such governments are the safest guardians both of public good and private rights." Closely linked with a solution for legislative abuses within the States was the corrective for that other vice, a lack of power to enforce the laws of the confederation government. Later on Madison suggested that the national government "have a negative, in all cases whatsoever, on the legislative acts of the States," considering this check "the least possible abridgment of the State sovereignties." The national veto was ultimately rejected in favor of judicial review, but the significance of Madison's drastic proposal is not diminished.

On April 8, 1787, a few weeks before the Convention delegates assembled in Philadelphia to frame a new constitution, James Madison, anticipating that "some leading proposition would be expected from Virgina," [19] wrote Governor Edmund Randolph concerning the central issue—federalism. Madison observed:

I hold it for a fundamental point, that an individual independence 'of the States is utterly irreconcilable with the idea of an

---

[19] Letter from James Madison to Edmund Randolph, April 8, 1787, in *The Writings of James Madison* (Hunt ed., 1901), II, 336, 337.

aggregate sovereignty. I think, at the same time, that a consolidation of the States into one simple republic is not less attainable than it would be inexpedient. Let it be tried then whether any middle ground can be taken which will at once support a due supremacy of the national authority, and leave in force the local authorities so far as they can be subordinately useful.[20]

By 1786 a consensus had developed in favor of more energetic central authority. The consensus was so overwhelming as to be virtually uncontested. "We all agree in the necessity of new regulations," George Mason told the Convention delegates on June 7, 1787, "but we differ widely in our opinions of what are the safest and most effectual." [21] Differences touching issues inherent in federalism were apparent as soon as Governor Randolph submitted the Virginia plan vesting in the central government authority "to legislate in all cases to which the separate States are incompetent. . . ." [22] Also lodged in the central government was the right of veto over acts of the several States. Suspicion was aroused: States-rights adherents, detecting in these proposals determination to destroy local authority, promptly introduced an alternative plan.

James Wilson, disassociating himself from those who would "swallow up" the States, pointed an accusing finger at Alexander Hamilton.[23] But Hamilton disavowed any such intention. "He had not been understood. . . . By an abolition of the States, he meant that no boundary could be drawn between the National & State Legislatures; that the former must therefore have *indefinite* authority. If it [national authority] were limited at all, the rivalship of the States would gradually subvert it." [24] In short, Hamilton's purpose and general objective was not to eliminate

---

[20] *Ibid.*, pp. 337–38.
[21] Farrand, *op. cit.*, I, 161.
[22] *Ibid.*, p. 21.
[23] *Ibid.*, II, 588.
[24] *Ibid.*, I, 323. (Emphasis added.) Yates' report of Hamilton's remarks is to the same effect: "I did not intend . . . a total extinguishment of state governments; but my meaning was, that a national government ought to be able to support itself without the aid or interference of state governments, and that therefore it was necessary to have full sovereignty." p. 328.

the States but to correct the congenital infirmity inherent in the
Articles of Confederation. The streams of national power, Hamilton insisted, must flow from that "pure original fountain" of all
legitimate authority—the consent of the people. A government
designed to meet great national purposes could not tolerate any
provision that would make its authority contingent on the existence of a state domain absolutely free from invasion. Later on in
The Federalist Number 22 Hamilton referred contemptuously to
the "enormous doctrine of a right of [State] legislative repeal"
and to the "gross heresy" that "a *party* to a *compact* has a right
to revoke that *compact*." [25]

Luther Martin and William Paterson, sponsoring the New
Jersey plan, opposed Randolph head on. They argued that national authority of such scope would destroy the States as independent units of government. The nationalists refused to budge.
If New Jersey, James Wilson retorted, "will not part with her
Sovereignty it is in vain to talk of Government." [26] To remove
this seemingly irreconcilable impasse, William Samuel Johnson,
with the assistance of Oliver Ellsworth of Connecticut, fashioned
the Connecticut Compromise, giving the States equal representation in the Senate.[27]

A crucial battle apparently had been won. The high caliber of
the delegates opposing the compromise, including Madison, Hamilton and Wilson, and the arguments used against it created the
impression that a basic federalist principle had been sacrificed.[28]
Jonathan Dayton of New Jersey dubbed the Connecticut Compromise "an amphibious monster." [29] In making the Senate "a
palladium of residuary sovereignty," seeds of rivalry would be
planted. Nationalists insisted that no government could be solid
or lasting unless representation is based on the people. Gunning

---

[25] *The Federalist* No. 22, p. 199. (Emphasis in original.)
[26] Farrand, *op. cit.*, I, 180.
[27] *Ibid.*, pp. 461–62.
[28] *Ibid.*, p. 490.
[29] *Ibid.*

Bedford of Delaware observed that there was "no middle way between a perfect consolidation and a mere confederacy of States." [30]

Ironically the nationalists' strenuous effort to safeguard national power by the legislative negative met with ignominious defeat the day after the Connecticut Compromise was adopted. If July 16, a Monday, seemed like "Black Monday," the next day must have been even gloomier. Madison, Wilson, Hamilton *et al.* had already tempered their more extreme desires. Now even Madison's "middle ground" seemed in jeopardy.

Not unnaturally those wishing to preserve the States as independent units of government regarded the Connecticut Compromise as a notable victory. A spirit of relaxation set in, enabling the friends of strong union to forge ahead and perhaps to regain the ground they had apparently lost.

As a partial substitute for Randolph's national veto over State action, Paterson and Martin fashioned what later became the supremacy clause, Article VI, Paragraph 2. [31] The Constitution and laws of Congress passed in pursuance thereof were declared to be *the supreme law of the land,* "any Thing in the Constitution or Laws of any State to the Contrary notwithstanding." Over strong protest, Madison also won approval of the provision calling for the Constitution's ratification by the people rather than by the State legislatures. The advance toward centralized government seemed alarming, stimulating the not unreasonable fear that the States were doomed. Delegates Robert Yates and John Lansing of New York left Philadelphia in disgust.

III

As the Constitution left the hands of the Framers, it contained no provision that smacked of the defect so disabling to effective

---

[30] *Ibid.*

[31] A. T. Mason, *The States Rights Debate* (1964), pp. 35–36.

government under the Articles, "State sovereignty, freedom and independence." The powers of the national government, although enumerated, were "undefined" and "indefinite." [32] Alert to possible inroads on the States, Hugh Williamson of North Carolina objected that the effect might be to "restrain the States from regulating their internal" affairs.[33] Indefinite power in the central authority would, Elbridge Gerry objected, "enslave the States." [34] Hamilton, Madison and Wilson stood firm, explaining that it was impossible to draw a line dividing State and national powers. "When we come near the line, it cannot be found. . . ." [35] "A discretion must be left on one side or the other. . . . Will it not be most safely lodged on the side of the National Government? . . . What danger is there that the whole will unnecessarily sacrifice a part? But reverse the case, and leave the whole at the mercy of each part, and will not the general interest be continually sacrificed to local interests?" [36]

A "middle ground," long thought of as sought after in vain, had apparently been found. Proposed for ratification was a national government of "indefinite" powers. The States would be retained insofar as they could be "subordinately useful." [37]

Antifederalists portrayed Article VI, Paragraph 2, the so-called supremacy clause (the germ of which, ironically, had been planted in the States-rights plan) and the "necessary and proper" provision—both dubbed "sweeping clauses"—as clearly designed to establish a "consolidated government." [38] Unity, they believed, had been substituted for union. James Wilson, noting that "consolidation" had yet to be defined, tried to clarify. If opponents of ratification meant, he explained, that the States would be subordinate to the national government when operating within its proper sphere, the truth of the charge must be conceded. But if

---

[32] Farrand, *op. cit.*, I, 323.

[33] *Ibid.*, p. 165.

[34] *Ibid.*

[35] *Ibid.*, p. 170.

[36] *Ibid.*, pp. 166–67.

[37] *The Writings of James Madison*, II, 338.

[38] Lee, *Letters of the Federal Farmer*, in *Pamphlets on the Constitution of the United States 1787–1788* (Ford ed., 1888), p. 282.

they meant that the States had been deprived of all independent existence, they were clearly in error.[39]

The Constitution itself presumes the continual existence of the States. The States are integral parts of the amending process. The Constitution guarantees to each State a republican form of government and pledges assistance, if requested, against invasion or domestic violence. The new system was to be considered approved when nine of the thirteen States ratified the document. All of these provisions indicated to advocates of ratification that the States would be more than mere administrative districts; they would play an important role in the operation of the national government itself.

Antifederalists were unconvinced. "A bill of rights," Jefferson wrote Madison from Paris, "is what the people are entitled to against every government on earth. . . ."[40] "There is no declaration of rights," George Mason noted; "the laws of the general government being paramount to the laws and constitutions of the several States, the declaration of rights, in the separate States, are no security."[41] The Constitution's supporters, Alexander Hamilton and James Wilson in particular, argued that a bill of rights was unnecessary and, if added, possibly dangerous. Anticipating Justice Harlan's current stress on institutional checks— federalism and separation of powers—as the major safeguards of freedom, Hamilton insisted that "the constitution is itself, in every rational sense, and to every useful purpose *A Bill of Rights*."[42]

Other supporters of the Constitution, notably George Nicholas, Edmund Randolph, Edmund Pendleton, John Marshall of Virginia, Oliver Ellsworth of Connecticut, Alexander Contee Hanson

---

[39] *The Debates in the Several State Conventions on the Adoption of the Federal Constitution* (Elliot ed., 1888), II, 455; see Birkby, "Politics of Accommodation: The Original Supremacy Clause," *Western Political Quarterly*, XIX (1966), 123.

[40] Letter from Thomas Jefferson to James Madison, Dec. 20, 1787, in *The Papers of Thomas Jefferson* (Boyd ed., 1955), XII, 18.

[41] G. Mason, *Objections of George Mason to the Proposed Constitution*, in *Pamphlets on the Constitution of the United States 1787–1788*, p. 329.

[42] *The Federalist* No. 84, p. 336.

of Maryland, James Wilson of Pennsylvania, pointed to the judiciary as the guardian of liberty. Ellsworth reassured antifederalists that if the Congress should exceed its powers, the judiciary is a constitutional check.

Antifederalists were not satisfied. Pressure mounted. Contending that courts would be handicapped for want of criteria against which to judge alleged violations of fundamental liberties, John Smilie of Pennsylvania declared that unless some criterion were established by which it could be easily ascertained how far the Congress might go and when they had transgressed their jurisdiction, this idea of altering or curbing government would be sound without substance.

In short the federalists had only *partially* succeeded in solving the gaping dilemma John Locke posed toward the end of his *Second Treatise*. When the people's chosen representatives are alleged to violate the trust imposed by the social compact and by "promulgated established laws," who is to judge the transgression? Locke's answer was that in the absence of a "judicature on earth to decide . . . God in heaven is judge"—presumably a Lockean euphemism for force. The federalists recognized that the hiatus in Locke's system had to be filled. They saw the need for *judges,* but they refused to provide *standards.* Without a Bill of Rights fixing the limits of national power in relation to the rights of individuals—and States—reliance on federalism and separation of power would be a vain hope. The prospect that judicial review alone would provide peaceable means for the redress of infringed rights was more apparent than real. Instead of averting recourse to revolution, the Constitution's failure to convert natural rights into judicially enforceable civil rights through the medium of a Bill of Rights made violent redress the more likely. Thus, rather than containing *"the means of its own preservation,"* the new national government contained the seeds of its own destruction.

Antifederalists insisted on carrying the solution to the Lockean dilemma one crucial step further. The mechanism of judicial review was not enough; also needed were standards, criteria—a Bill of Rights.

Madison finally agreed to sponsor amendments in the first Congress, if for no other reason "than that [they were] . . . anxiously desired by others."[43]

In presenting his proposals, Madison, now Jefferson's convert, accepted as his own the argument Jefferson had propounded as having "great weight" with him—the "legal check" which the Bill of Rights puts in the hands of the judiciary. "If they [a bill of rights] are incorporated into the constitution," Madison argued, in language Justice Harlan apparently overlooks, "independent tribunals of justice will consider themselves in a peculiar manner the guardians of those rights; they will be an impenetrable bulwark against every assumption of power in the legislative or executive; they will be naturally led to resist every encroachment upon rights expressly stipulated for in the constitution by the declaration of rights."[44]

The antifederalist campaign was both a great success and an enduring disappointment. Gained were constitutional safeguards for individual liberty—freedom of speech, press, religion, right of assembly and procedural guarantees for persons accused of crime. The primary objective—constitutional protection for the States, a line or marker specifically safeguarding local authority against Federal encroachment—was lost. Achieved was a constitutional redundancy—the tenth amendment: "the powers not delegated to the United States by the Constitution, nor prohibited by it to the States, are reserved to the States respectively, or to the people." Despite the Tenth Amendment the national government is supreme in the exercise of its delegated and implied powers. "It was impossible," Madison told the first Congress, "to confine a Government to the exercise of express powers; there must necessarily be admitted powers by implication, unless the constitution descended to recount every minutia."[45]

---

[43] Letter from James Madison to Thomas Jefferson, Oct. 17, 1788, in *The Papers of Thomas Jefferson,* XIV, 18.

[44] "Speech Placing the Proposed Bill of Rights Amendments Before the House of Representatives," June 8, 1790, in *Annals of Congress,* I (1789–91), 457.

[45] *Ibid.,* p. 790.

The reaction of States-rights advocates revealed profound disgust. Instead of "substantial amendments," Pierce Butler complained, Madison had proposed "a few *milk-and-water* amendments . . . such as liberty of conscience, a free press, and one or two general things already well secured. I suppose it was done to keep his promise with his constituents, to move for alterations," Butler speculated concerning Madison's strategy, "but if I am not greatly mistaken, he is not hearty in the cause of amendments." [46] In 1790 the Tenth Amendment was recognized for what it is—a gold brick.

The States-rights failure in 1790 was compounded in 1868 by the adoption of the Fourteenth Amendment. Won also in that amendment's spacious provisions was the proposal that had been close to Madison's heart: "No State shall violate the equal rights of conscience, or the freedom of the press, or the trial by jury in criminal cases." [47]

Those who feared national encroachment had to be content with a constitutional tranquilizer, the Tenth Amendment. Its purpose, Chief Justice Marshall declared, was to quiet "the excessive jealousies which had been excited." [48] In interpreting national power, Marshall never referred to the Tenth Amendment as a limitation. For him its language merely restated the supremacy clause. Within these limits the Tenth Amendment was and is significant. The fears motivating its Framers were genuine.

IV

The Constitution, framed in general language, was susceptible of widely divergent and not wholly unreasonable interpretations. Madison's statesmanship represents a remarkable embodiment of the alternatives. At the Philadelphia convention he was a staunch federalist; later he helped to lay the foundation of "dual

---

[46] Letter from Pierce Butler to James Iredell, Aug. 11, 1789, in McRee, *Life and Correspondence of James Iredell* (1857), II, 265.

[47] *Annals of Congress*, I (1789), 452 [1789–1824].

[48] *McCulloch* v. *Maryland*, 17 U.S. (4 Wheat.) 159, 199 (1819).

federalism." [49] In the debate of 1791 on establishment of a national bank he conceded that *"interference with the powers of the States was no constitutional criterion of the powers of Congress. If the power was not given, Congress could not exercise it; if given, they might exercise it, although it should interfere with the laws or even the constitution of the States."* [50] In 1819, however, Madison deplored Chief Justice Marshall's alleged determination to convert a limited into an unlimited government. There is certainly a reasonable medium between expounding the Constitution with the strictness of a penal law or other ordinary statute and expounding it with a laxity which may vary its essential character, and encroach on the local sovereignties with which it was meant to be reconcilable. *The very existence of these local sovereignties is a control on the pleas of a constructive amplification of the powers of the General Government.* [51]

Marshall disagreed. "It has been said," he reasoned, "that they [the States] were sovereign, were completely independent, and were connected with each other only by a league." [52] Prior to 1789 the Chief Justice conceded the truth of this proposition. "But when these allied sovereigns converted their league into a government, when they converted their congress of ambassadors . . . into a legislature, empowered to enact laws on the most interesting subjects, the whole character in which the States appear, underwent a change. . . ." [53] Striking at the jugular vein of the States-rights argument, Marshall continued:

It has been contended, that if a law passed by a State, in the exercise of its acknowledged sovereignty, comes into conflict with a law passed by congress in pursuance of the constitution, they

---

[49] Edward S. Corwin, who coined the term, states its postulates as follows: "1. The national government is one of enumerated powers only; 2. Also the purposes which it may constitutionally promote are few; 3. Within their respective spheres the two centers of government are 'sovereign' and hence 'equal'; 4. The relation of the two centers with each other is one of tension rather than collaboration." "The Passing of Dual Federalism," *Virginia Law Review*, XXXVI (1950), 4.

[50] *The Writings of James Madison* (Hunt ed., 1906), VI, 28. (Emphasis added.)

[51] *Ibid.*, VIII, 451–52 (1908). (Emphasis added.)

[52] *Gibbons* v. *Ogden*, 22 U.S. (9 Wheat.) 1, 82 (1824).

[53] *Ibid.*

affect the subject, and each other, like equal opposing powers. But the framers of our constitution foresaw this state of things, and provided for it, by declaring the supremacy not only of itself, but of the laws made in pursuance of it.[54]

Furthermore the "necessary and proper" clause gives Congress a discretionary choice of means for carrying its enumerated powers into execution. The Tenth Amendment does not limit this freedom of selection. Thus Marshall established not only the proposition that national powers must be liberally construed, but also the principle that the Tenth Amendment does not create in the States an independent limitation on national authority.

Other critics attacked Marshall's robust nationalism. "The government has been fundamentally altered by the progress of opinion," Hugh Swinton Legaré of South Carolina wrote in 1828. "Instead of being any longer one of enumerated powers and a circumscribed sphere, as it was beyond all doubt intended to be, it knows absolutely no bounds but the will of a majority of Congress. . . . That argument . . ." Legaré concluded, "cannot be sound which necessarily converts a government of enumerated into one of indefinite powers, and a confederacy of republics into a gigantic and consolidated empire." [55]

After Marshall's death in 1835 the course of American federalism was significantly altered. As if in answer to fears of consolidation President Jackson appointed Roger Brooke Taney as Chief Justice Marshall's successor. During the next generation (1835–64) the Court, under Taney's leadership, redefined federalism in terms more favorable to the States. An important incidental result was a greatly enlarged role for the Supreme Court.

Under the revised federalism the Constitution was a compact of sovereign States, not an ordinance of the people. "Dual federalism" means two mutually exclusive, reciprocally limiting fields of power—that of the national government and of the States. The two authorities confront each other as equals across a precise

---

[54] *Ibid.*, p. 92.
[55] Legaré, *Kent's Commentaries*, in *Writings of Hugh Swinton Legaré* (1845), II, 102, 123, 131.

constitutional line, defining their respective jurisdictions. Said Chief Justice Taney, "It is unquestionably no easy task to mark by a certain and definite line . . . and to fix the precise point . . . where the paramount power of Congress terminates, and that of the State begins. The constitution itself does not attempt to define these limits." [56]

Drawing the line which the Framers refused to draw, the Taney Court enforced nation-State equality. Within the powers allegedly reserved by the Tenth Amendment the States were sovereign. Final authority to determine the scope of State and national power rested with the Supreme Court, a body presumably standing aloof from the sovereign pretensions of both the national government and the States, not, as Marshall had insisted, merely an instrument of the national authority. In cases involving a clash of sovereignties Marshall asked one question: Does Congress have the power? Taney asked two questions: Does Congress have the power, and do the States have any rights precluding congressional action?

"As the constitution itself does not draw the line," Chief Justice Taney observed, "the question is necessarily one for judicial decision, . . . depending altogether upon the words of the constitution." [57] Supreme Court justices thus assumed the responsibility for doing what the Framers and the first Congress had deliberately left undone. With this assertion of the sovereign prerogative of choice there was but a short step from national supremacy to judicial supremacy.

V

In practice judicial interpretation of Federal-State relations has precipitated three major crises. The first occurred near the end of Chief Justice Taney's long regime, the second came in the middle 1930's, and the third confronts us today. Distrustful of

---

[56] *License Cases,* 46 U.S. (5 How.) 590, 671 (1846). See also the opinions of Justices McLean, p. 685, and Daniel, p. 713.

[57] *Ibid.,* p. 671.

any further drive toward national unity, Chief Justice Taney ruled in the Dred Scott Case [58] that Congress could not abolish slavery even in the territories. Slavery was a matter reserved *exclusively* to the States. Taney's failure to recognize slavery as a problem national in scope demanding national authority to deal with it helped to bring on the Civil War. Union victory was reflected in the revolutionary Thirteenth, Fourteenth and Fifteenth amendments, designed, as Justice Miller declared, radically to change "the whole theory of the relations of the State and Federal governments to each other and of both of these governments to the people." [59] In its determination to prevent this transformation the Court suggested that Federal-State relations are immune to the formal amending process.

Government attempts to control large business corporations operating across State boundaries occasioned America's second crisis in federalism. By switching from the doctrine of national supremacy to that of dual federalism and back again, the Supreme Court defeated both State and national attempts to regulate business enterprise. Ultimately at both levels "Uncle Sam" was, as Justice Stone said in 1936, "tied . . . in a hard knot." [60] State regulations were vetoed by application of the doctrine of national supremacy, the Court holding that since the problem was national, corrective action must come from Congress. When

---

[58] *Scott* v. *Sandford,* 60 U.S. (19 How.) 393 (1856).

[59] *Slaughter-House Cases,* 83 U.S. (16 Wall.) 36, 78 (1872). Justice Miller, in reaching a decision which defeated the objectives of the radical Republican Congress, was understandably apologetic.

The argument we admit is not always the most conclusive which is drawn from the consequences urged against the adoption of a particular construction of an instrument. But when, as in the case before us, these consequences are so serious, so far-reaching and pervading, so great a departure from the structure and spirit of our institutions; when the effect is to fetter and degrade the State governments by subjecting them to the control of Congress, in the exercise of powers heretofore universally conceded to them of the most ordinary and fundamental character; when in fact it radically changes the whole theory of the relations of the State and Federal government to each other and of both these governments to the people; the argument has a force that is irresistible, in the absence of language which expresses such a purpose too clearly to admit of doubt.

Ibid., p. 78.

[60] A. T. Mason, *Harlan Fiske Stone: Pillar of the Law* (1956), p. 426.

Congress responded to this invitation, State power was inter-
posed. National action was regarded as an invasion of the domain
reserved to the States. The Tenth Amendment was applied as if it
read "all powers not *expressly* delegated are reserved." In 1918
judicial amendment of the Tenth Amendment enabled the Supreme Court to defeat congressional authority to regulate child
labor under the commerce power.[61] The Court divided five to four.
By interpolating "expressly" in the Tenth Amendment [62]—the
very word the Congress of 1789 had deliberately refused to insert
—five Supreme Court justices put manufacturing, agriculture and
employer-employee relations beyond the reach of national authority. The constitutional theory of "dual federalism" had become a thin disguise for the economic dogma of laissez faire.

"Dual federalism" as an instrument of judicial government
reached its climax in a series of decisions upsetting New Deal
legislation. In one term, 1935–36, eleven congressional statutes
fell under the judicial ax. The redundancy of the Tenth Amendment—"powers not delegated are reserved"—then became a noto-
rious judicial device for defeating the power to govern. In a
notable dissent of 1936 Justice Stone discredited this judicial
perversion in language of unmatched vehemence.[63] Several weeks
later, still pondering the subject, he wrote to Charles A. Beard,
"Have you ever found in your researches . . . any indication that
the framers of the [Tenth] Amendment intended the reserve
powers of the States to constitute a limitation of the power of
Congress?" [64] Beard's search served only to confirm Stone's belief
that no such limitation had been intended. "I have always held,"
the Justice wrote the historian, "that the framers of the Constitu-

---

[61] *Hammer* v. *Dagenhart,* 247 U.S. 251 (1918).
[62] Said Justice Day:
> In interpreting the Constitution it must never be forgotten that the
> Nation is made up of States to which are entrusted the powers of local
> government. And to them and to the people the powers not *expressly*
> delegated to the National Government are reserved. . . . The power of
> the States to regulate their purely internal affairs by such laws as seem
> wise to the local authority is inherent and has never been surrendered
> to the general government.

Ibid., p. 275. (Emphasis added.)
[63] *United States* v. *Butler,* 297 U.S. 1, 78 (1936).
[64] See A. T. Mason, *Harlan Fiske Stone: Pillar of the Law,* p. 410.

tion intended to create a strong government, adequate to deal with every situation. I think they would have been surprised, even after the Tenth Amendment, to learn that the Constitution reserved a legislative field to the States. It granted power to the national Government and, in the vernacular of the farmer, 'the tail goes with the hide.' " [65]

In 1936 six Supreme Court justices, bent on slaying the New Deal, had again inserted "expressly" before the word "delegated." The judiciary, portrayed by Hamilton in *The Federalist* Number 78 as "the weakest of the three departments of power," predicting "that it can never attack with success either of the other two," became in fact the dominant power. Justice Roberts, the swing man, was "the most powerful man in the United States. . . ." [66]

In 1940 Justice Stone, speaking for a unanimous Court, set the Tenth Amendment in the context of history.

Our conclusion is unaffected by the Tenth Amendment. . . . The amendment states but a truism that all is retained which has not been surrendered. There is nothing in the history of its adoption to suggest that it was more than declaratory of the relationship between the national and state governments as it had been established by the Constitution before the amendment or that its purpose was other than to allay fears that the new national government might seek to exercise powers not granted, and that the states might not be able to exercise fully their reserved powers. . . . From the beginning and for many years the amendment has been construed as not depriving the national government of authority to resort to all means for the exercise of a granted power which are appropriate and plainly adapted to the permitted end. [67]

Striking hard at the Court's misguided view of American federalism, Stone had observed in 1936:

Interpretation of our great charter of government which proceeds on any assumption that the responsibility for the preservation of

---

[65] *Ibid.*, pp. 410–11.

[66] Rodell, *Nine Men: A Political History of the Supreme Court from 1790 to 1955* (1955), p. 221.

[67] *United States* v. *Darby Lumber Co.*, 312 U.S. 100, 123–24 (1940).

our institutions is the exclusive concern of any one of the three branches of government, or that it alone can save them from destruction is far more likely, in the long run, "to obliterate the constituent members" of "an indestructible union of indestructible states" than the frank recognition that language, even of a constitution, may mean what it says.[68]

VI

After more than a hundred and fifty years, judicial reading of federalism has brought about a third major constitutional crisis. The Supreme Court's 1954 decision outlawing racial segregation in public schools [69] evoked the familiar cry of States rights and judicial usurpation. Proposals for Federal aid to education, usually a State rather than a national function, raise the specter of Federal dictation of educational policy and content. In a series of four rulings [70] beginning in 1962, the justices stepped into another area heretofore reserved to the States, commanding that election districts bear some reasonable relation to population distribution. After generations of tolerance and neglect the Supreme Court has finally begun to enforce higher standards for State police officers.[71] The Court's critics, invoking States rights, object that the police have been handcuffed. A more reasonable reaction is that the justices have merely decided that the time had come to enforce the high standards we have long professed.[72] All these problems had become national in scope. No remedy was forthcoming from the States, but judicial attempts to deal with them at the national level raised the States-rights issue and stirred passionate feelings against the unity which judicial assertion of national power and responsibility seemed to portend.

---

[68] *United States* v. *Butler,* 297 U.S. 1, 87–88 (1936).

[69] *Brown* v. *Board of Education,* 347 U.S. 483 (1954).

[70] *Reynolds* v. *Sims,* 377 U.S. 533 (1964); *Wesberry* v. *Sanders,* 376 U.S. 1 (1964); *Gray* v. *Sanders,* 372 U.S. 368 (1963); *Baker* v. *Carr,* 369 U.S. 186 (1962).

[71] *Wolf* v. *Colorado,* 338 U.S. 25 (1949).

[72] *Mapp* v. *Ohio,* 367 U.S. 643 (1961). See Griswold, "The Long View," *American Bar Association Journal,* LI (1965), 1017.

Meanwhile a battle continues within the councils of the judiciary concerning basic constitutional principles—federalism and the Bill of Rights—and the Court's responsibility toward them. Justice Harlan deplores the majority's apparent drive to incorporate provisions of the Bill of Rights into the equal protection and due process clauses of the Fourteenth Amendment [73]—at the expense, he charges, of federalism and separation of powers.

For Justice Harlan the decisions asserting judicial responsibility for "one man, one vote" "cut deeply into the fabric of our federalism," representing judicial entry into an area "profoundly ill-advised and constitutionally impermissible." [74] The extension to accused persons in State courts of the safeguards available to them in Federal jurisdiction is denounced by Harlan as "historically and constitutionally unsound and incompatible with the maintenance of our federal system. . . ." [75] Judicial censorship of obscene and indecent literature trenches, Harlan complains, on the "prerogative of the States to differ on their ideas of morality," denying both nation and States the advantage of having fifty laboratories of experimentation for trying out "different attitudes toward the same work of literature." [76]

Justice Harlan's wide-flung strictures revive the eighteenth-century debate between federalists and antifederalists concerning whether a bill of rights was necessary as a supplement to the protection afforded by federalism and separation of powers; he apparently ignores the argument Jefferson made in behalf of the Bill of Rights—the legal check it places in the hands of the judiciary. Rejuvenated is a variant of "dual federalism," the assertion that certain subject matter, notably the administration of criminal justice, is peculiarly within the State's domain. It is "the very essence of our federalism," Justice Harlan declares,

---

[73] *Pointer* v. *Texas,* 380 U.S. 400, 408 (1965) (concurring opinion).

[74] *Reynolds* v. *Sims,* 377 U.S. 533, 624 (1964).

[75] *Pointer* v. *Texas,* 380 U.S. 400, 409 (1965) (Harlan, J., concurring).

[76] *Roth* v. *United States,* 354 U.S. 476, 505–6 (1957) (separate opinion); see *Memoirs* v. *Massachusetts,* 86 Sup. Ct. 942, 953 (1966) (Harlan, J., dissenting).

"that the States should have the widest latitude in the administration of their own system of criminal justice." [77]

On April 5, 1965, shortly before he doffed judicial robes to become Ambassador to the United Nations, Justice Goldberg made a point-by-point reply to "Brother Harlan." [78] The "incorporation" theory, Justice Goldberg argued, far from being discredited, had made notable progress. Now included among the Fourteenth Amendment's guarantees against infringement by the States are the liberties of the First, Fourth, Fifth, Sixth and Eighth amendments. Nor did Justice Goldberg accept Justice Harlan's easy transition to civil liberties of Brandeis' claims for the advantages of federalism. "While I agree with Mr. Justice Brandeis," Goldberg observed tartly, "that 'it is one of the happy incidents of the federal system that . . . a State may . . . serve as a laboratory; and try novel social and economic experiments,' . . . I do not believe that this includes the power to experiment with the fundamental liberties of citizens safeguarded by the Bill of Rights." [79]

Finally Justice Goldberg did not believe that Harlan's restrictive views of judicial responsibility would advance any legitimate State interest. Said Goldberg, "To deny to the States the power to impair a fundamental constitutional right is not to increase Federal power, but, rather, to limit the power of both Federal and State governments in favor of safeguarding the fundamental rights and liberties of the individual." [80]

The 1963 decision guaranteeing a Florida indigent, Clarence Gideon, his constitutional right to counsel illustrates Justice Goldberg's point. Since *Gideon* v. *Wainright*,[81] twenty-six States have instituted vital reforms in their criminal procedures. "I didn't start out," the triumphant Gideon observes, "to do any-

---

[77] *Hoag* v. *New Jersey*, 356 U.S. 464, 468 (1958).
[78] *Pointer* v. *Texas*, 380 U.S. 400, 410 (1965) (concurring opinion).
[79] *Ibid.*, p. 413.
[80] *Ibid.*, p. 414.
[81] 372 U.S. 335 (1963).

thing for anybody but myself, but this decision has done a helluva lot of good. . . ." [82] Nor have the steps taken to secure more equitable representation, in response to judicial command, weakened the States, or encouraged, as Justice Harlan anticipated, "inertia in efforts for political reform through the political process." [83] In time, reapportionment, now in progress on a broad front, may better equip the States to meet twentieth-century needs.

In June, 1965, Justice Harlan's persistent campaign for judicial self-restraint to stem the rising tide of judicial guardianship of civil liberties, at the alleged expense of federalism, won support from Justice Black, heretofore a fierce antagonist. The case was *Griswold* v. *Connecticut.*[84] Justice Douglas, speaking for the Court, invoked amendments One, Three, Four, Five, Six, Nine and Fourteen. In none, however, was there a specific bar against Connecticut's anticontraceptive statute. Douglas found the constitutional killer in the right of privacy, in "penumbras, formed by emanations from those guarantees that help give them life and substance." [85] Joined by Chief Justice Warren and Justices Brennan and Goldberg, Justice Douglas asserted that the constitutional right of privacy of married persons is "older than the Bill of Rights—older than our political parties, older than our school system." [86]

"We do not sit," Justice Douglas observed, "as a super-legislature to determine the wisdom, need, and propriety of laws that touch economic problems, business affairs, or social conditions. This law, however, operates directly on an intimate relation of husband and wife and their physician's role in one aspect of that relation." [87] The implication is that the Court does sit as a super-legislature in the latter field.

Justice Black denies that the Founding Fathers intended the

---

[82] *Time,* Dec. 17, 1965, p. 39.
[83] *Wesberry* v. *Sanders,* 376 U.S. 1, 48 (1964) (dissenting opinion).
[84] 381 U.S. 479 (1965).
[85] *Ibid.,* p. 484.
[86] *Ibid.,* p. 486.
[87] *Ibid.,* p. 482.

Supreme Court to have "such awesome . . . powers"; [88] he condemns as shocking any doctrine that would "make of this Court's members a day-to-day constitutional convention." [89] "I like my privacy as well as the next one," the eighty-year-old Justice commented feelingly, "but I am nevertheless compelled to admit that government has a right to invade it unless prohibited by some specific constitutional provision." [90] "Considerations of 'natural justice,'" he warned, "are no less dangerous when used to enforce this Court's views about personal rights than those about economic rights." [91] General application of the constitutional right of privacy would "amount to a great unconstitutional shift of power to the courts," [92] tending to break down doctrines of major concern to Justice Harlan—separation of powers and federalism.

This dramatic break, this "discordant symphony of a free society" [93] at a high level, foreshadows exciting years ahead. For Justice Harlan judicial sensitivity to State invasion of the Bill of Rights, even in the face of the sweeping provisions of the Fourteenth Amendment, threatens the federal balance. Echoed are the fears that troubled Justice Miller in 1873—gnawing concern lest such judicial censorship "fetter and degrade the State governments." Arguing, as did Justice Miller, in terms of the consequences that must follow the 1964 "one-man-one-vote" decision, Harlan observed:

No thinking person can fail to recognize that the aftermath of these cases, however desirable it may be thought in itself, will have been achieved at the cost of radical alteration in the relationship between the States and the Federal Government, more particularly the Federal Judiciary. Only one who has an overbearing impatience with the federal system and its political process will believe that that cost was not too high or was inevitable.[94]

---

[88] *Ibid.*, p. 519 (concurring opinion).

[89] *Ibid.*, p. 520 (concurring opinion).

[90] *Ibid.*, p. 510 (concurring opinion).

[91] *Ibid.*, p. 522 (concurring opinion).

[92] *Ibid.*, p. 521 (concurring opinion).

[93] Recorded conversation of Adlai Stevenson with Arnold Michaels, June 19, 1956.

[94] *Reynolds* v. *Sims,* 377 U.S. 533, 624 (1964) (dissenting opinion).

Harlan apparently believes, as did Justice Miller, that the Fourteenth Amendment left Federal-State relations unchanged. Justice Black's concern, although not entirely distinguishable from Harlan's, focuses on the danger of judicial supremacy. Recalling the early 1930's, Black warns against using the due process formula to enforce personal preference. Before 1937 the Justices asserted and achieved judicial dominance by embellishing provisions of the Constitution with an economic dogma—laissez faire. In the 1960's Black suggests that the majority, deeply concerned about personal rights, enthroned the "specific" provisions of the Bill of Rights to enforce a political doctrine—the right of privacy. Thus, Justice Black, himself formerly cast as a judicial activist, now ironically asserts the doctrine of "self-restraint" strongly proclaimed before 1937 by Justice Stone.

The trend toward national unity under judicial sponsorship and auspices has been in response to necessity, not motivated, as sometimes supposed, by doctrinaire considerations or desire to fetter and degrade the States. "It is ludicrous to preclude judicial relief," Justice Douglas commented in *Baker* v. *Carr*, "when a mainspring of representative government is impaired." [95] "The majority of the people of Tennessee have no 'practical opportunities for exerting their political weight at the polls . . . ,' " Justice Clark noted.[96] Without judicial intervention the people of Tennessee would, he said, "be saddled with the present discrimination in the affairs of their State government." [97] The Federal courts stepped in because of the failure of the States to discharge their primary responsibility for a system of criminal justice that protects all rights, State and Federal, at all stages of a proceeding. Justice Brennan suggests that "if the States shoulder this

[95] 369 U.S. 186, 249 (1962) (quoting Judge McLaughlin in *Dyer* v. *Kazuhisa Abe*, 138 F. Supp. 220, 236 [D. Hawaii 1956]).

[96] *Baker* v. *Carr*, 369 U.S. 186, 258–59 (1962) (concurring opinion).

[97] *Ibid.*, p. 259. Justice Clark cited John Rutledge's (later Chief Justice) belief, stated in the Federal Convention of 1787, that "a chief function of the Court is to secure the national rights," and that "to be fully conformable to the principle of right, the form of government must be representative." *Ibid.*, p. 261 (referring to Farrand, *op. cit.*, I, 124).

burden, . . . the friction and irritants that presently exist . . . between the State and Federal courts will rapidly disappear." [98]

In the abstract it would have been better perhaps if the encroachments on individual freedom represented in Connecticut's anticontraceptive statute, largely unenforced, could have been corrected by the State legislature. But this was not done. As in school desegregation, reapportionment and administration of criminal justice, failure of the States to protect individual liberties or to undertake corrective measures to make themselves responsive and responsible drove the Court to enter untrod fields, raising again the States-rights issue of judicial usurpation.

Chief Justice Warren has repeatedly recognized that the national government has on occasion become too deeply enmeshed in matters properly within the prerogatives of the States. But, he explains, the fault lies more often than not with the States themselves: "When the State governments fail to satisfy the needs of the people, the people appeal to the Federal Government. Whether the question is one of the advancement of human knowledge through research, of law and order, or of the right of all persons to equal protection of the law, the Federal Government need become involved only when the States fail to act." [99]

After the Court in 1937 abandoned judicial pre-eminence and recognized, as Madison declared in *The Federalist* Number 51, that "dependence on the people is the primary control on government," it seemed logically to follow that the Court should assert responsibility for preserving an open society. Free government demands freedom of expression; responsible government requires equitable representation. In the assertion of a special responsibil-

---

[98] Brennan, "Some Aspects of Federalism," *New York University Law Review*, XXXIX (1964), 959.

[99] Mason and Beaney, *The Supreme Court in a Free Society* (1959), p. 310. See also Address by Chief Justice Warren to the California Bar Association in San Francisco, Sept. 25, 1963, in *New York Times*, Sept. 26, 1963, p. 29, col. 5. Speaking before the annual meeting of the American Law Institute, May 18, 1966, Chief Justice Warren expressed concern over some of the thirty-four bills pending in Congress: "Some of them go a long way and may radically change the relationship between the Federal and State governments." *New York Times*, May 19, 1966, p. 1, col. 3.

ity for the enforcement of the Bill of Rights now incorporated in the Fourteenth Amendment,[100] the present Court is fulfilling the expectations voiced by Jefferson, Madison, Hamilton and Marshall.[101] Despite this authoritative support it has aroused the cry of States rights—judicial usurpation.

The most compelling authentication of our "indestructible union of indestructible States," achieved by resort to the sword and judicial decision,[102] has not resolved the issue of federalism. A debate capable of generating heat for so long cannot be reasonably considered lacking in the essential fuel of controversy on either side. The explanation of this neverending wrangle may lie in the Constitution itself and in the nature of the government it establishes. Chief Justice Marshall was accustomed to reiterate the telling reminder, "We must never forget, that it is a *Constitution* we are expounding." [103] Like an oracle, it speaks ambiguously. Neither friends nor enemies of the proposed constitution could be certain about the nature of the government it ordained. Antifederalists, trying to defeat ratification, argued with conviction that it would lead to "consolidation." Hamilton, an ardent consolidationist, signed reluctantly on the common-sense ground that it is impossible "to deliberate between anarchy and Convulsion on the one side, and the chance of good to be expected from the plan on the other." [104]

What was said on both sides in the ratifying debates is more ambiguous than the document itself. In their series of essays designed to sway a widely divergent constituency it was not unnatural that Hamilton and Madison should blur hotly controverted issues. When John Taylor set out to prove that Chief Justice Marshall had, through spurious interpretation, converted a compact of sovereign States into a consolidated empire, he drew

---

[100] Justice Goldberg lists the relevant cases in *Pointer* v. *Texas,* 380 U.S. 400, 410 (1965) (concurring opinion).

[101] See Brant, "Edmund Cahn and American Constitutional History," *New York University Law Review,* XL (1965), 225.

[102] *Texas* v. *White,* 74 U.S. (7 Wall.) 700 (1869).

[103] *McCulloch* v. *Maryland,* 17 U.S. (4 Wheat.) 159, 200 (1819).

[104] Farrand, *op. cit.,* III, 646.

indiscriminately from both Hamilton's and Madison's numbers of *The Federalist*.[105] Chief Justice Marshall enlisted the support of

[105] Madison's most significant concessions to States rights occur in *The Federalist* Nos. 39 and 45. In the latter essay he wrote, "The States will retain, under the proposed Constitution, a very extensive portion of active sovereignty. . . . The powers delegated by the proposed Constitution to the Federal government are few and defined. Those which remain to the State governments are numerous and indefinite." *The Federalist* No. 45, pp. 326, 328 (Wright ed., 1961). As we have seen, Hamilton and James Wilson successfully combatted this view of national power, and Madison himself, in presenting the Tenth Amendment to the first Congress, seemed in agreement.

In *The Federalist* No. 9, p. 128 (Wright ed., 1961), Hamilton declared that "The proposed Constitution, so far from implying an abolition of the State governments, makes them constituent parts of national sovereignty, by allowing them a direct representation in the Senate, and leaves in their possession certain *exclusive* and very important portions of sovereign power." (Emphasis added.) Yet John Taylor was wary: "The ambiguity of this sentence arises from the interpolation of the words national sovereignty. . . ." Taylor, *New Views of the Constitution of the United States* (1823), p. 65. Thus while "Mr. Hamilton seems to *intimate,* that the constitution has created two sovereignties . . . each invested with exclusive powers, [he has made one sovereign over the other] . . . by the representation [of the inferior sovereignty] in the Senate." *Ibid.,* pp. 66–67. (Emphasis added.)

Taylor suggested that Hamilton planted the seeds of nullification by saying in *The Federalist* No. 28, pp. 225, 226 (Wright ed., 1961):

Power being almost always the rival of power, the general government will at all times stand ready to check the usurpations of the State governments, and these will have the same disposition towards the general government. . . . [The people] . . . are in a situation, through the medium of their State governments, to take measures for their own defence, with all the celerity, regularity, and systems, of independent nations. . . .

In *The Federalist* No. 31, p. 239 (Wright ed., 1961), Hamilton declared flatly that "the State governments, by their original constitutions, are invested with complete sovereignty." In *The Federalist* No. 32, pp. 241, 243 (Wright ed., 1961), Hamilton was

willing here to allow, in its full extent, the justness of the reasoning which requires that the individual States should possess an independent and uncontrollable authority to raise their own revenues. . . . I affirm that (with the sole exception of duties on imports and exports) they would, under the plan of the convention, retain that authority in the most absolute and unqualified sense; and that an attempt on the part of the national government to abridge them in the exercise of it, would be a violent assumption of power, unwarranted by any article or clause of its Constitution. . . .

The necessity of a concurrent jurisdiction in certain cases results from the division of sovereign power. . . .

In *The Federalist* No. 33, pp. 245–46 (Wright ed., 1961), Hamilton undercut the basis of Marshall's jurisprudence, as well as his own, saying: "The declaration itself [authorizing the national legislature to make all laws which

America's political classic—that "great authority," he called
it—to demonstrate that Federal judicial power must extend to
Supreme Court review of State-court decisions arising under the
Federal constitution or laws of the United States.[106] Yet Spencer
Roane resorted to this same resourceful arsenal for the ammuni-
tion he used to blast Marshall's alleged usurpations.[107]

VII

Extreme exponents of States rights would turn the clock back;
they would scuttle the Constitution and return us to the mon-
strous *imperium in imperio* so convincingly discredited in the
years both before and after 1776. Their proposals seem absurd,
yet debate—one of the normal "wastes of democracy" [108]—must
be tolerated. Distrust of power at all levels, of whatever orienta-

---

shall be necessary and proper], though it may be chargeable with tautology
or redundancy, is at least perfectly harmless."

Small wonder Taylor could write that "the principles I am advocating are
forcibly sustained in [*The Federalist*]. . . ." *New Views of the Constitution
of the United States*, p. 75. Small wonder, too, that America's political
classic has been dubbed a "split personality." See Adair, "The Authorship
of the Disputed Federalist Papers" (pts. 1–2), *William and Mary Quarterly*,
I, 3d 97 (1944), 235.

[106] *Cohens* v. *Virginia*, 19 U.S. (6 Wheat.) 120, 187–88 (1921).

[107] Roane, "On the Lottery Decision," *Richmond Inquirer*, June 8, 1821,
reprinted in *The John P. Branch Historical Papers* (1906), II, 170.

In *Cohens* v. *Virginia* Marshall wrote, "These States are constituent parts
of the United States; they are members of one great empire—for some
purposes sovereign, for some purposes subordinate." 19 U.S. (6 Wheat.) at
185. In *Gibbons* v. *Ogden* Marshall, conceding the States' power to impose
inspection laws, referred to these laws as "a portion of that immense mass
of legislation . . . not surrendered to the general government; all which can
be most advantageously exercised by the States themselves." 22 U.S. (9
Wheat.) at 89. See also *Willson* v. *The Black-bird Creek Marsh Co.*, 27 U.S.
(2 Peters) 152 (1829). Even in *Charles River Bridge* v. *Warren Bridge*, 36
U.S. (11 Peters) 341 (1837), Chief Justice Taney was not wholly lacking in
support drawn from John Marshall. Taney was able to cite four precedents
drawn from the Marshall era: *United States* v. *Arrendondo*, 31 U.S. (6
Peters) 462 (1832); *Beatty* v. *Knowler*, 29 U.S. (4 Peters) 93 (1830);
Providence Bank v. *Billings*, 29 U.S. (4 Peters) 314 (1830); *Jackson* v.
Lamphire, 28 U.S. (3 Peters) 173 (1830). The Providence Bank case
supplied quotable words from Marshall's opinion. See Garvey, "The Constitutional Revolution of 1837 and the Myth of Marshall's Monolith," *Western
Political Quarterly*, XVIII (1965), 27.

[108] A. T. Mason, *Brandeis: A Free Man's Life* (1946); p. 382.

tion, is still the American watchword. Eternal vigilance is still the price of liberty. Power concentrated in Washington and in the President is not an unmitigated blessing. Thomas Jefferson declared that "the jealousy of the subordinate governments is a precious reliance." [109] A century and a half later Louis D. Brandeis thanked God for "the limitations inherent in our federal system." [110] The methods of the welfare state have not reached such a peak of perfection as to make them immune to discussion and criticism. We still need to bear in mind John Randolph's trenchant caveat: "You may cover whole skins of parchment with limitations but power alone can limit power." [111] Conflict between Federal and State authority means "vibrations of power," and this, Hamilton said, is "the genius of our government." [112]

Hamilton and Madison considered the States essential not only as serviceable units of government but also as safeguards against the abuses of national authority. As Madison wrote in *The Federalist* Number 14:

It is to be remembered that the general government is not charged with the whole power of making and administering laws. Its jurisdiction is limited to certain enumerated objects, which concern all the members of the republic, but which are not to be attained .by the separate provisions of any. The subordinate governments, which can extend their care to all those other objects which can be separately provided for, will retain their due authority and activity. Were it proposed by the plan of the convention to abolish the governments of the particular States, its adversaries would have some ground for their objection; though it would not be difficult to show that if they were abolished the general government would be compelled, by the principle of self-preservation, to reinstate them in their proper jurisdiction. [113]

[109] Letter from Thomas Jefferson to James Madison, March 15, 1789, in *The Papers of Thomas Jefferson*, XIV, 660.

[110] *Brandeis: A Free Man's Life*, p. 621.

[111] Bruce, *John Randolph of Roanoke* (1922), II, 211.

[112] Letter from Alexander Hamilton to Rufus King, June 3, 1802, in *The Works of Alexander Hamilton* (Lodge ed., 1904), X, 437, 439.

[113] *The Federalist* No. 14, p. 152 (Wright ed., 1961). For Madison's concessions to States rights see *The Federalist* Nos. 39, 45. Hamilton goes equally far in *The Federalist* Nos. 9, 28, 31–32.

The States-rights debate will continue. Nationalists should be
the last to suggest a moratorium. Informed explorations of the
record—and the compelling verdict of history—redound overwhelmingly to their advantage. Nevertheless Jefferson's admoni-
tion of 1821 is applicable—as much to the national government
and the States as to Congress, the Executive and the Court. The
"healing balm" of our Constitution, he said, is that "each party
should prudently shrink from all approach to the line of demarcation, instead of rashly overleaping it, or throwing grapples ahead
to haul to hereafter." [114] That the Constitution drew no "line of
demarcation" limiting national power vis-à-vis the States does
not detract from the wisdom of Jefferson's advice. The Tenth
Amendment may be a "truism," but it remains a compelling
reminder of America's search for union without unity.

---

[114] Letter from Thomas Jefferson to Spencer Roane, June 27, 1821, in *The
Writings of Thomas Jefferson* 190 n.1. (Ford ed., 1899), X. Compare
Jefferson's opinion of May 3, 1790, on Federal-State relations in the
Georgia Land Grants Controversy:
> The right of the general government is, in my opinion, to be main-
> tained. The case is sound; and the means of doing it as practicable as
> can ever occur. But respect and friendship should, I think, mark the
> conduct of the general towards the particular governments; and expla-
> nations should be asked, and time and colour given them to tread back
> their steps, before coercion is held up to their view. . . . I should think
> it better than that the first measures, while firm, be yet so temperate as
> to secure their alliance and aid to the general government. Might not
> the eclat of a proclamation revolt their pride and passion, and throw
> them hastily into the opposite scale?

The Papers of Thomas Jefferson, XVI, 407–8. Compare Hamilton's language in *The Federalist* No. 36, p. 262 (Wright ed., 1961): "As neither [the
federal nor state governments] can *control* the other [in the objects of
taxation] each will have an obvious and sensible interest in this reciprocal
forbearance."

In 1944 Justice Frankfurter, propounding the views now strenuously
espoused by Justice Harlan, wrote:
> The interpretations of modern society have not wiped out State lines.
> It is not for us to make inroads upon our federal system either by
> indifference to its maintenance or excessive regard for the unifying
> sources of modern technology. Scholastic reasoning may prove that no
> activity is isolated within the boundaries of a single State, but that
> cannot justify absorption of legislative power by the United States
> over every activity.

Polish National Alliance v. *NLRB*, 322 U.S. 643, 650 (1944).

SELECTED BIBLIOGRAPHY

Jensen, Merrill. *The New Nation: A History of the United States During the Confederation 1781–1789*. New York: Alfred A. Knopf, 1950.

Kenyon, Cecelia M. "Men of Little Faith: The Anti-Federalists on the Nature of Representative Government." *William and Mary Quarterly*, xii (1955), 3–143.

Main, Jackson Turner. *The Antifederalists: Critics of the Constitution*. Chapel Hill: University of North Carolina Press, 1961.

McDonald, Forrest. *We the People: The Economic Origins of the Constitution*. Chicago: University of Chicago Press, 1958.

Rutland, Robert. *The Birth of the Bill of Rights*. Chapel Hill: University of North Carolina Press, 1955.

Swindler, W. F. "The Current Challenge to Federalism." *Georgetown Law Journal*, LII (1963), 1–41.

Wright, B. F. *Consensus and Continuity, 1776–1787*. Boston: Boston University Press, 1958.

GEORGE CAREY
Georgetown University

FEDERALISM:
HISTORIC QUESTIONS
AND CONTEMPORARY MEANINGS
A DEFENSE OF
POLITICAL PROCESSES

ALTHOUGH IT IS UNLIKELY that the whole of the "conventional wisdom" on American federalism can be stated with precision, there is a high probability that the student of American government will be told the following:

1. Our Founding Fathers "invented" federalism. This invention was the result of compromise made necessary because the Philadelphia Convention could not produce an acceptable and viable constitution, the very task assigned to it, unless some accommodations or compromises were made regarding the status and powers of the States vis-à-vis those of the national government. This is the principal explanation for equal representation of the States, guaranteed by an express constitutional provision, in the Senate. The various "plans" submitted to the convention demonstrate that the Constitution is in reality the product of compromises between the "large" States (that supported the Virginia plan) and the "small" States (that supported the New Jersey plan). Great significance is attached to the Connecticut Compromise in explaining the working out of a federal system at Philadelphia.

2. Federalism can be defined as a division of powers between the State and national governments, a *vertical* distribution of powers, as distinct from a *horizontal* distribution embodied in the doctrine of separation of powers. At this juncture the Tenth Amendment will be introduced as proof positive that a vertical division of powers, although implicit in the structure of the Constitution emerging from the Convention, was clearly deemed a constitutional principle of fundamental importance by the people of America at the time.

3. There have been severe tensions in our constitutional system which arise directly from this vertical distribution of powers. The varied interpretations of the "necessary and proper" clause, the role and function of the Supreme Court in adjudicating disputes between the national and State governments, the meaning attached to the major provisions of the Fourteenth Amendment in conjunction with the process of "selective incorporation" and the interpretations (both congressional and judicial) of the delegated powers, for example, the commerce power, give some indication of the nature, depth and scope of the tensions and conflicts since the founding of the Republic. But if these do not suffice to convince the student of the problems surrounding vertical distribution of powers, he can be directed to examine the countless acts of "nullification" of national legislation by States,[1] both northern and southern, or to the writings and speeches of some of the most prominent American theorists and politicians—Jefferson, Calhoun, Taylor, Madison, Lincoln, Douglas. If all this fails (God forbid!), the student has only to be directed to his daily newspaper, where he will meet head on any number of George Wallaces.

At this point one might well ask, Why belabor the obvious? For two reasons, both of them important for what I wish to prove. First, as I will show at some length, much of what we say about federalism in the United States is pure myth. Recognition that it is myth gives us some insight into the nature and possible solu-

---

[1] Many acts of nullification by the States were not directed at national legislation. Rather they were directed at and prompted by Federal court decisions.

tions for those tensions which have plagued us throughout our relatively brief history.

In brief: "No, Virginia (the girl, not the State), we did not invent federalism. Sorry. What is more, Virginia, there can never be any Federal system such as that ascribed to the United States."

Second, tensions arising from conflict over the scope of State and national authority were simply inevitable. Any individual with his wits about him at the time of our founding could have anticipated them. Indeed, as even a cursory reading of *Elliot's Debates* reveals, some did. From our twentieth-century vantage point we can point out to students of constitutional governments and to constitution-makers the complexity of a federal system so that they may better understand or avoid the tensions that we, the presumed inventors of federalism, have encountered.

After explicating these points, I want to set forth only those two lines of argument most frequently encountered both as justification for federalism and as "guides" for determination of the proper boundary lines between the State and national governments. Then in a more positive vein I shall propose some general principles that might be fruitful in reducing tensions in our federal system. Finally I shall show that a legalistic approach is more than unsatisfactory in light of these proposed principles.

I

Anyone who reads the pertinent sections of *The Federalist* will soon discern that our Founding Fathers probably had only the sketchiest idea of what is today called federalism.[2] The term "federal," as used by the Founders, did not mean what it has come to mean, but rather "confederal" or even "confederational." There was general agreement at Philadelphia that, whatever the end product of their labors, the confederal or confederate system to be established could *not* be so defective in national strength as the Articles of Confederation.

---

[2] See in this connection Martin Diamond's contribution to *Essays in Federalism*, ed. George C. S. Benson (Claremont, Calif.: Institute for Studies in Federalism, 1961).

Political scientists now speak of a unitary form of government, as opposed to a confederate form. A federal form is something between the unitary and confederate forms. It combines a certain amount of central autonomy (assuming thereby characteristics of the unitary form), while simultaneously providing for a degree of local autonomy (characteristic of a confederate form). Certain matters can be regulated by both the local and central authorities. Modern doctrine visualizes two overlapping circles, the one encompassing powers "reserved" to the States, the other powers delegated to the national government. The circles "overlap" on powers shared by the two jurisdictions, for example, the power to tax.

In *The Federalist* Number 39, certainly one of the more important and relevant papers on the matter of federalism, *the word "federal" is used in a manner synonymous with that of our current conception of "confederate," and the word "national" closely resembles our understanding of a "unitary" form of government.* One quotation will serve to demonstrate this. In explicating and then answering one of the objections to the Constitution, Madison wrote:

'But it was not sufficient,' say the adversaries of the proposed Constitution, 'for the convention to adhere to the republican form. They ought with equal care to have preserved the *federal* form, which regards the Union as a *Confederacy* of sovereign states; instead of which they have framed a *national* government, which regards the Union as a *consolidation* of the States.'

Shortly thereafter he wrote:

. . . In order to ascertain the real character of the government, it may be considered in relation to the foundation on which it is to be established; to the sources from which its ordinary powers are to be drawn; to the operation of those powers; to the extent of them; and to the authority by which future changes in the government are to be introduced.

Let us follow Madison through these "tests" of the real character of the government.

A. On the "foundation" test the union is clearly seen to be federal. The sovereign States, acting in their individual capacities, must, according to the terms of the proposed constitution,

ratify (albeit through special conventions convened for this purpose) as States. Therefore Madison regarded the act of ratification as "federal" (confederate) in nature:

That it will be a federal and not a national act, as these terms
are understood by the objectors—the act of the people, as forming
so many independent States, not as forming one aggregate nation
—is obvious. from this single consideration: that it is to result
neither from the decision of a *majority* of the people of the Union,
nor from that of a *majority* of the States. It must result from the
unanimous assent of the several States that are parties to it . . .

B. On the test of "sources from which its [the proposed national government's] ordinary powers are to be drawn" Madison
described the system as "mixed." The government is "national"
with respect to the House of Representatives because it "will
derive its powers from the people of America; and the people will
be represented in the same proportion and on the same principle
as they are in the legislature of a particular State." But it is
"federal" (confederate) in regard to the Senate, since it "will
derive its powers from the States as political and coequal societies; and they will be represented on the principle of equality in
the Senate, as they now are in the existing Congress."

C. On the test of the operation of powers of the proposed
national government Madison spent but one paragraph in ac-
knowledging that the proposed constitution establishes a "national" (unitary) government because it will act directly upon
the people and not through any intermediate political structure.
Here we come near to the heart of some of our past and present
difficulties.

D. On the "extent" of the powers of the newly created Government, is it federal or national in character? Madison wrote:

But if the government be national with regard to the *operation*
of its powers, it changes its aspect again when we contemplate it
in relation to the extent of its powers. The idea of a national
government involves in it not only an authority over the individual citizens, but an indefinite supremacy over all persons and
things, so far as they are objects of lawful government. Among a
people consolidated into one nation, this supremacy is completely

vested in the national legislature. Among communities united for particular purposes, it is vested partly in the general and partly in the municipal legislatures. In the former case, all local authorities are subordinate to the supreme; and may be controlled, directed, or abolished by it at pleasure. In the latter, the local or municipal authorities form distinct and independent portions of the supremacy, no more subject, within their respective spheres, to the general authority than the general authority is subject to them, within its own sphere. In this relation, then, the proposed government cannot be deemed a *national* one; since its jurisdiction extends to certain enumerated objects only, and leaves to the several States a residuary and inviolable sovereignty over all other subjects.

Note well that Madison, if he had held our modern conception of federalism, could have said: "We have proposed a system that is, in many ways, a combination of the unitary and confederate form. We will call this form 'federal.' " At precisely this point he could have suggested that the government was to be based upon some innovative principles of vertical distribution of powers. It is significant that he did not do so.

And finally to (*E*). Let us once again quote extensively from Number 39:

If we try the Constitution by its last relation to the authority by which amendments are to be made, we find it neither wholly *national* nor wholly *federal*. Were it wholly national, the supreme and ultimate authority would reside in the *majority* of the people of the Union; and this authority would be competent at all times, like that of a majority of every national society to alter or abolish its established government. Were it wholly federal, on the other hand, the concurrence of each State in the Union would be essential to every alteration that would be binding on all. The mode provided by the plan of the convention is not founded on either of these principles. . . .

The proposed Constitution, therefore, even when tested by the rules laid down by its antagonists, is, in strictness, neither a national nor a federal Constitution, but a composition of both.

Having applied his tests, what did Madison conclude? I think, the following, which must be read in conjunction with the development of my second point below. Let *N*, national, stand for unitary government. Let F, federal, equal confederate form of government. For Madison, as I suspect for others of his time, N plus F equalled something of a question mark or, at most specific, a "composite" form of government. Subsequent generations of Americans have had to fill out the character of this composite form. Our Founders left us with many perplexing and unanswered questions.

For a complete understanding of the nature of our tensions we must turn to another aspect of the Framer's thought. *The Federalist* essays provided no "constitutional morality" to instruct with any great precision as to the relative spheres of authority for the State and national governments. To be sure any number of statements convey a crude idea—for example, purely local matters should be handled locally; national matters, nationally. Madison in Number 45 seemed to have such a formula in mind when he wrote that the powers of the national government

. . . will be exercised principally on external objects, as war, peace, negotiation, and foreign commerce; with which last the power of taxation will, for the most part, be connected. The powers reserved to the several States will extend to all the objects which, in the ordinary course of affairs, concern the lives, liberties, and properties of the people, and the internal order, improvement, and prosperity of the State.

So also did Hamilton in Number 33, although he was mighty stingy in specifying powers reserved to the States. As a matter of fact, throughout the early years of the Constitution and to this day, the "national-local" rule of thumb has been appealed to as a standard for determination of the relative spheres of national-State jurisdictions.

But such a rule, on its face reasonable, falls far short of providing answers. Just as one can argue convincingly that specification of necessary and proper powers would be a virtual impossibility, so too, exact determination and specification of what is a local matter as distinct from a national matter is far too difficult and subtle a task to be handled in a written constitution.

If it is not sensible to divide substantive powers using the national-local rule, is it possible to specify some procedure whereby disputes between the two jurisdictions (State and national) can be resolved? The answer is theoretically, "Yes." But because the Framers had no conception of federalism as we understand the term, we search in vain for any precise constitutional morality as to who is to decide in the event of conflict between the two governments. The answers in *The Federalist* vary. For example:

(Number 39) . . . In controversies relating to the boundary between the two jurisdictions, the tribunal which is ultimately to decide, is to be established under the general government.

(Number 46) . . . The ultimate authority, wherever the derivative may be found, resides in the people alone, and that it will not depend merely on the comparative ambition or address of the different governments, whether either, or which of them, will be able to enlarge its sphere of jurisdiction at the expense of the other. Truth, no less than decency, requires that the event in every case should be supposed to depend on the sentiments and the sanction of their common constituents. . . .

. . . Ambitious encroachments of the federal government on the authority of the State governments would not excite the opposition of a single State, or of a few States only. They would be the signals of general alarm. Every government would espouse a common cause. A correspondence would be opened. Plans of resistance would be concerted. One spirit would animate and conduct the whole.

How to explain the failure of the Founders to provide some definite morality concerning the settlement of disputes between the two jurisdictions? I would surmise that just as the modern concept of federalism was unknown to them, so too was any conception of divided sovereignty. Put otherwise the Founders could no more conceive of a political system with *divided sovereignty* than my good Jesuit friends can conceive of a world without God.

Such a speculation is certainly not unreasonable. Hobbes and Locke, among many others, had maintained essentially the same proposition, namely, that sovereignty is indivisible. So too had later theorists of diverse persuasions, like, for example, Calhoun and John Stuart Mill. In sum there is every reason to believe that the notion of divided sovereignty was not simply unheard of but no part of the ethos. *Elliot's Debates* demonstrate that the most effective antifederalist arguments center on the very proposition that sovereignty cannot be divided.

The antifederalists were sniffing in the right direction. The whole idea of divided sovereignty is on the face of it absurd. It is a chimerical idea unless the parties involved, as is sometimes the case in marriage, develop through prolonged and subtle interchange some understanding of what their spheres of authority are —the wife decides to buy a new car, and the husband chooses the color. No wonder then we lack an established morality with respect to the relative powers of the State and national governments, for the Founders could not possibly have devised a political system that would both divide sovereignty and operate effectively. In conflictive situations either the State or the national government must have its way. There is no escaping this fact.

Having this in mind, we should not be surprised in the slightest that our contemporaries talk about "cooperative" federalism, "creative" federalism or for that matter any other kind of federalism. Why should we expect any political leader or scholar to speak otherwise? They can no more handle the problems associated with divided sovereignty than could their forebears. The problems are simply insoluble when the two jurisdictions find themselves in a state of conflict.

Predictably and logically in a country which considers the written constitution as central to its governmental system, very many of the studies of federalism are legalistic in nature. If in fact sovereignty cannot be divided—*one* authority prevails, the other yields—and if one wishes, as most do, to provide peaceful and orderly solutions to conflict of authorities, then, in the absence of the most miraculous political skills to effect accommodation, one turns to processes of law, to the courts whose business it has been for centuries to decide conflicting claims, and specifically in the instant case, to the Supreme Court, which, since

McCullough v. *Maryland,* has resolved conflicts of national and State laws.

Such legalistic studies of national-state relations have merit. However, they do serve to take our eyes off the ball, because they preclude consideration of the full potentialities and merits of the crazy-quilt structure we call "federal." We can put the matter this way: The Constitution gives broad freedom with respect to the vertical distribution of powers. There are few rules concerning the substantive division of powers and practically none concerning adjudication of conflict. We should, I think, be thankful for all of this. We are entitled and even obligated to make of federalism pretty much what we will. How best can we proceed about this task?

II

A. It could be argued that in drawing the appropriate boundary lines between jurisdictions we ought to place a high premium on efficiency.

Obviously any such contention would be extremely difficult to prove, for there is the difficult question of whether "efficiency" has any meaning, operational or otherwise. Suppose we agree that it comes down to "maximum output" for "minimum input." Next we confront the problem of measurement. Usually, because of the complex nature of the operation being studied, there can be no satisfactory decision on *what* and *how* to measure.

Some political scientists have suggested that centralization, which would involve at the extreme elimination of State and local governments, would provide greater efficiency. A "milder" or less extreme form of this position is that county, township and special districts ought to be either eliminated or unified in some fashion. One of my contemporaries in graduate school built a physical model of the overlapping jurisdictions in Indianapolis, Indiana. I must confess it was most impressive, extending with multicolored plastic sheets from floor to ceiling. After viewing it, one could not argue that our Federal system, as it presently operates, promotes efficiency.[3]

Also the increasingly large proportion of our population that can be termed "highly mobile" would be unlikely to deem our federal structure efficient. A morning or afternoon spent standing in line to obtain a valid driver's license because there are no reciprocal agreements in driver qualifications among many States hardly symbolizes efficiency of any sort. Countless such examples could be cited.

On the other hand the Federal government does, because of its accessibility to the best sources of revenue, take most out of our pockets. What is returned in the grant-in-aid programs is significantly less than the total contribution.[4] There is, in other words, an "overhead" or "cover" charge. Whether this charge would be greater or less if the same or similar functions were performed by the State or local governments is certainly debatable. Yet in our considerations of this and like questions we have tended to paint ourselves into a corner. More precisely there is no a priori reason to believe that the present substantive division of power and functions between State and national government promotes efficiency. Partly because of an overly legalistic approach to federalism, we have overlooked and ignored—granting efficiency to be our prime goal—prudential approaches to questions of State-national relations.

B. If perchance too much emphasis has been placed on the efficiency argument, few if any will fault me for directing their attention to the "freedom" or "liberty" line of thinking. While the efficiency and freedom arguments in justification of our present federal system do merge, sometimes almost imperceptibly, they differ significantly in thrust.

---

[3] We must recognize that no political society to date has regarded efficiency as its end value. Thankfully so, most would say.

[4] Obviously, some individuals get back more than they contribute. This is one of the very objects of many of our grant-in-aid programs. What I am saying, however, is this: X amount of dollars are extracted from the people for these programs. X minus the overhead is then redistributed according to formula.

The freedom line runs something as follows: There are problems of a peculiarly local nature that are best settled or handled at the local level. I can't prove that this is the case, nor can all of our survey data in either the comparative or American government areas, because there has been a distinct tendency to ask questions of a "random" sample that are discrete and of such nature as to preclude any investigation of this dimension.

That a great number of Americans find this argument appealing is beyond dispute. Just as many feel that various "functional" interests (labor, business, etc.) ought to have a great say with respect to legislation affecting their respective interests, so too there is a strong belief in all sections of the country that the "geographic" dimension ought to be taken into account. How many times, for instance, have we heard from the lips of perfectly decent and honorable southern whites that northern whites "do not understand the racial problems of the South"? Or, for but another example, don't many, including the highest elected officials, believe that the metropolitan areas in which they live have unique problems or at least problems more acute than other areas of similar composition and size?

How can we use our structure to maximize the freedom of either individual citizens or localities? How best can we insure the retention of the widest possible latitude of choice in handling "local" problems? Certainly a strong case can be made that Negroes in the South were for a long time deprived of basic freedoms because we as a people at one time believed in allowing a great autonomy to State and local units. The formula that is attractive to so many, "local problems should be handled locally," has operated in the past, from the vantage point of both the average American Negro and those sympathetic with his plight, to deprive a significant portion of our population in certain geographic areas of freedoms enjoyed by the majority of the population residing in other areas. On the other hand once (for whatever reason, including "civil rights") control is taken away from local or State authorities, there is no arresting the process of centralization.

The problems involved in using maximization of freedom as a principle for demarcating State-national jurisdictions seem insurmountable. Why? If we try to attack the problem substantively, to mark out those substantive powers best exercised by the respective governments, our task seems hopeless from the outset. If we attempt to approach the problem procedurally, that is, to specify what institutions or combinations of institutions should make a determination in specific cases as to how best freedom can be maximized, we will soon find ourselves ensnarled in endless controversies over the meaning and nature of the Constitution, controversies which can never be authoritatively settled. Also we may safely assume that much of the debate over how a decision should be made will really be predicted or based on the achievement or preservation of a highly valued substantive end. Witness the Lincoln-Douglas debates.

III

I do not mean to imply from what I have said thus far that there is no hope for the alleviation of tensions which have necessarily surrounded the operation of our Federal system. If federalism in its present-day meaning is to serve the function of maximizing the values of efficiency and/or freedom, State-local-national relations and conflicts must be handled with a high degree of flexibility. What is meant by "flexibility"? Principally the following:

A. We must not assume that there are "given" or predetermined answers to the conflicts that inevitably occur. This is not to deny that there are meaningful divisions of power between the national and State governments. The national government has a fairly well defined area of exclusive jurisdiction. Madison, as we have seen, drew lines that are somewhat meaningful. But at best he only dealt with half of the matter. He did not specify with precision the formula (nor indeed did any of the Founding Fathers) for the settlement of disputes on those matters and in those areas where controversy has actually abounded in our republic.

B. There should be, if we place a high value on efficiency and maximization of freedom, strong guarantees that in the resolution of conflict between State and national authorities or in their mutual efforts to solve a common problem the involved local or State interests are allowed to participate effectively in the decision-making process. Why? For at least the following two reasons: First there is a greater likelihood that the local peculiarities of circumstance can be taken into account, and second a knowledge of such local peculiarities will almost certainly lead to the emergence of alternative solutions and policies regarding the problems at hand.

What, however, is effective participation? Again most probably we cannot ever hope to answer this. Few would subscribe to the application of Calhoun's doctrine of "concurrent majorities," wherein each significant geographical interest would possess a veto on any given matter affecting it. Perhaps in a very genuine sense we have as a nation already provided for this effective participation through our formal and informal structures and procedures. At the "informal" level we must recognize the importance of political parties in sluicing into our structure and deliberations representation of purely local interests. Critics of our party system are more than likely to argue that parties perform this function to excess. At the formal level States and localities form the base of our representational and electoral structures and processes. It might well be that we have gone as far as we can in our purely political processes to insure such participation.

C. We should, to be prudential in the advancement of our goals, have some means readily available for the correction of egregious errors once a problem has presumably been "solved" or once we have embarked upon a given policy that proves to be highly unsatisfactory.

And (*D*) the means for adjustment and/or adjudication of conflict, once a decision has been made with respect to any given issue or policy, must somehow be made "proportionate" to the "depth" and "scope" of the controversy or problem. This would mean, among other things, that those (and here we are assuming that the national government or its agencies will in reality make the binding decisions in national-State matters), who make the laws and set down broad policy will allow administrators a great deal of flexibility so that unforeseen circumstances and conditions stemming from geographical differences can be handled without recourse to the legislative process.

The doctrine of separation of powers embodies within it a presumption that certain functions of government ought to be divided. Just as the legislative assembly cannot possibly be expected to interpret its own laws whenever an individual case arises under these laws, so too must there be some agency (executive and/or judicial) that will draw the fine lines and make the necessary subtle adjustments in matters pertaining to the problems arising from our federal structure. We can and probably should expect Congress and the President in their lawmaking capacities to set forth the broad goals and outlines of policy within which such adjustments are to be made. More: We should expect the branches to alter or abolish programs that seem unfeasible or unworkable. However, prudence would dictate that a certain amount of latitude or "shimmy" be allowed.[5]

These relatively broad standards set forth to maximize efficiency and freedom and to reduce tensions inherent in the Federal system are not as well defined as they might be. Nor are they exhaustive. I would submit, however, that a majority of thoughtful individuals would after a fashion probably subscribe to the principles they embody. In fact for many these crude standards might seem either bland or airy. So much the better for what I have to say next.

IV

As noted earlier, much of our study of federalism in the United States is legalistically oriented. There are telling criticisms of this approach. To the extent that such an approach orients our think-

---

[5] Most of our grant-in-aid programs probably operate along the lines I have suggested. When they do depart from this general standard, we once again find ourselves in political turmoils.

ing about national-State-local problems, it serves to inhibit it and most probably results in the maximization of tensions in the political system.

First, and this is an empirical matter, do the people of our republic really pay any attention to the Supreme Court's decisions in national-State controversies? In asking this I do not mean to stress the fact that most people are ignorant of the substance of the Court's decisions.[6] Rather, when the Court does come down hard on the States or localities, using perforce in most cases the "equal protection" or "due process" clauses of the Fourteenth Amendment, do the people—or for that matter the local authorities—obey? Although all the evidence is not in on this matter, there is some reason to believe, particularly with respect to the desegregation and prayer decisions, that there has been less than full and/or willing compliance.

But resistance to the Court's decisions is no valid reason in and of itself to be highly critical of the Court. Few if any would deny that it must play some role in the resolution of conflict between the national and State governments. But what role? How? On what grounds?

I would submit for consideration that the Supreme Court and lower federal courts have encountered resistance in these areas for two reasons. First the courts, unlike our "political organs" of government (Congress, the President, and even the bureaucracy), are in a very poor position, because of the very nature of the judicial process, to treat the problems arising from federalism in the flexible manner described above. Second and more important the Supreme Court in these very touchy and sensitive areas has seen fit to peg its decisions to the Constitution. I will dwell only on this second point.

To the extent that the Supreme Court insists on relying on the Constitution for resolution of conflicts in the areas I have mentioned, we have no reason to believe that it will operate in such a

---

[6] Some political scientists and sociologists make a good living simply by periodically reminding us about the political ignorance of the American people.

manner as to maximize those values usually associated with federalism (as we today understand the term) like diversity, efficiency, freedom or what have you. On the contrary what we are most likely to encounter in the Court's decisions are *ex cathedra* pronouncements about what the authors of the Bill of Rights "really" intended, or what the somewhat vague and elusive concepts of "equal protection" and "due process" "really" mean. And when we begin to accept this approach, I submit, we have already lost sight of the prudence and flexibility so necessary for a viable federal system of government. Hence we should not be surprised at a certain amount of resistance at the local levels to the Court's decisions. Because a majority of the residents in any given locality do not want their children in the public schools to say prayers voluntarily, should we then say that such voluntary prayers are constitutionally forbidden in all public schools, regardless of the religious composition and preferences of the parents? Is this a prudential or flexible solution to the problem? Another example: Many who are known to be quite sympathetic with the Court's rulings on integration are now beginning to have doubts. Not doubts about the morality or justice of the decisions, but rather in the broader context of asking, Do such decisions help or hinder the desired advancement of the Negro in American society? Many, even those keenly interested in the cause of "civil rights," would argue at this time that what the Negro child needs most is a first-class education that will enable him to compete in our highly competitive society. The question then of whether the schools are integrated or not is secondary and tangential. But we are compelled to ask, Has not the Supreme Court boxed us in?

My point throughout has been simply this: To the extent that such judicial decisions rest upon distinctly constitutional grounds, no matter on what exact provision, our political leadership, much in the habit of trying to accommodate and placate various interests, loses the flexibility necessary to make incremental decisions or needed adjustments that might well serve to achieve desired goals more quickly and with less friction. Yes, I readily grant, the Supreme Court can, to use an old football idiom, reverse its field. But such reversals—and the Court has made them before—are quite costly in more ways than one. Aside from involving a certain amount of delay (which in some cases has been costly to our society) and creating unnecessary tensions, they also serve to undermine the prestige and status of the Court.

But we have lost more than the ability to handle State-Federal problems in a flexible manner through our excessive emphasis upon legalisms. This emphasis has served, as I mentioned earlier, to inhibit rational dialogue concerning those issues associated with our federal system. Why so? The root cause, it seems to me, resides in the existence of a written constitution and the reverence we are accustomed to pay to it. Surely those familiar with the origins of our republic would not argue that a written document of some sort was not absolutely necessary if the Colonies were to unite on an effective basis. Above all, unlike England, we had not evolved through slow and subtle processes institutions, rules and traditions in the political and social sphere that would serve to obviate the need for a written document. But because of our need for a constitution we should not be distracted from recognizing its significance in the subsequent development of our republic and the disputes over its meaning that have and will continue to plague us.

How does a written constitution inhibit us in the manner I have suggested? Precisely because it nourishes and cultivates a mentality, attitude or "mind set" that believes our basic constitutional questions have been or can be settled by reference to the basic document and its amendments. In other words such an approach encourages us to go back to that contract which specifies the obligations of one party to another, much in the same manner that individuals haul out their warranties when their cars or appliances break down. And once one makes up his mind on the crucial issue of who should decide when a dispute does arise (or who defers to his presumed intellectual superiors on this point), we know that a very critical decision has been made. Insofar then as we regard the resolution of national-State conflict

as the peculiar province of the Court, we are necessarily chan-
nelled into or "bounded" by a legalistic framework. I hope to
have shown, however, that these legalistic parameters (in many
instances leaning heavily on questionable interpretations of constitutional provisions) are not suited to the problems associated
with our Federal system.[7] There is nothing in the Constitution,
The Federalist or any of our basic documents even suggesting
that subsequent generations of Americans should not handle
questions arising from this vertical distribution of powers in a
prudent manner. Indeed the Preamble to our Constitution is
proof of this.

   And, I conclude, the sooner we come to recognize this fact, the
better off we are going to be.

BIBLIOGRAPHICAL NOTES

   I will confine myself to the early period and give only references to
primary materials that will introduce the student to the problems surrounding our federal system.

   There is much in *Debates on the Adoption of the Federal Constitution,* ed. Jonathan Elliot (5 vol.), important for an understanding of
early thinking about State-Federal relations. The student should look
over these debates himself to pick out the pertinent materials. *Documents Illustrative of the Formation of the Union of the American States,*
ed. Charles C. Tansill, is a readily accessible one-volume compilation of
the "notes," including Madison's, taken at the time of the Philadelphia
convention. *The Federalist,* of course, should be read in its entirety, although some portions—as I have indicated in the text—are more pertinent than others. John C. Calhoun's *A Disquisition on Government* and
A Discourse on the Constitution and Government of the United States
are required reading for a student interested in this area. The so-called

   ---

   [7] The English probably have a more viable and efficient federal system
than we do. And it may well be that their success is due in some measure to
the fact that the notion of dual sovereignty never corrupted their thinking.
At any rate there are no inhibitions introduced in their decision-making
process regarding distribution of powers between the central and subordinate governments.

Resolutions of the States of Kentucky and Virginia relative to the Alien and Sedition Acts are also must reading. So too are the responses of the various States to the Virginia Resolution. These works are readily available in almost any comprehensive compilation of documents. John Taylor's works are highly relevant, particularly his *Constitution Construed, and Constitutions Vindicated.* Portions of Joseph Story's multivolume work, *Commentaries on the Constitution of the United States,* should be read in conjunction with Calhoun and Taylor. Finally the best of early congressional thinking about the problems associated with federalism as taken from the *Annals* is to be found in *A Second Federalist,* ed. Charles Hyneman and George Carey.

VALERIE EARLE
Georgetown University

CREATIVE FEDERALISM:
POLITICS AND
POLICY FOR
URBAN PROBLEMS

THROUGH MUCH OF the flood of literature dealing with urban problems—whether one is reading the hearings of congressional committees on the war on poverty, crime control, water and air pollution, or sociological studies of urban minorities, or the work of political scientists on local government and intergovernmental relations, or reports in the press dealing with the probable effects of recent local elections, such as that of Mayor Richard Hatcher in Gary, Indiana,[1] one question recurs, one concern is expressed almost uniformly: How to get decisions, when so many forces seemingly work against their being made?

A very important component of the forces working to make difficult the taking of decisions on urban problems is the large number of independent governmental jurisdictions existing within the metropolitan areas of the United States.[2] Many people

[1] Mayor Hatcher's concerns, not surprisingly, are jobs, education, housing, an improved welfare program. Yet the largest employer in his city is an absentee employer, and both the county and the State control or significantly influence the raising and spending of money for education, public housing and welfare.

[2] The annual publication of the U.S. Department of Commerce, *The Statistical Abstract of the United States,* provides current information on the number of such units.

argue that effective action is not possible short of some means of circumventing the separate jurisdictions, perhaps by imposing a level of metropolis-wide government, perhaps through the special-district device, or perhaps through a council of governments, voluntarily undertaken or stimulated by Federal grant requirements which make mandatory cooperation in planning and may in time make mandatory a considerable degree of joint action.

Although such cooperation seems to make good sense, local governments and those who run them have been plainly reluctant to yield any part of their authority to decide, even if only to decide to do nothing. The "hot summers" of recent years may spur a change of mind on this score, but it is probably safe to argue that joint planning and action will become reality only if Federal grant administrators become sufficiently insistent that such action is a condition precedent to the making of a grant; if dynamic leadership (perhaps "charismatic" is the more appropriate word) arises from within the urban complex; if the proper vehicle (a council of governments perhaps) is found; and if the States for whom many have entertained little hope for a very long time can galvanize themselves (and turn up the necessary revenues) to act and to prod and to help their local governments to act.

All of these may in the end be required. It is the central argument of this essay that the single essential requirement is not any of the above, but rather the development of political community in the metropolitan areas of the country. Without this none of the above can achieve very much; without it perhaps none can even occur.

In a recent seminar discussion of the council of government approach to the solution of metropolitan problems, a number of public officials, Federal and local, elective and appointive, made very clear their overwhelming concern to find the magical formula by which to prompt cooperation.[3] The lecturer, a professor

---

[3] The discussion took place in the spring of 1967 at the Washington, D.C., Center for Metropolitan Studies as one of a number of seminar discussions on urban problems.

of government, had described the history of "ABAG" (the Association of Bay Area Governments, San Francisco) which, formed some years ago, has grown to include most of the local governments in the area and so far has withstood some fairly severe divergence of interest among the members. No explanation was offered—or could be—for the survival of the Association, although its employment of a fulltime director, energetic, imaginative and perceptive (at least in understanding that his job and the "job" of the Association were largely undefined and could be formed by him), was clearly of some importance.

An official of the Department of Transportation put the first question. "Professor, do you think you can evolve a methodology for encouraging formation of regional governments, or associations of government? I'd like to know something about that." Then a question and comment by a local government official: "Who decides which government gets what under the supermarket offerings in the Model Cities program, and other such recent Federal acts? What is the relationship between applicants and grants? Does the regional body review all applications and decide which has high priority, which should be combined? We've got a Council of Governments here, but it doesn't do this kind of thing." (With some inference that the thought of its trying would not be unqualifiedly welcome.) A rejoinder by the Department of Transportation: "I'd hate to referee those fights." And a worried comment from the director of the Council of Governments, "How do we program all this for more than one government?"

The last question was asked, although in different words, by several who were interested in knowing how it might be possible to move from regional planning of highways and sewage disposal systems (comparatively old hat) to regional planning of housing, schools, urban development.[4]

---

[4] This is not to argue that conflicting interests do not any longer affect the Federal-State highway and sewage plant programs, but rather that these long-established grant programs have, because of age and the comparatively settled character of the technology involved, faced and resolved a large number of problems. One can argue that in the two programs there is nothing very new under the sun. In contrast the urgency about beginning

The "Professor" had no answers. He volunteered the prediction that the requirement in recent Federal legislation for regional planning as a condition for receiving Federal grants, reinforced by Title II of the Model Cities Act, offering incentives for regional cooperation in the drawing of a plan, might remake the character of the Federal system.[5] He hastily added that he had in the past mistakenly thought that other developments would significantly alter American federalism.

Two familiar themes interweave throughout the preceding exchange. There is first aspiration to rational decision, made through rational forms and processes: In metropolitan areas, people do not live and work in the compartments described by government boundaries; hence public decisions affecting them cannot be made rationally by local governments, but only by some mechanism reflecting the scope of the crosshatch pattern of living and working.[6] There is also the driving impulse to get on with the job, to get decisions made and projects begun, an urgency about progress in resolving urban problems.

---

to find solutions for problems of housing, education, economic opportunity, urban renewal—and racial inequality is a very large element in the urgency —and the thoroughly unsettled state of social and economic technology necessary for solutions make these rapidly developing areas of public policy extremely complex, and the politics of intergovernmental program development and administration is filled with surprises.

[5] In the stated desire to remake American federalism, there is the implicit assumption that, in its present state, federalism "makes no sense," that is, State and local boundaries are artificial and anachronistic, and the multiplicity of local jurisdictions ensures an endless pulling and hauling among interests, to the detriment of the good or rational public program. The thesis of Morton Grodzins, that this untidiness, is a strength— or, as Grodzins put it, the vices of the system are its virtues—is therefore rejected by those who hold this view of rationality. See Grodzins, *The American System—A New View of Government in the United States,* ed. Daniel Elazar (Chicago: Rand McNally & Co., 1966), p. 7. Title II of the Demonstration Cities and Metropolitan Development Act of 1966 (PL 89–754) begins with the words: "The national welfare is directly dependent upon sound and orderly development and reorganization of metropolitan areas. The task is handicapped by the complexity of governmental services required, the multiplicity of governmental jurisdictions and agencies, and the inadequacy of existing administrative arrangements for intergovernmental cooperation."

[6] From such a position one may easily move to the argument that the "compartments" represented by States obstruct rationality.

By inference there is anxious conjecture that rationality will lose out to the very strong impulse to get things done; but in the long run everything will come unstuck *unless* rationality becomes the prime goal.

I

RATIONALITY AND POLITICS

The thought becomes very clear that once again there is the real possibility that "rationality" and "politics" (or political processes) will be defined as though mutually exclusive. The logic of areawide government is so overpowering that at almost any moment "everyone" must see and accept it—or reject or ignore it at very considerable peril. So reason many specialists in urban affairs. That peril to important and widely held interests might be involved in the launching of a new government to displace, at least in some significant degree, existing governments—that rationality in some meaning could then be involved in reluctance to undertake the launching—these are facts of life safely ignored by academics but not by politicians.[7]

The thesis that good government is government without politics is an old one. In municipal government much of the drive for new forms, that is, commission government, the city manager, came from those who argued that *form* made all the difference, or that form could absolutely control and direct force (assure good decisions by eliminating, by a rabbit-out-of-hat technique one supposes, the influence of all the bad political forces).

So also much of the rationalization for the special district is drawn from the premise that it is desirable and possible to get a function, like education, out of politics. Get education out of the hands of the mayor and council members and deliver it over to the philosopher kings in educational administration, in the PTA's

---

[7] For example, of the twelve papers given at the Inter-University Faculty Seminar on Metropolitan Studies of the Washington Center, Spring, 1967, only three dealt with politics and the policy process. The interests of the academics involved were clearly in something other than politics.

and in the specially selected school boards and you will assuredly have a quality product. That the meaning of "quality product" is not settled and may never be, and that the means of attaining quality are not agreed upon and may never be, have been demonstrated countless times, very recently in Washington, D.C., where, it is fair to assume, someone supposed that to provide for appointment of the school board by a body of judges was bound to give an unusual degree of detachment from the corrupting influence of politics and a consequent capacity to perceive and settle upon the true, the right and the good. The decision in Hobson v. Hanson, cited below, asserts in substance that the Washington, D.C. School Board has been highly responsive to "the establishment's" political views, and insensitive to the public good in denying equal educational opportunity to the inner city. On April 22, 1968, the President signed into law P.L. 90–292 Act of Congress providing for an electoral D.C. school board.

In the general study of public administration the removal of politics from the sphere of the administrator was a dominant goal up to the Second World War.[8] Then perhaps because so many academics were drawn into government bureaucracies, there gradually came awareness that at least high-level administrators could not escape some involvement in politics, in policy debate. Neither the President nor Congress was prepared to leave them alone, both President and Congress wished to draw upon their experience, and they themselves earnestly desired to have a dialogue with President and Congress, in part because of their commitment to achievement of policy goals, in part because of their instinct for survival.[9]

That the "ideal" of government without politics is still alive is shown quite clearly in much of the writing and talking about the Planning-Program-Budgeting System (PPBS). When Arthur

---

[8] See Dwight Waldo, *The Administrative State* (New York: Ronald, 1948), esp. chap. x.

[9] See, for example, Norton Long, "Power and Administration," *Public Administration Review* IX (Autumn, 1949), pp. 257–264.

Smithies wrote of PPBS, he emphasized its usefulness in facilitating the making of difficult choices, necessary because "any government is limited by the scarcity of resources." PPBS should make possible choosing "with as full knowledge as possible of the implications of alternatives . . . [PPBS] involves the application of new analytical techniques as an aid to the exercise of the human judgment on which choices must ultimately rest." [10] In sum Smithies claimed for PPBS that it can provide more rigorous analysis by which to determine the probable outcome of diverse courses in public policy. He did not assert that the selection of a particular course is *determined* by what the analysis shows. For example, that course X is cheaper than course Y *may* determine the businessman's conduct, but public policy is not exclusively concerned with this kind of efficiency.

In its edition of Thursday, July 6, 1967, *The Washington Post,* in an editorial entitled "Nobler and Cheaper," asserted:

Rational budgeting and cost effectiveness may well turn out to be the most radical and disruptive political idea in the next decade of city government. . . . The past effect of the famous programming-budgeting system in Defense is as nothing compared with its future effect upon the city halls.

In Washington's District Building, for example, the budget is an annual monument to the irrational element in public administration. . . . Accurate cost analysis would instantly show that the city's crowded orphanage, Junior Village, is not only far more harmful to children than any of the numerous alternatives, but a good deal more expensive as well. . . . Cost analysis would further demonstrate that almost any other way of spending the mental health funds would be more beneficial than to put them into a great swollen custodial institution like St. Elizabeth's. . . . At last we may see Congress driven to adopt sound policy for the city, not because it is nobler but because it is cheaper and more effective.[11]

---

[10] "Conceptual Framework for the Program Budget," in *Program Budgeting—Program Analysis and the Federal Budget,* ed. David Novick, abridged version of a Rand study (Washington, D.C.: Government Printing Office, 1965), p. 4.

[11] P. A18.

From the foregoing the following erroneous conclusions concerning the use of PPBS can fairly be drawn: (1) That it provides exact measurements of the harm done children and the mentally ill by confinement in an overcrowded institution and entirely accurate comparison with the outcomes of other means of providing for these groups. (2) That PPBS can describe what is more effective policy—as though the definition of effective were beyond argument. (3) That PPBS can indicate that course which is cheapest—but cheapest in terms of what? Human life? Happiness? Dollars? Social strife? (4) That PPBS will indicate with compelling force what the course of action must be.

The assumption that Congress, if only it can be brought to drop its wrongheaded ways for PPBS, will be shown what is cheaper and will then adopt that policy is made quite clear. But if Congress were really interested in what is cheaper in terms of dollars spent, above all else, it could opt for sterilization of mothers who produce more than one illegitimate child likely to end up in Junior Village or on the swollen ADC rolls, or even for all members of those groups in the population among whom the rate of illegitimacy is highest, and for "mercy killing" of the mentally defective.

In their essay "Problems, Limitations, and Risks," in *Program Budgeting*, edited by David Novick, Professors Melvin Anshen and Roland N. McKean wrote of the Department of Defense design of its program budget in 1961: Having asked the question, "What is the Department trying to do?" DOD found a "viable and acceptable answer . . . in such categories as Strategic Retaliatory Forces, Continental Air and Missile Defense Forces, Airlift and Sealift Forces, and Research and Development. . . . It is by no means clear that comparable and acceptable answers are readily forthcoming for the rest of the federal government. As the political campaign in progress in the fall of 1964 suggested, 'What is Government for?' can be a question of philosophy about which strong disagreements boil." [12]

---

[12] Novick, *op. cit.*, p. 220.

Although more sophisticated than the *Post* editorial writer, Professors Anshen and McKean are equally confident that PPB can surmount those strong disagreements in philosophy. A problem in public policy is not to be resolved by

Solomonic wisdom. If there is a "right" answer, it will be discovered only through study of the logics and logistics of the federal decision process. . . . The existing organization structure and existing decision processes may not significantly assist, in fact, may only obfuscate. . . . The bureaucratic structure that is now in being . . . is largely the product of an historic response to political pressures and expedient adjustments thereto, or, in some instances, to haphazard acts of creation for the most part unresponsive to the planned analysis of needs of efficient decision design. Considering the circumstances of its invention, there is little reason for the bureaucratic structure to reflect a logical decision-determined architecture. In fact, out of the existing structure and its operating habits, must be expected resistance and opposition, corresponding to the familiar human disposition to protect established seats of power and procedures made honorable by the mere facts of existence and custom.[13]

II

THE LOGIC OF METROPOLITAN GOVERNMENT

Although the preceding was written to describe the promise of PPBS and the resistance to be expected from those whose positions were created in consequence of "political pressures and expedient adjustments thereto" rather than logic and a rational perception of good decisions, it might well have been written by any of a number of students of metropolitan government.

Rational, that is, areawide, transportation systems, housing plans, educational systems, recreations programs are usually described as givens upon which all men agree when they see clearly, think rationally and act disinterestedly and benevolently.[14]

But what is logical for the suburbanite about giving up what he

[13] *Ibid.*, p. 221.

[14] To paraphrase Walter Lippmann, *The Public Philosophy* (Boston, Little, Brown & Co., 1955), p. 42.

knows, warts and all, for what he cannot know, can hardly speculate about? The toughest problems are in the central city; their effects upon the suburbs are as yet indirect. Within the central city there may not be visible an adequate supply of political leaders who have demonstrated the capacity to get things done despite the conflict of diverse interests, or by managing to harness them through satisfying all somewhat and alienating none totally.[15] No one knows whether the intelligence, the political skills, the personal strengths of character of inner-city leaders would be sufficient to a role of responsible leadership in a self-governing, thoroughly pluralist community.

The suburbanite may see quite clearly that his family and his property enjoy a known degree of protection in what is, but that this situation would almost surely change if governmental arrangements were to change. He may be deeply persuaded of a moral obligation to help the less fortunate, but equally persuaded that there are, there must be, ways of helping other than by making family and status vulnerable to unpredictable, quite likely uncontrollable, decision-making bodies. A leap into metropolitan government—or even into an influential council of metropolitan governments—could endanger the good life parents want for children and for themselves. That moral obligation is involved in assuring the good life for one's dependents is unarguable; that the good life includes for most a good education, decent housing, health, safety of person and property *now* is equally unarguable.

The suburbanite may be willing to pay higher taxes to finance programs for the center city and its disadvantaged inhabitants (some will argue that he can and should pay more, much more); he may be willing to increase his contribution in money and

---

[15] Because of its lack of home rule Washington, D.C., provides an especially acute example of a city in which little or no "general purpose" leadership has developed; rather there have been leaders who could claim to represent special groups. The reorganization accomplished in late 1967, although it does not provide home rule, may have brought to the District a quality of top leadership which can make a difference, even perhaps to the point of facilitating a transition to home rule.

service to private voluntary organizations seeking to alleviate center city problems. So long as these alternatives remain, why should he commit himself to an experiment in governmental form?

The gloomy prediction that, given the fragmentation of governmental jurisdictions, essential services in the metropolis would inevitably collapse has not been fulfilled. Fragmentation absent—they *might* be better, depending entirely upon who makes decisions in response to whom. They might also, from the point of view of the better off, be worse—as some residents of Washington, D.C., assuredly would assert to be the case were Judge Skelly Wright's recent decision on public schools in the District of Columbia to have areawide force.[16]

III

Politics and Community Interest

The words above, ". . . depending entirely upon who makes decisions in response to whom," suggest the key element in the solution of metropolitan or any other problems, that is, politics. One of the most widely recognized modern definitions of politics —who gets what, when and how—is so unabashedly rooted in a conception of decision as the product of conflict, so matter of fact in acceptance of the constancy of struggle for power as to put off a wide variety of people, not excluding, unfortunately, many political scientists.[17] With Aaron Wildavsky one must lament that it appears almost to be necessary to go out of the field of political science to find an appreciation of the primacy of politics.[18]

---

[16] *Hobson* v. *Hanson*, U.S. Federal District Court for the District of Columbia, Civil Action 82–66. Also see J. Skelly Wright, "Public School Desegregation: Legal Remedies for De Facto Segregation," *New York University Law Review*, XL, No. 2 (April, 1965), p. 305. Judge Wright makes the argument for disregarding local government boundaries where necessary to accomplish desegregation.

[17] Harold Lasswell, *Politics: Who Gets What, When, How* (New York: McGraw-Hill Book Co., 1936).

[18] Aaron Wildavsky, "The Political Economy of Efficiency: Cost-Benefit Analysis, Systems Analysis, and Program Budgeting," *Public Administra-*

Perhaps a return to the ancient derivation of the word may not only alleviate the apprehension of many who cannot bear to see struggle and conflict as basic continuing parts of life, but may also emphasize that aspect of politics which so clearly is of the very essence in beginning to make progress on metropolitan problems—that politics is the single word descriptive of all the diverse activity of the polity, the polis, the city-state, the *community*. To separate "politics" from "community" was an impossibility for Aristotle's political man. Group theorists and the more recent political theorists to the contrary, it has been and remains bedrock in the Western political tradition that politics is activity carried on by those who have a community of interest—some degree of community about some kind of interest—while at the same time having divergence about other kinds of interests. The sense of community has been strong enough to compel agreement or accommodation.

It is very clear that fragmentation of governments in a metropolitan area is not the major factor accounting for divergence of interests and for conflict protecting interests, as the engineering of a single metropolitan-wide government would not create effective community. A higher degree of homogeneity of social, economic and cultural ways ought to enhance a sense of community. Metropolitan government could be an unexpected payoff from a genuinely effective war on poverty in the center city but not the other way round. An increased supply of political skills among suburbanites and center-city residents ought also to make possible a larger sense of community.

To rephrase, consciousness of common good in which all share is the basis of effective cooperation. That consciousness can hardly be a significant element influencing decisions so long as the center city is populated by a growingly alienated, long-disad-

tion Review XXVI (December, 1966), pp. 292–310. Wildavsky remarks, "One is driven to a philosopher like Paul Diesing to find the case for the political: '. . . The political problem is always basic and prior to the others. . . .' There is hardly a political scientist who would claim half as much." P. 308. The reference is to Diesing's book, *Reason in Society* (Champaign: University of Illinois Press, 1962), p. 228.

vantaged minority, which, each summer, riots in savage and
mindless fashion, thereby alienating many of the majority. To
speak of a common good may seem either absurdly romantic or
cruelly hypocritical to both the black and brown minorities and
to the white majority. Daniel Moynihan's words, that the United
States has set goals "unique in history: not only to abolish
poverty and ignorance, but also to become the first genuinely
multi-racial and we hope in the end non-racial democracy the
world has ever seen," may seem to describe a very remote if not
unattainable end.[19]

Certainly governments, particularly the Federal government,
have for some time undertaken to alleviate the conditions of life
in the center city, more importantly to bring ghetto dwellers into
the mainstream of American life. Many critics of these efforts
view them as too little and too late, and certainly they are in
some measure. An important element accounting for the ineffec-
tiveness of public programs has been disagreement among the
experts in the various fields—education, housing, health, crime
control, the opening up of economic opportunity—as to what
kinds of programs can accomplish the greatest lasting improvement in the shortest possible time.

These disagreements among experts have not remained merely
expert in character. Not surprisingly they have spilled over into
public discussion, into the arena of political debate, where they
inevitably take on a political character, that is, positions are
taken in response to constituent interests, and the outcome of
debate may reflect, not the preponderance of expert opinion, not
even the most insightful view of moral values, but quite simply
the wish of the strongest interest present. In short when debate
becomes as heated, as emotional, as the present debate about the
conditions of life of city dwellers, elements of reason, of calm
choice among alternatives, of a goodwilled and goodhumored
commitment to experiment and to alter course as appears necessary, to compromise, are likely to become minimal. The decision

---

[19] "A Crisis of Confidence?" *The Public Interest*, No. 7 (Spring, 1967),
p. 10.

is the product of fright, of anger, of moral and political black-mail. It *may* turn out to be a good decision, but the chances are materially reduced.

That is why the nurturing of political skills among the people of a metropolitan area becomes critical so that they may resist both the beguilingly "scientifically correct" proposals of one or another expert and the angry threatening of minority and major-ity groups; so that they may strengthen their understanding of accommodation and their recognition that diverse solutions may work, in one combination or another; so that they may renew their commitment to what works rather than to sterile principle.

IV

DECISION MAKING: THE FUNCTION OF EXPERTS

A number of examples of agonizing and perplexing differences among the experts in fields of policy important in urban areas can be cited. These differences make difficulties for the politician and for the citizen.

Of the public programs regarded as critical for improvement of the urban minority, none outranks education; the experts differ sharply on how the school may overcome a disadvantaged home life.

The premise of Judge Skelly Wright's recent decision in the suit brought by Julius Hobson in Washington, D.C., is that separation or segregation, even when not in consequence of law but rather of residential patterns, is unequal and discriminatory and therefore unconstitutional.[20] By way of supporting evidence

---

[20] In Volume I of the Report of the U.S. Commission on Civil Rights, *Racial Isolation in the Public Schools* (Washington, D.C.: Government Printing Office, 1967), Professor Allan Wilson's study, *Educational Conse-quences of Segregation in a California Community,* is cited as demonstrat-ing that student environment in the school has a stronger relationship to the performance of Negro students than to that of white students. Family environment has a stronger effect upon white students than upon Negroes, *Report,* pp. 85–86. But Wilson's study is also cited as demonstrating that social class is the single factor most closely related to academic achieve-ment of children in the early grades, p. 81. On pages 89–90 the Commission

he offered per capita expenditures in schools in predominantly Negro neighborhoods, which were lower than in schools in white neighborhoods. The lower expenditure per child was a fact easily proved; that it was moreover a detriment to the children in these schools most people would accept. But that the de facto segregation was in itself repressive is not a demonstrated fact, however often one may make reference to the doctrine of *Brown* v. *Topeka*, in which the Supreme Court itself made almost casual reference to Gunnar Myrdal's very large work. It can be argued that in a democratic society to separate on the basis of skin color by law is, by law, by public act, to *grade* citizens by color of skin; this is intolerable, or should be, to all. When the legal requirement of segregation is removed, it can be argued (although not proved) that the situation becomes very different.

Judge Wright's assertion that the difference in per capita spending is proof of the cynicism of the power structure is political argument, perhaps quite true, perhaps not at all true. It is not proof that separation marks children for life. Nonetheless the opinion stands as additional support to the contention of the Brown case that it is fact that segregation is per se injury. It stands moreover as a barrier to any remedy for lower expenditures per child in the slum schools other than the mixing of children by busing, or educational parks, or the like, throughout the District. Given the predominance of Negroes in the population of the District, one may ask how much of a remedy the Skelly Wright prescription can be, short of throwing open all the schools of the metropolitan area to all the children of the area, which Judge Wright did not order to be done.

One additional example in the field of education of difference among experts: The Fall, 1966, report to the Office of Education prepared by Professor James Coleman entitled "Equality of Educational Opportunity" unequivocally declared that "the pupil-teacher ratio . . . showed a consistent lack of relation to achieve-

---

concludes that research has not yet given clear answers to the question of whether the racial composition of a school has an effect upon achievement distinct from that of social class.

ment among all groups under all conditions." Professor Peter Rossi has also contended that "by and large class size has no effect on the learning of students, with the possible exception of classes in the language arts." Nevertheless in the spring of 1967, in announcing a new program "Operation Keep Moving," the Office of Economic Opportunity listed as the first point in the program a reduction of pupil-teacher ratios in elementary grades to that of the Head Start ratio, 15 to 1.[21]

As Daniel Moynihan has written, to accomplish a ratio of 15 to 1 in elementary grades across the nation would require an expenditure in a range not far removed from that needed for a guaranteed family income of $1,000 per year. To be sure, the experts are needed to speak to the question of how much the lower pupil-teacher ratio might accomplish, but the experts do not agree. In the end a political decision must be made as to the comparative values the people wish to assign to either a lower pupil-teacher ratio or a guaranteed family income. For that decision people must speak to people, must make judgments about situations in which they find themselves and in which their neighbors find themselves. The experts can only help; they can't decide.

Another important area of public function for urban dwellers is that of crime control. The experts here are of a variety of kinds, sociologists, psychologists, statisticians, practicing police officers, lawyers.

If one were to read reports of crimes without reference to who commits them, the point would be missed that by far the largest incidence of crime is in the 15 through 34 age group of male Americans. As the President's Commission on Law Enforcement and Administration of Justice stated in its recent report, this has been so ever since crime statistics were kept.[22] The greatest increase in the population of the United States being precisely in the young adult group, it may be that the excess in the increase of

---

[21] Moynihan, *op. cit.*, p. 7.
[22] *The Challenge of Crime in a Free Society* (Washington, D.C.: Government Printing Office, 1967), p. 5.

crime over the increase in population has been very much exaggerated, so that, as James Wilson put it, "What appears to be a crime explosion, may in fact be a population explosion." [23] Since there is uncertainty about the causes of crime in any group, Wilson's faintly amused words may need to be taken more seriously than most would wish: "The only sure way we know of fighting crime is birth control." [24]

In *The Economics of Delinquency* Belton Fleisher concluded that economic factors, especially family income, have a strong effect on delinquency rates. He estimated that a $500 annual increase in income for families in high-delinquency areas (presumably not middle-class suburbs, where, so the newspaper accounts reveal, the rate of delinquency is uncomfortably high) would cut juvenile arrests by about 5 per 1,000 population. The political nature of the decision whether to put public funds into family income or into lower pupil-teacher ratios becomes ever clearer.[25]

James Wilson underscores that Fleisher's analysis shows race to be statistically insignificant in comparison with economic level in disposing persons toward crime. Wilson has also written that, quite to the contrary of what many believe, that urban policemen discriminate against the Negro by arresting him for every "infraction, however minor," it is more likely that the police "will 'discriminate' against him by not arresting him for many crimes, including some serious ones." [26] If this is true, how can Wilson be so certain that race is statistically insignificant? [27]

The Task Force reports and the final report of the President's

[23] "Crime in the Streets," *The Public Interest*, No. 5 (Fall, 1966), p. 32.

[24] *Ibid.*

[25] Belton M. Fleisher, *The Economics of Delinquency* (Toronto: Quadrangle Books, Burns and McEachern, 1966).

[26] Wilson, *op. cit.*, p. 29.

[27] Wilson's rueful comment that crime is not a problem about which American liberalism has had much to say, excepting to support civilian review boards and to criticize the FBI, and his conclusion that unless the liberal becomes more to the point in his reflections about crime, liberalism "will become a notable victim of crime in the streets" may have pointed relevance.

Commission document widespread deficiencies in the enforcement of law and the administration of justice which tend to vitiate due process for all accused of crime, but most particularly for the poor.[28] Here again is a problem on which the expert voices become diverse. Particularly since recent Supreme Court decisions on confessions, many policemen have complained that their already difficult job has been made impossible. Although the standing of these complaints is often questioned because it is said that too many policemen have little regard for the rights of suspects, the complaints cannot simply be disregarded. After all the practitioner is an expert who has something of value to tell us about his work. A member of the faculty of Georgetown Law Center in the spring of 1967 described a research project in which a serious exploration of revision in the role of defense counsel was being undertaken. The purpose of the project was to determine whether it would be desirable for defense counsel to concentrate upon rehabilitative services rather than on defense. At almost the same time the Supreme Court of the United States had begun to require the extension to juvenile defendants of some of the more formal aspects of due process in criminal proceedings, particularly that with respect to counsel for defense at critical stages.[29]

As a third instance of public policy of critical importance for urban dwellers about which there are important differences among experts as to what ought to be done, one may cite welfare or public assistance. Some extremely heated arguments continue about the extent to which public assistance ought to be displaced by a guaranteed family income.[30] Subjects of debate also include the desirability of having uniform Federal regulations rather than varying State and local regulations on such matters as residence requirements in determining eligibility, the level of pay-

---

[28] See especially Task Force on the Administration of Justice, *Report: The Courts* (Washington, D.C.: Government Printing Office, 1967).

[29] *Kent* v. *U.S.*, 383 U.S. 541 (1966), and *In Re Gault*, 387 U.S. 1 (1967).

[30] See, for example, *The Guaranteed Income,* ed. Robert Theobald (New York: Doubleday & Co., 1966).

ments and the quite basic matter of adequate and appropriate training and certification for social workers.[31]

The most emotional controversy centers upon the ADC program, which at the outset in 1935 contributed to the support of children 88 per cent of whose fathers were dead or disabled. In 1962 only 7 per cent of the children on ADC rolls were involuntary dependents, that is, children whose fathers were dead or disabled. For the 93 per cent of ADC cases whose fathers were unknown or who had disappeared, the *voluntary* dependents, public funds were less enthusiastically voted.[32] In fairness it must be made clear that there was little or no desire to penalize children as voluntary dependents; there seemed to be considerable doubt that their mothers should be subsidized to continue to have children on such a hapless basis.

It is not simply politicians who have difficulty in finding the answer to the problem of illegitimate or abandoned children. In his report on the Negro family Daniel Moynihan argued that the matriarchal character of Negro family life, the roots of which lie deep in the wretched history of the Negro in America, contributes powerfully to a pattern of irresponsibility, if not criminal conduct, on the part of the Negro male, which in turn tends to emphasize the dominance of the Negro woman, and so on in a vicious circle.[33] For this thesis blows were rained upon his head by a variety of Negro and white intellectuals and politicians, and one may judge from Moynihan's recent contribution to the *Annals* of the American Academy of Political and Social Sciences that his memory of the debate is still alive and painful.[34] But it is a far

---

[31] See chap. vii, "The Social Work Syndrome," in Gilbert Steiner, *Social Insecurity—The Politics of Welfare* (Chicago: Rand McNally & Co., 1966).

[32] *Ibid.,* p. 114.

[33] *The Negro Family: The Case for National Action,* Office of Policy Planning and Research, U.S. Department of Labor, March, 1965. Reprinted in Lee Rainwater and William L. Yancey, *The Moynihan Report and the Politics of Controversy* (Cambridge: The M.I.T. Press, 1967).

[34] *Social Goals and Indicators for American Society,* Vol. I (May, 1967). Moynihan's essay, "Urban Conditions: General," contains the following sentences: ". . . it is essential that all concerned with the development of a system of urban social indicators be prepared in advance to find themselves accused of having betrayed some of those very causes with which they have

cry from the eloquent defense of Negro family life by Dr. Martin
Luther King to the advice given young Negro girls by a New
York State certified social worker, Mrs. Ruby Evans.

Speaking in October, 1965, partly with reference to public
comment on the Moynihan report, Dr. King said:

The Negro family for three hundred years has been on the tracks
of the racing locomotives of American history and was dragged
along mangled and crippled. . . . American slavery is distinguished from all other forms because it consciously dehumanized
the Negro. . . . The shattering blows on the Negro family have
made it fragile, deprived and often psychopathic. This is tragic
because nothing is so much needed as a secure family life for a
people seeking to pull themselves out of poverty and backward-
ness. . . . The dark side of the picture appears almost to make
the future bleak, if not hopeless. Yet something says this is not
true. . . . The Negro was crushed, battered and brutalized, but he
never gave up. He proves again life is stronger than death. The
Negro family is scarred, it is submerged, but it struggles to
survive. . . . Superficial people may superciliously expect it to
function with all the graces and facility of more advantaged
families. Their unfeeling criticism may hurt, but it will not halt
progress. If the Negro is called upon to do the impossible, he may
fail in the eyes of those ignorant of his tortured history, but in his
own eyes the Negro knows he is imperceptibly accumulating the
resources to emerge fully as a total human being. . . . A hundred
times I have been asked why we allowed little children to march
in demonstrations, to freeze and suffer in jails, to be exposed to
bullets and dynamite. The questions implied that we have a want
of family feeling or recklessness toward family security. The
answer is simple. Our children and our families are maimed a
little every day of our lives. If we can end an incessant torture by
a single climactic confrontation, the risks are acceptable. . . . I
do not think that the tiny nation that stood in majesty at
Concord and Lexington, that electrified a world with the words of

been most allied. . . . [American social scientists] are problem-prone and
reform-minded and inevitably come to be seen as allies by those about
whose problems they are most concerned. These latter, having social
scientists on their side, easily came to assume that social science will be.
This does not always happen, a fact not easily forgiven. Knowledge is
power, and in contemporary society social scientists are often in the
position of handing power about in an almost absent-minded way . . . to
those whom they would consider the very worst contenders." Pp. 160–61.

the Declaration of Independence, will defame its heritage to avoid a responsibility. That is why I believe not only in the future of the Negro family but in the future of the family of man.[35]

Mrs. Evans, a staff member of the United Planning Organization, Washington, D.C.'s, poverty agency, said to an audience of about thirty girls: "I don't advocate birth control at all. It's part of being a woman to get babies . . . and a girl doesn't think about the child that might come into the world when she's in love with a boy." A *Washington Post* story quoted her as believing that there is some hint of racial implications in the attitudes normally exhibited by social agencies toward unwed Negro girls and in the fact that white social workers "generally are giving contraceptives to Negro girls." [36]

It would be quite easy to find examples of similar differences in the advice offered by experts in a large number of other policy areas for coping with urban problems, including urban renewal and public housing. The examples given, however, should demonstrate that there is no "expert" answer, no final scientific solution, but only diverse courses holding out a variety of pluses and minuses. Citizens must decide which they will choose.

V

DECISION MAKING: THE RESPONSIBILITY OF CITIZENS

It was not the purpose of the preceding section to disparage the experts, the professionals, who work upon urban problems; it would almost surely be entirely accurate to say that no more complex, painful and urgent problems confront us or ever have confronted us.

Nor was it intended to suggest that, given the complexity of urban problems, we should "wallow in the very chaos of complexity, rather than to begin the task of unraveling and analyzing, and, ultimately, of acting. . . . But to move from the recognition

---

[35] Reprinted in Rainwater and Yancey, *op. cit.*, pp. 402-9.
[36] *The Washington Post*, July 23, 1967, p. D3.

of infernal complexity to the refuge of damnably inaccurate simplicity is surely heresy. Much has to be done. All of it is difficult, tangled and anxious-making. Still it must be done; there's no escape in the world of sociological fakery." [37]

What is to be done must be decided by citizens and their representatives. There is no one to save them from the sovereign prerogative of choice. And the choice should be based upon as careful an assessment of facts found rather than those *believed* to be found as is possible. Given the *fact* of deprivation in the schools of the center city, why not pour in money to reduce crowding, to pay teachers more so as to help attract the best and help persuade them to give their best, to provide teaching aids, to make the school a center of community life for adults and children alike? Why, on the basis of *believed* but not demonstrated fact, simply command that the children attend integrated schools, as though this alone would do all that is possible to overcome a deprived home?

The rejection of sterile principle—the avoidance of polarized positions arrived at in consequence of perplexity, frustration, moral indignation—should be the goal of urban political processes. And fully as much weight in the development of public policy should be given to those programs which can help to develop skills in the political process as to those which shore up the severely overtaxed financial resources of State and city government and which undertake to alleviate deprivation and suffering now.

The Federal government should continue the grants-in-aid now existing to deal with urban problems; it should almost certainly add to such programs. It should undertake periodic careful examination of these programs and their effectiveness. It should adequately fund the Model Cities and war on poverty programs. It should adopt some form of the proposal made by Walter Heller and others for sharing revenues with States and perhaps local

[37] William Ryan, "Savage Discovery: The Moynihan Report," *The Nation,* Nov. 22, 1965. Reprinted in Rainwater and Yancey, *op. cit.,* pp. 457–66.

governments on an unconditional basis. It should look to its own organization and procedures to facilitate effective use of available Federal programs by State and local governments; the metropolitan expediter could be a useful addition to the Federal bureaucracy.

But with equal enthusiasm, imagination and generosity, it should put its efforts into such programs as the community action aspect of the war on poverty. With all of the strains imposed by the various forms of community action which have occurred since passage of the Economic Opportunity Act, with all of what appear to be the absurd and yet maddeningly irritating cries from the poor that, once elected by them, their representatives cease to be representative, with the graft, the excessive salaries which have undoubtedly prevailed in some community action agencies, community action represents an effort to involve in cooperative action those not previously involved (whatever the reasons), to challenge them, to give them responsibility, to compel them to find out how things look to others. Such a proposal as Senator Ribicoff's for Federal funding of neighborhood corporations to deal with aspects of housing and business opportunities could be a similarly useful experience.[38]

VI

CREATIVE FEDERALISM: EXTENDING THE STORE OF POLITICAL TALENTS

I have written above that the Federal government should turn its attention "with equal enthusiasm" to those efforts which may cultivate and extend political skills. It is the thesis of this essay that without such skills, decent, effective, sensible solutions cannot be found, most particularly with respect to problems which are fraught with emotion, which carry for some a heavy sense of guilt, for others a savage sense of injustice done them.

If urban man cannot become Aristotle's political man, if he cannot soon come to recognize, whatever his vantage point, a

---

[38] See *The Congressional Record,* Jan. 23, 1967, pp. S709–10.

community of interests and purposes, then indeed American cities may burn to the ground, may be desolated, and urban man cease to be recognizable as man.

SELECTED BIBLIOGRAPHY

Barton, Weldon. *Interstate Compacts in the Political Process.* Chapel Hill: University of North Carolina Press, 1967.
Break, George F. *Intergovernmental Fiscal Relations in the United States.* Washington, D.C.: Brookings Institution, 1966.
Committee for Economic Development. *A Fiscal Program for a Balanced Federalism.* New York: The Committee, 1967.
Committee for Economic Development. *Modernizing Local Government.* New York: The Committee, 1966.
Committee for Economic Development. *Modernizing State Government.* New York: The Committee, 1967.
Elazar, Daniel. *American Federalism: A View from the States.* New York: Thomas Y. Crowell Co., 1966.
Heller, Walter. *New Dimensions of Political Economy.* Cambridge: Harvard University Press, 1966.
Pechman, Joseph. *Federal Tax Policy.* Washington, D.C.: Brookings Institution, 1966.
Sanford, Terry. *Storm over the States.* New York: McGraw-Hill Book Co., 1967.
Tax Foundation, Inc. *Facts and Figures in Government Finance,* 14th biennial edition. New York: The Foundation, 1967.
Wildavsky, Aaron, ed. *American Federalism in Perspective.* Boston: Little, Brown & Co., 1967.

PART II

FEDERALISM
IN OTHER COUNTRIES

INTRODUCTORY ESSAY

As the following essays demonstrate, the societies in which there may be an impulse to a federal form of government may be diverse, and the legal and political institutions with which federalism is compatible may take a variety of forms.

A reading of these essays makes possible one immediate generalization—that, far more than upon constitutional or legal prescription, the maintenance of federalism depends upon political process, institution, tradition.

As Professor Kantor writes, the impulse toward union without unity has been strong in a number of Latin American states since independence, won in the early nineteenth century. Elaborate constitutions to the contrary, no federal system has persisted in any meaningful sense of a division of significant governmental powers between levels of government. Although substantial disparity in the size, population and resources of the constituent units and natural barriers which make communication difficult are important explanatory factors, they cannot wholly account for the failure of federalism to take root. As Professor Cerny points out, Prussia was by far the wealthiest and most powerful of the German constituent states, yet federalism (of a kind not wholly satisfactory to all Germans) endured. Moreover the present German states are largely artificial creations, deriving from but not identical with the earlier states and by no means commanding the same degree of local attachment or patriotism. Yet again these artificial states appear viable as entities and as parts of the federal union. Certainly there are natural barriers in the English-speaking countries—the Australian desert, for example —but they have not sufficed to prevent union.

The essays dealing with the United States, Canada and Australia and with the West German Republic emphasize common motivations underlying the establishing of a federal system. Professor Cerny's comments upon the nineteenth- and early twentieth-century identification of federalism in the German mind with bureaucracy and with Prussian domination provide an interesting contrast with the common identification in American minds of federalism with individual freedom and liberalism.

Of greater interest than common motivations, these essays suggest the range of governmental institutions and processes with which federalism may live.

In Canada, Australia and West Germany the second house of the legislature is comparatively unimportant, compared with the American Senate, but not in the same fashion in all three countries or for the same reasons. Professor Livingston makes the point for Canada and Australia that parliamentary government does not tolerate a strong second house: The government is directly responsible to the lower house, and in addition, since effective government in a parliamentary system requires a well organized party, the second chamber tends to be party-oriented rather than region-oriented, even though its composition is formally based upon representation of geographic areas. The Canadian second house, being appointed by the governor-general on the advice of the prime minister and the cabinet, has tended to become a "kind of retirement benefit for senescent politicians." One must then look elsewhere for significant representation of regional interests in the central government.

American students may ponder the question of whether representation of State interests in the government at Washington depends upon the constitutional guarantee of equality of representation in the Senate, where the practice of instructing Senators disappeared more than a century ago, or upon a complex combination of many institutions with political practices.

The West German Bundesrat, composed of instructed delegates from the states, which are not represented equally, is not a powerful legislative body but has succeeded in maximizing the powers given it so that it may accurately be described as "the most effective instrument for the Länder governments to influence the policy-making process of the federation." Professor Cerny's description of the composition and work of standing committees in the Bundesrat and the referral of proposals to Länder cabinets for the purpose of giving instructions to Bundesrat delegates helps to explain the significance of the state role in national decisions.

Although the Bonn constitution divides governmental powers between the federation and the states vertically, that is, by subject matter in the manner familiar to Americans, it also divides them horizontally, since it continues the practice of earlier German federal systems of keeping a major part of the administration of national policies in state administrative agencies. Certainly at its founding such an arrangement would have rendered the American Federal system highly vulnerable to a decline of the national government. Leonard White has commented that the acts of the first Congress in establishing national administrative agencies in the field were a major contribution to the development of a strong national government. Even in the twentieth century, almost two hundred years later, it would make very little sense to propose that national legislation on civil rights be implemented by the States.

Although in the English-speaking countries the written constitution and judicial review have been regarded as intertwined institutions, the Bonn constitution (which, in recognition of the unfinished character of the German state pending reunification, Germans prefer to speak of as the Basic Law) apparently anticipated no more significant role for the Federal Constitutional Court than had been given the courts in the Hohenzollern Reich or the Weimar Republic. Professor Cerny explains this primarily in terms of an allocation of powers to the national government so extensive as to permit it to move into areas of social and economic policy as thought necessary. Thus one source of a large number of American constitutional cases, the dispute over the scope of national powers affecting commerce, taxing and spending versus the scope of State police powers, has been nonexistent in the German federal systems. Yet the present West German Federal Constitutional Court has handed down some decisions affecting the growth of American federalism.

American students may contrast the emphasis given in Professor Mason's essay in Part I of this collection to judicial protection of individual rights with the emphasis in the Livingston and Cerny essays upon structure, allocation of power and political process. The three essays prompt reflection upon the question whether, in the words of the present Mr. Justice Harlan, federalism and separation of powers are "the root of our constitutional system," "our free society," or whether a Bill of Rights, judicially enforced, is the "principal guarantee of personal liberty."

The forms of cooperation among the states and between the national government and the states provide an additional area for interesting speculation. In all four countries the constituent units have found it desirable to agree upon common policies and to establish special bodies to administer these policies, bodies which Professor Cerny describes as a third level in the federal system. To the argument that if the states cooperate because they cannot achieve a particular purpose singly, then the purpose has become national in character and should be dealt with by the national government, Professor Cerny responds that the availability of the "third-level" solution makes possible another alternative to that of a single policy imposed on all by the national government or separate and inadequate state policies.

By all odds the most interesting form of cooperation between the national government and the states occurs in the area of revenue sharing. Here the variety of arrangements worked out or being proposed is striking, as are also the effects of these arrangements upon governmental powers and functioning. To possess powers without the revenues required to exercise them is to be impotent. Americans were concerned in 1787 about the allocation of adequate taxing powers to both the national government and the States, and they have retained this concern, as demonstrated at Bonn in their insistence that the Germans alter their original proposal that revenues be collected and distributed by a national fiscal administrative system. Not even the fact that in the German proposal certain revenues were to be earmarked for the states, certain for the national government and certain to be shared seemed sufficient to guarantee to the Americans that the states would be financially independent.

But whether national revenues have increased more rapidly than national functions, as is the case in the United States, Australia, and Canada, or not, the practice of sharing—through grants-in-aid, or a return of national revenues after collection to the States, as proposed by Walter Heller, or annual negotiation on the respective national and state shares of specified tax sources—has become central to the character of federalism, and its effects are widespread upon programs, institutions and political processes.

To conclude on a note struck at the beginning of this introductory essay, it is the political process which is determinative of the nature and development of federalism.

WILLIAM S. LIVINGSTON
The University of Texas

CANADA, AUSTRALIA AND
THE UNITED STATES:
VARIATIONS ON A THEME

Mᴀ PURPOSE is to examine the experience of federalism in the three major English-speaking federations in order to identify points of similarity and difference in that experience. I do not seek to derive broad generalizations about the nature or dynamics of federalism, even though the similarity of developments does sometimes suggest hypotheses that give that appearance. In each of the three countries the practices and institutions of federalism have been shaped by the demands of a local situation, and although the three bear considerable resemblance to one another, the development in each case has been a response to local needs and a local environment. Whether the dynamics of federalism are the product of its own inherent imperatives or of the environmental forces of the particular national setting is a question that will not be resolved here. The evidence surveyed suggests a little of each.

I

THE ENVIRONMENT
OF FEDERALISM

The three countries are roughly equal in size but quite different in population, that of the United States being more than ten times that of either Canada or Australia.[1] This disparity is largely due to the fact that large areas of the Canadian north and the Australian interior are virtually uninhabitable. The disparity in population makes for a different political life in the three countries and also helps explain the disparity in the number of component units that comprise the three federations. Australia consists of six states and Canada of ten provinces, while the United States, with its much larger population, comprises fifty different units, again called States. With regard to the homogeneity of the population one can arrange the federations on a kind of scale: Australia is at one extreme, with the greatest homogeneity; the United States is somewhere in the middle; and Canada is at the other extreme, displaying the greatest heterogeneity. Unlike Australia and the United States Canada was virtually an invention for bringing together two quite different nationalities, the French and English, and the history of Canadian federalism has been very largely a history of efforts to reconcile the different values and aspirations of these two groups, which comprise the Canadian nation. The differences in social composition have meant that the political life of the three countries is quite different in character. The State-based federalism of America has served as a vehicle (or cloak) for a competition of regional or sectional interests. In Australia, with its greater social homogeneity, politics has been based much more directly on class differences and the clash of economic interests and only exceptionally on State or sectional diversities. In Canada, while the spread of

[1] Areas in square miles: Australia, 2,974,581; Canada, 3,845,774; United States (including Hawaii and Alaska), 3,623,995. Populations (1964 estimates): Australia, 11,135,000; Canada, 19,361,000; United States, 191,000,000. Council of Foreign Relations, *Political Handbook and Atlas of the World, 1965,* ed. Walter H. Mallory (New York: Harper & Row, 1965).

the country encompasses a variety of sectional and economic differences, the basis of political life has always been the differences between the French- and English-speaking communities.

II

THE ORIGINS OF FEDERALISM

Although the three federations were created at different times and in response to different perceptions of need, they did have a number of things in common, things which above all led them to the adoption of a federal union, but which also helped shape the character of that union. It may be useful to begin, therefore, with a few comments on the similarity of these formative influences.

In the first place all three were settled by people from the British Isles, with the one very large exception of the French Canadians, who preceded the British in Canada. More important, however, were British values and British political and constitutional traditions which the colonists carried with them. In the United States more than in Canada and Australia the influence of British models was both affirmative and negative. In a number of respects Americans in the eighteenth century, deliberately or without thinking, adopted and perpetuated governmental practices brought from Britain—the organization of the legislature, the character of local government, the organization and practices of the judiciary and so on. On the other hand the Americans deliberately abandoned some British practices of which they disapproved, establishing a system of separated powers, a republican government, a federal rather than a unitary system, a limited executive and a written constitution with a Bill of Rights. In the other two countries—with the major exception of Quebec —British models were more consistently followed; and in each of the three it can be said that the familiar institutions were transported and put into effect and only later modified by local conditions. Perhaps the most important of these influences, one that is clearly evident in each of the three, is the strong conviction about free government under law. The sense of freedom that had been developed in Britain over the long centuries was perhaps the most cherished right that Britishers carried with them overseas, and the liberal tradition, "under the impulse of individualism, legalism and *laissez faire*," [2] as J. A. Corry has described it, became a fundamental value of each new society.

Each new nation, moreover, quite unlike the mother country, adopted a formal and written constitution—no doubt a necessity when constructing a federal system with a distribution of powers provided by law. Beyond this each of the three federations expected the courts to police the system and to guard the boundaries of the distribution of authority. The consequence has been that the development of federalism in each of the three has been significantly, although not of course exclusively, lodged in the hands of judicial bodies at state, national and imperial levels.

All three federations came into existence through the bringing together of previously separate units. That is to say, in all three cases federalism meant an alternative, not to a single, centralized, unitary state, but to the continued separation of the component parts. The point is not so obvious as it may sound, for this conception of the alternatives fundamentally affects the psychological setting of federalism in the Anglo-American federations in a way that is not found elsewhere. The typical Continental conception of federalism, for example, treats it as an alternative to complete unity and tends to consider that federalism is merely a form of decentralized unitary government.[3]

Finally it can be said that in each federation people hoped to derive from the new association advantages which they could not get while separated. Indeed the advantages they sought were very similar in all three, although they varied appreciably in importance from place to place. In each case there was a mixture

[2] J. A. Corry, "Constitutional Trends and Federalism," in A. R. M. Lower, F. R. Scott *et al., Evolving Canadian Federalism* (Durham: Duke University Press, 1958), p. 95.

[3] See Hans Kelsen, *General Theory of Law and the State,* trans. Wedberg (Cambridge: Harvard University Press, 1946), p. 316. Rudolf Schlesinger, in *Federalism in Central and Eastern Europe* (New York: Oxford University Press, 1945), although he does not argue this point, does supply historical and theoretical evidence that appears to support it. See chaps. i–iii, *passim.*

of motives, and it is very doubtful that any one of them dominated over the rest.[4] One advantage was clearly the greater
military security of the peoples involved. In the United States
this took the form of an apprehension about European politics,
for it was feared that the new nation, weak and divided under its
Articles of Confederation, would fall prey to the dynastic and
political intrigues of European power politics. In Canada, surprisingly enough to many Americans, the apprehension concerning national security turned toward the United States, which in
the period of Canadian confederation was emerging from a great
Civil War which had heightened an already vigorous sense of
American nationalism. Canada had already been subjected to
two American invasions and a threat of war over the Oregon
boundary, and there was a widespread sense among Canadians
that federation would not only protect Canada against American
aggression but might also serve as a vehicle for Canadian emula-
tion of the rapid American development and expansion in the
first half of the nineteenth century. In Australia the military or
security consideration was perhaps less obvious, but there too
federation meant greater security. The turn of the century produced a widened interest in the Pacific world and the appearance
of a modernized Japan which had recently fought a war with
China and was soon to fight one with Russia. Hence the Australians felt that their continent would be more secure if its component territories were united into a single nation.[5]

Beyond the military aspects, however, there were other consid-

---

[4] A recent book by William H. Riker, *Federalism: Origin, Operation,
Significance* (Boston: Little, Brown & Co., 1964), argues that in each of
these three federations the concern with military security was the primary
motive for federal union. Although the author concedes the existence of
other factors, his emphasis on security concerns seems to me excessive. See
pp. 16–28.

[5] See, for example, C. Hartley Grattan, *The Southwest Pacific to 1900*
(Ann Arbor: University of Michigan Press, 1963), p. 358, and Riker, *op.
cit.*, pp. 27–28. Even so, the concern for security appears to have been minor
in the Australian federation movement. See Ernest Scott, *A Short History
of Australia* (8th ed.; Melbourne: Oxford University Press, 1950), pp.
314–15; A. G. L. Shaw, *The Story of Australia* (London: Faber & Faber,
1960), chap. xii; and Grattan, *op. cit.*, chap. xvii.

erations that led each of the three toward federal union. A great deal of the argument in the United States turned on the economic advantages that federation would produce, and the same considerations were influential in both Canada and Australia. Increased control over the economy, the reduction of interstate barriers to trade, the need to create a national system of communications, the enhanced administrative efficiency of a "national" government—all these things impelled the adoption of a closer form of union, and in each of these spheres each country hoped to achieve something from federation that it feared it could not obtain without it.

Despite these similarities in background, however, each nation was born in its own time and in response to circumstances that uniquely shaped its character and destiny as a federal system. In 1787 the United States contrived the first modern federal system, molded largely by its own experience in the preceding century. The American Federal system led the way and provided a model which the other two might follow or reject. One did the one, and one did the other.

Eighty years later Canada federated, largely in response to the example that the United States provided. But America at that time was engaged in a Civil War, which was often described as a battle between two points of view over the character of federalism and which was frequently attributed by the Canadians to faults in the American Federal structure. The Canadians were determined that in their union there should be no opportunity for the hypertrophy of States rights, which they saw as the root cause of the American difficulties. Hence they reacted strongly against the American model, conceiving that the American Constitution had lodged far too much power in the States. They included in their system, therefore, a number of devices designed to redress the balance, and they called it a confederation rather than a federal union. The most obvious manifestation of this reaction was the reversal of the distribution of powers in Sections 91 and 92 of the British North America Act of 1867. Whereas the Americans had listed the powers that were granted to the national government and reserved everything else to the States, the Canadians reversed this technique by listing in Section 92 the powers that were assigned to the provinces and in Section 91 reserving everything else to the Dominion. In this way they believed that the great emphasis that had been given to the States by the reserved powers of the American Constitution would be placed upon the Dominion in the Canadian system. To make the point more obvious they abandoned the American term "State" and called their own units "provinces." Beyond this, moreover, they provided that the lieutenant-governor, who was the official head of the provincial government, should be directly appointed and instructed by the Dominion government and that the Dominion cabinet should be given the power to disallow (that is, veto) acts of the provincial legislatures. Sir John Macdonald, the Conservative leader who more than any other man influenced the form of the Canadian constitution, was quite determined that the system should be stronger and more highly centralized than that of the United States. When the constitutional conferences finished their work, Sir John breathed deeply:

Here we have adopted a different system. We have strengthened the General Government. We have given the General Legislature all the great subjects of legislation. . . . We have thus avoided that great source of weakness which has been the cause of the disruption of the United States.[6]

But Sir John, it turned out, had misjudged his work. A federal constitution tends to be what the judges, rather than what the founding fathers, say it is; and the judges of the Canadian constitution—notably the Judicial Committee of the Privy Council—by a particular technique of interpretation, produced in Canada constitutional problems no less difficult than those in the United States.

A generation later Australia formed her federal system, and just as Canada had reacted against the American model, Aus-

---

[6] Province of Canada, Parliament, *Confederation Debates* (Quebec, 1865), p. 33.

tralia reacted against the Canadian, reverting to the system employed in America. There were several reasons for this shift of emphasis. Canada was already encountering difficulties in the interpretation of her "reversed" distribution of powers. As interpreted by the courts, the Dominion was slowly being strangled by a broadened interpretation of certain clauses in Section 92, particularly that one granting to the provinces exclusive control over "property and civil rights." [7] There was also a widespread feeling in Australia and elsewhere that Canada, for the reasons mentioned above, was not truly a federal system but a kind of hybrid confederation. The Australians, on the other hand, were ready to accept the more prestigious and more solidly established American model. Indeed that model was by now a far different one from that which the Canadians had observed in the middle of the century. The strong centralized thrust of the early days and of the Civil-War era had given way to a greater emphasis upon laissez faire and had produced the rise of what came to be called dual federalism. The scepticism of the Canadians toward American States rights no longer seemed so important.

Thus the Australians consciously rejected a great many of the variations on the American model that the Canadians had adopted. This was particularly true as regards the distribution of powers: The new national government's powers were expressly listed, and the residual powers were assigned to the states. There was created, moreover, a very broad range of concurrent jurisdiction, much more like the American practice than the Canadian.

Australian terminology illustrates this same reaction. The component units were again called states instead of provinces, and the head of the state government was called a governor instead of a lieutenant-governor. State governors, moreover, were appointed directly by the crown, that is, by the responsible state government itself, rather than by the national government of the Commonwealth. No provision at all was made for national disallowance of state legislation. Appeals from state courts might be

---

[7] Section 92.13.

carried directly to the Privy Council in London, whereas in Canada they had to go first to the Canadian Supreme Court. The Australians believed—no doubt correctly—that one of the reasons for the difficulties the Canadians had encountered in the interpretation of their constitution was that the federal distribution of powers was ultimately subject to the decisions of the Privy Council in London. The Australians were determined that the final judgment on such matters in their own federation would be lodged in their own courts; hence it was provided that all questions involving the distributions of powers between the Commonwealth and the states or among the states themselves should go to the High Court of Australia, and no appeal could be carried to the Privy Council except upon the High Court's certificate.

Finally the Australians, benefiting from the Canadian experience, included in their constitution an amending clause (Section 128) which would enable them to alter the constitution rather than leaving such questions to the Imperial Parliament in London. The failure to provide an amending clause in the British North America Act was in fact a mistake from which the Canadians have not recovered even today.

III

THE STRUCTURE OF CONSTITUTIONAL POWER

In addition to the formal differences among the three federations with regard to distribution of powers there are certain other, more subtle and intricate differences in the federal structures.

The Canadian and Australian federations were developed within the system of understandings provided by the British Crown and the British constitutional tradition. This meant that the royal prerogative was still operative, that the principles of parliamentary government with a responsible executive still obtained, and that government offices tended to be appointive rather than elective. The two British federations retained the system of responsible government provided by the British model, whereas the United States reacted strongly against that model and contrived a direct popular election and a fragmentation rather than a concentration of governmental power. Since the American Constitution departed so decisively from the British pattern, more of its contents had to be addressed to the arrangements of executive, legislative and judicial institutions. Federalism was only a part of the Constitution.

In Australia and Canada it was unnecessary to make elaborate provisions for the executive-legislative relationship, for this was based on the well understood patterns of the British constitution. Consequently both the Australian and Canadian constitutions said a great deal about that which was new, namely, the federal system, and very little about that which was based on traditional understandings, namely, the responsible system of parliamentary government.

The United States Constitution rests on the principle of limited government, that is, the government is authorized to perform only those functions expressly assigned to it and not prohibited to it. This is true not merely of the federal distribution of powers but of the whole constitutional structure; the principle of limited government runs throughout. It is perhaps most clearly evident in the Bill of Rights, with its elaborate prohibitions on the national government, and in the Fourteenth Amendment, with its less elaborate but no less comprehensive limitations on State governments.

In Australia and Canada there is no such principle. The constitutions begin instead with the assumptions of parliamentary omnicompetence derived from the understandings of the mother system in Great Britain. Neither the Canadians nor the Australians saw this as incompatible with federalism, although the latter were quite sensitive to the fact that they were introducing a novel element into a federal constitution.[8] The result, however, was that in the two British constitutions all power was distributed.

---

[8] On the interests, motives and forces that led to federation in Australia see the works cited by S. R. Davis and C. A. Hughes in *Federalism in the Commonwealth,* ed. W. S. Livingston (London: Cassell, Hansard Society, 1963), pp. 29–31. For a similar guide to the Canadian confederation movement see Alexander Brady in *ibid.,* pp. 11–15.

That is to say, instead of having both state and national governments operating within an elaborate set of limitations and prohibitions, the constitution allotted all governmental power to one
government or the other. Thus the question is never, Can the
thing be done? but only, Which government can do it? The sole
exception to this is Section 92 of the Australian constitution,
which somewhat mysteriously provides that "trade, commerce
and intercourse among the States . . . shall be absolutely free,"
which apparently does considerably restrict both states and
Commonwealth.[9]

Another significant difference in the distribution of powers is
that the Australian and United States constitutions provide for a
much broader area of concurrent powers than does the Canadian.
In both the United States and Australia the powers of the national government are enumerated and all other powers are reserved to the states, save those that are expressly prohibited. In
Australia, however, almost all the powers of the Commonwealth
are exercised concurrently with the states, that is to say, the
powers assigned in Section 51, which contains most of the Commonwealth powers, are not exclusive but are to be exercised
jointly by both governments. A few additional powers of the
Commonwealth are declared to be exclusive,[10] but these occupy
far less of the area of governmental authority than does the list
of concurrent powers in Section 51.

In the United States there is no specific provision regarding the
exclusiveness of the powers assigned to the national government
in Article 1, Section 8, and the only inference that can be drawn
about the exclusiveness of those powers is from the existence of
corresponding prohibitions on the States with regard to some of
them. For example, the United States is empowered to make

---

[9] On Section 92 see the brief comment by J. D. B. Miller in *Australian
Government and Politics* (London: Gerald Duckworth, 1954), pp. 128–29.
For more elaborate analysis see the papers cited by Davis and Hughes, *op.
cit.,* p. 36.

[10] Principally in Section 52, regarding the seat of the government and the
Commonwealth public service, and in Section 90, regarding customs duties.

treaties, to maintain an army and navy and to issue coins and paper money, and the States are elsewhere prohibited from doing these things.[11] But where no prohibition is provided, concurrency of jurisdiction is left to be inferred. The actual extent to which the powers of the national government in the United States are exclusive has never been satisfactorily determined either by scholars or by the courts. What one can say is that presumably by intent, and clearly by interpretation, the area in which both governments can act is a broad one and has been rapidly increasing in the last twenty-five or thirty years.[12] In fact both governments in America have a tremendously broad authority to regulate and act upon a great variety of subjects and activities within the society, although the acts of the two governments are justified for quite different reasons. As the Constitution has grown through practice and interpretation, the area of concurrent jurisdiction has been greatly broadened to the point where the limitations on the States, like the limitations on the national government, have been significantly diminished. One can almost say nowadays that there is nothing left in the Federal system itself that constitutes a limitation on the national government. One can also say that the States can do virtually anything they wish to do, limited by the Federal system only in that they may not levy taxes upon national institutions or seek to apply discriminatory regulations to interstate commerce.

In Canada the situation is quite different. The assignment of powers to the Dominion in Section 91, like the assignment of powers to the provinces in Section 92, is exclusive. It will be recalled that the enumerated powers were granted to the provinces in Section 92 and all other powers reserved to the Dominion

---

[11] Article I, Section 10.

[12] See, for example, the wealth of illustrative materials in W. Brooke Graves, *American Intergovernmental Relations* (New York: Charles Scribner's Sons, 1964), and the carefully reasoned analysis by Morton Grodzins, "Centralization and Decentralization in the American Federal System," in *A Nation of States,* ed. Robert A. Goldwin (Chicago: Rand McNally & Co., 1963), pp. 1–23.

by Section 91; but in an effort to make clearer what had been
reserved to the Dominion the authors of the constitution proceeded to list the powers that had been intended to be reserved,
although it was said in the constitutional document that the list
in Section 91 was intended to be illustrative and not comprehensive. This turned out to be a serious mistake, as the British North
America Act came under the interpretation of the Judicial Committee of the Privy Council, for by the turn of the century the
committee came to the position that the Dominion possessed no
general reserved powers except in times of national emergency
and that the illustrative list of powers in Section 91 did in fact
constitute very nearly the whole of the authority of the Dominion Parliament.[13] Both lists of powers—in Section 91 and in
Section 92—are exclusive, and since there is no principle of
limited government, all the powers of government are divided
into two comprehensive and mutually exclusive categories. There
is, however, one set of exceptions to this proposition, provided for
expressly in Sections 93 through 95, which authorize both provinces and Dominion to exercise a concurrent jurisdiction in a
limited number of areas, principally agriculture, immigration and
old-age pensions.

Comparatively and in summary it may be said that Australia
and the United States have a broad area of concurrent jurisdiction in the distribution of powers; this area of concurrency is
provided by specific statement in the Australian constitution but
has been developed without express provision in the United
States Constitution through practice and judicial interpretation.
In Canada, on the other hand, with the exceptions noted above
all powers are exclusive. In consequence, therefore, the Australian and the United States constitutions have provided national-
supremacy clauses by virtue of which a state act in conflict with
a national act is void to the extent of the conflict. In Canada
there is no supremacy clause except as regards the very limited

---

[13] Although this interpretation was more fully elaborated later on, it is
quite clear in Lord Watson's opinion in *A.G. Ontario* v. *A.G. Canada*, A.C.
348 (1896).

area in which concurrency of jurisdiction is provided in Sections 93 through 95.[14] One is left to speculate on the possibility that if a supremacy clause had been included in the British North America Act, the distribution of powers might have been protected against the distortions induced within it by the austere and remote judgments of the Judicial Committee.

IV

FEDERALISM AND PARLIAMENTARY GOVERNMENT

The most dramatic and most interesting thing about Canada and Australia is the attempt to combine a federal constitution with the practices of parliamentary government. In each case a British people, imbued with and accustomed to the techniques of parliamentary government by virtue of their British background, found themselves in a situation where they were divided by great distances into communities which had long developed a self-conscious particularity of their own.

The resort to a federal system for uniting these separated territories was a natural proposal, but it was equally natural that British colonies should retain their familiar British parliamentary institutions. Although the Canadians made the first attempt to combine the two, the Australians were far more self-conscious and daring as regards the combination. In the years leading up to 1900 they made a very careful search of the precedents and practices of other countries and quite deliberately built their constitution by an eclectic selection of institutions from other lands. The debates of the Australian conventions are full of soul searching regarding the combination of federalism with parliamentary government.[15] The experience of Canada did not at that

---

[14] The British North America Act of 1951 authorized the Dominion to provide old-age pensions concurrently with the provinces. The Act provided, however, that in case of conflict the *provincial* law should prevail over the national.

[15] On the compatibility of federalism and parliamentary government see the reservations voiced in the Australian convention of 1897. *Official Report of the National Australasian Convention* (Adelaide, 1897), pp. 27–31, cited in K. C. Wheare, *Federal Government* (4th ed.; London: Oxford University Press, 1963), p. 80. See also Sir John Quick and Sir Robert Garran,

time seem to be so obvious a precedent, for the Canadian constitution was not thought to be a clearcut federal system, even by
the Canadians themselves, and the Australians were reverting to
the more clearly federal American model and abandoning those
elements in the Canadian constitution that were felt to be less
than federal. In any case the Australian people had always been
much more consciously experiment-minded. Australia during the
nineteenth century had become a laboratory of Victorian radical-
ism and experimental democracy, and the Australians brought to
the task of constitution making a sense of adventure and a
willingness to experiment that did not mark the Canadian constitutional discussions in the 1860's.

Federalism is a cumbersome, difficult and expensive system of
government. It requires a particular kind of political sense for
successful operation. Parliamentary government, no less than
federalism, has its own internal imperatives and propensities, and
those of federalism and those of parliamentary government are
not always compatible with one another. The interesting thing
for the student of federalism is to see how the one affected and
modified the other and to examine in these two countries the
interaction between the two principles.

Above all parliamentary government presumes and encourages
a concentration of power, while the whole thrust of federalism is
toward the fragmentation of it. The question then is how has each
affected the other in the Canadian and Australian experience.

1. The Party System

In Canada and Australia political parties, like many other
things, have acquired a form and practice somewhere between
those of Great Britain and those of the United States. They

Annotated Constitution of the Australian Commonwealth (London: Australian Book Co., 1901), p. 166. Also J. A. McCallum, "How Fares Parliamentary Government in the Federal System?" in *Federalism in Australia*,
ed. Geoffrey Sawer (Melbourne: Cheshire, 1949), pp. 109-34. Of interest also
is a polemical book by A. P. Canaway, *The Failure of Federalism in
Australia* (London: Oxford University Press, 1930), which argues that the
two are wholly incompatible and that federalism makes responsible government impossible.

afford a good point at which to observe the interaction of the two principles. The parliamentary system, as developed in Great Britain, rests upon certain assumptions about the party system, namely, that it be well disciplined, that it be coherent and centralized, and that it be responsible. Indeed parliamentary government is frequently equated with the responsible party system. Federalism in America, on the other hand, has both nurtured and been nurtured by a highly fragmented system of political parties in which a great variety of factions parade under the labels of the national two-party system. Parties in Australia and in Canada are neither so highly centralized as in Great Britain nor so undisciplined as in the United States, and one may argue, although at the risk of a *post hoc propter hoc* conclusion, that the diminution of discipline in the Commonwealth parties is due to the federal character of the system and that the greater centralization than obtained in the United States is due to the exigencies of British parliamentarism.

In both countries party coherence is greater than is known in either Republican or Democratic party, and indeed at any one level of organization the political party evinces a strong and disciplined coherence; but in both Canada and Australia one observes a considerable disjuncture in party organization between the national and the state levels, a disjuncture that has no counterpart in the great national parties of the United Kingdom.

There is also evident in Canada (rather more than in Australia) a tendency to throw up state-based minor parties which have had a considerable persistence over the years. It may be suggested, therefore, that the countervailing tendencies of federalism and parliamentary government have produced in both Australia and Canada party systems typical neither of the traditional federalism of America nor of the traditional parliamentarism of Great Britain, but standing somewhere in between—better disciplined than the one, less centralized than the other.[16]

---

[16] For analyses of the party system in Australia see Louise Overacker, *The Australian Party System* (New Haven: Yale University Press, 1952),

2. The Second Chamber

In both federations the upper chamber of the national legislature—in each case called the Senate—was organized so as to
represent the regional interests that made federalism appropriate.
In Australia, perhaps because of its greater fidelity to the American model, the six states are represented equally in the Senate. In
Canada, however, owing to the greater differences in size and
population among the provinces, the Senate is based upon the
equal representation of four regions, namely, Quebec, Ontario,
the West and the Maritime Provinces. The provinces in the last
two regions receive a specific allotment of Senate seats.[17] Newfoundland is separately represented owing to its much later
accession to the federation.

In neither of the British federations has the upper chamber had
the importance it has had in the United States. This relative
unimportance is directly attributable to the parliamentary system, for parliamentarism makes a strong second chamber impossible. In the first place, the government is directly responsible to
the lower house of the legislature, which excludes the upper house
from the principal arena of political power. Second, the government must be based upon a well organized party, sufficiently
coherent to enable it to get its program through the parliament,
which means that the upper chamber tends to be party-oriented

and S. R. Davis, *The Government of Australian States* (Melbourne:
Longmans, Green, 1960). On federalism and the party system see Miller,
op. cit., pp. 53 ff. There is no comparable study of parties in Canada, but
the following are most useful: *Party Politics in Canada,* ed. Hugh G.
Thorburn (Toronto: Prentice-Hall, 1963), and *Politics: Canada,* ed. Paul
Fox (Toronto: McGraw-Hill Book Co., 1962). On federalism and the party
system see Robert MacGregor Dawson, *The Government of Canada* (2nd
ed.; Toronto: University of Toronto Press, 1954), pp. 529–30 and 572–77,
James Jupp, *Australian Party Politics* (Melbourne: Melbourne University
Press, 1964), and the items mentioned in note 51 below.

[17] Ontario and Quebec each have 24 seats. The western region seats are
divided equally among British Columbia and the three prairie provinces (6
each), and the maritime seats are divided thus: Nova Scotia and New
Brunswick 10 each and Prince Edward Island 4. Newfoundland has an
additional 6 seats, making a total of 102.

rather than state- or region-oriented. Beyond this, moreover, in the twentieth century the popular election of the lower house and the fact that the lower house controls the purse strings of government inevitably give it a far greater political importance. Interestingly enough Professor Wheare argues this point the other way around, that is, that the separation of powers in the United States enhances the power of the United States Senate, since there is no principle that government is responsible to the lower house.[18] There is no incompatibility between these two arguments; the point in each is that the separation of powers and a strong second chamber go together, and parliamentary government and a weak second chamber go together.

In any event the present hypothesis is that the introduction of parliamentary government in a federal system inevitably leads to the decline of the second chamber and to the weakening of whatever representation of state interests that chamber is intended to provide.

The Australian Senate has only rarely served the interests of the states. From almost the very beginning it has been a party-based chamber, and an analysis of Senate votes discloses a consistent pattern of party orientation and only rarely a pattern of state or regional orientation.[19] In Canada the problem is compounded by the peculiar organization of the Senate itself. It is not elected but is appointed by the governor-general on the advice of the prime minister and cabinet. Its members enjoy a life tenure, and it has often been used as a kind of retirement benefit for senescent politicians. The result is that its average age and its average effectiveness are respectively greater and lesser than those of almost any legislative body in the democratic world; consequently it has seldom played a significant part in the political or federal system.

---

[18] Wheare, *op. cit.*, pp. 89–90.

[19] This point can be illustrated by several studies; as good as any for the present purpose is the analysis of votes on constitutional amendments in the writer's *Federalism and Constitutional Change* (Oxford: Clarendon Press, 1956), chap. iii.

3. Composition of the Cabinet

In both Canada and Australia there has taken place what is sometimes called the federalization of the cabinet, as a result of which the cabinet has virtually supplanted the senate as a representative institution and has itself become an instrumentality of federalism.

In Canada the prime minister, in constituting a cabinet, must follow certain quite rigid rules designed to insure the representation of sectional, functional and provincial interests. Every province must have at least one member (when the party system permits); Quebec has four members, one of whom must be English-speaking, and both Montreal and Quebec City must be included among the four; Ontario gets five members, with the North, the West and Toronto all represented; several ministries are traditionally assigned to certain sections of the country—agriculture to the prairies, fisheries to the maritimes, and so on. The rigidity of these requirements has been somewhat on the decline since the Second World War, but they have by no means disappeared, and the result is that the cabinet in Canada, as Alexander Brady has suggested, is often noted more for its representativeness than for its competence.[20] Moreover, when the Dominion and the provincial government are under the control of the same political party, the provincial government tends to regard "its" member of the cabinet as a special representative of the provincial interest at the national level.

In Australia a similar though less insistent principle may be observed. The requirements are far less rigid, and there is no fixed rule that can be spelled out in detail as in Canada; but every Australian prime minister tries to include in his cabinet some representation from each of the six states, and any state that receives no such representation is likely to protest loudly.[21]

---

[20] Alexander Brady, *Democracy in the Dominions* (3rd ed.; Toronto: University of Toronto Press, 1958), p. 83.

[21] See S. Encel, *Cabinet Government in Australia* (Melbourne: Melbourne University Press, 1962), pp. 116–17. Also an article by K. A. McKirdy comparing Australian and Canadian practice, "The Federalization of the

Although the rule is less traditional and less rigid, there is none-theless a striking correlation in the over-all figures between the state's share of cabinet posts and the state's seats in parliament.[22] This suggests that the composition of the cabinet is based upon a combination of principles, deriving in part from the electoral success of the party and in part from its distribution among the several states.

4. Independent Agencies

The fractionizing of power that is part of the character of federalism also opens the way for the creation of independent decision-making bodies which appear to be perfectly compatible with federalism but quite out of harmony with the assumptions of the parliamentary system. The development in the United States of independent regulatory commissions and other autono-mous decision-making entities, more or less outside the control of both the national and the State governments, is quite in keeping with the American constitutional principle of the diffusion of power. The development of such autonomous centers of power in a parliamentary system, however, appears to be clearly incom-patible with the fusion-of-power principle that lies at the heart of parliamentary government, at least in the British form. In both Canada and Australia, however, there is evidence—in the latter case overwhelming evidence—that the same kind of imperative has produced the same kind of autonomous centers of power.

In Canada there is frequent resort to royal commissions for recommendations on problems of a special difficulty, and there has been a gradual development of Dominion-Provincial Confer-ences, by now well established, for the regular fiscal bargaining that takes place between the national and provincial govern-ments.[23] These conferences, begun about the turn of the century

Australian Cabinet, 1909–1939," *Canadian Journal of Economics and Politi-cal Science,* XXIII (1957), 216–26.

[22] Encel, *op. cit.,* p. 118, table 9.

[23] See Wilfrid Eggleston, *The Road to Nationhood: A Chronicle of Dominion-Provincial Relations* (Toronto: Oxford University Press, 1946), and Dawson, *op. cit.,* chap. vi.

on an intermittent ad hoc basis, have come to be meetings at which actual decisions are made regarding fiscal relations.

In Australia a still more significant and obvious set of institutions has developed, again largely in the fiscal sphere. The first of these to be adopted was the Federal Loan Council, which came into existence by virtue of the Financial Agreement of 1927 and the subsequent constitutional amendment of 1928.[24] The Loan Council, which comprises representatives of both states and Commonwealth, now has complete control over all public borrowings, and although the Commonwealth has usually been able to dominate its decisions, it is nonetheless a wholly independent body controlled by neither Commonwealth nor states.

The Commonwealth Grants Commission, although an agency of the national government, stands largely independent of the cabinet and makes recommendations on the whole array of ordinary grants-in-aid annually offered by the Commonwealth to the states. The recommendations of the commission are regularly accepted by the Commonwealth government, which means in effect that in this important area also an independent agency has been created.

Third, there has developed over the years a practice by which the premiers of the states meet annually with the prime minister of the Commonwealth for the discussion of whatever matters are appropriate. The meetings of this so-called premiers' conference are not held in public, but there is a great deal of speculation and comment on what takes place. The most important thing is an annual negotiation and decision on the compensatory grants from the Commonwealth to the states in lieu of the income taxes lost by the states under the uniform tax scheme adopted shortly after the Second World War. The premiers' conference, like the Grants Commission and Loan Council, has thus come to be an independent institution, making significant governmental decisions, outside the regular control of the cabinet, despite the fact that this is a parliamentary system presumably operating according to the principles of responsible party government.

---

[24] Section 105A.

Finally, one may mention the development of a whole complex of quasi-judicial institutions called generically the "arbitration courts." In the Commonwealth and in each state there is a court with a very broad jurisdiction over labor-management relations, including the power to fix a minimum or "living" wage. These institutions take the form of judicial bodies, but the decisions that they regularly make are in fact policy-oriented, and thus the arbitration courts also illustrate the influence of the diffusion-of-power principle upon the parliamentary system.[25]

Parliamentary government presumes a concentration of authority; federalism presumes the reverse. When the two are combined, an amalgam is produced which represents influences and institutions derived from each.

V

The Growth of Federalism

Federalism is inevitably a dynamic and ever changing system, and no attempt at assessing similarities and differences among federal nations can ignore patterns of growth and development. An examination of these patterns in the three countries reveals a surprising similarity, for in each of the three the principal vehicles for development have been the same, namely, judicial interpretation of the constitution and the evolution of new financial relationships. The ways in which these techniques of development have been employed, however, have varied considerably.

1. Judicial Interpretation

In each of the three federations a written constitution spelled out the distribution of authority between the component units and the general government, and in each case the written constitution took the form of a law superior to the authority of either government. Thus, since the distribution of powers was part of

---

[25] A useful brief summary of their working can be found in Miller, *op. cit.*, pp. 110–14.

the supreme law, the task of interpreting and delineating it was thrust upon the judiciary. The courts were expected to serve as arbiters of the distribution and guardians of the boundaries between the two governments. In point of fact the role of the courts has been very much the same in each of the three countries.

The authoritative interpreter of the Constitution in the United States has been the Supreme Court. In Canada the corresponding function was performed by the Supreme Court of Canada, subject to the ultimate decision of the Judicial Committee of the Privy Council, until the final abolition of appeals to the committee in 1949. In Australia the early years of the federation witnessed a running controversy between the High Court of Australia, which tended to follow the more liberal techniques of interpretation of the United States Supreme Court, and the Judicial Committee of the Privy Council, which followed a much more literal and restrictive interpretation. The final decision in matters relating to Australian federalism was settled upon the High Court of Australia in 1907, but with a nice sense of historical irony the High Court in 1920 reversed its position and adopted the interpretive techniques of the Judicial Committee.[26]

There are several points upon which judicial interpretation of the three constitutions can be compared. Among the most obvious of these is that curious doctrine known as dual federalism. The doctrine meant two things. It was, first, a set of assumptions about the character of federalism by which the system was conceived as comprising two exclusive sovereignties, each having full and total authority in its own assigned sphere and neither having power to infringe upon the sphere allotted to the other. Second, it was a judicial doctrine by which courts held that the possession of powers by one government constituted an external and inde-

---

[26] The complex developments thus so briefly summarized may be examined in more detail in Geoffrey Sawer's chap. ii on "Constitutional Law" in G. W. Paton, *The Commonwealth of Australia: the Development of Its Laws and Constitution* (London: Stevens, 1952), esp. pp. 61–76. Useful also is Sir W. Ivor Jennings, *Constitutional Laws of the Commonwealth*, Vol. I. *The Monarchies* (Oxford: Clarendon Press, 1957), chap. v.

pendent limitation upon the exercise of powers by the other government.

In the United States dual federalism was usually, although not consistently, employed by the Supreme Court from the late nineteenth century to 1937 to bar the national government from using powers so as to effect a regulation of something not expressly granted by Article 1, Section 8, of the Constitution and therefore by inference held to be reserved to the States by the Tenth Amendment.[27] In short the Tenth Amendment was said to limit Article 1, Section 8. The Court employed this doctrine primarily in matters of economic regulation, while in questions of morals or health it was perfectly willing to allow the Congress to act, although logic would have precluded congressional action on prostitution and impure food just as it did on minimum wages and child labor. The doctrine was abandoned in 1937.[28]

In the early years of the Australian federation, there was a vigorous dispute between the High Court of Australia and the Judicial Committee of the Privy Council over the technique of interpreting the Australian constitution. The judges of the High Court had made a careful study of American precedents, and since their federation had been modeled on the American, they tended to incorporate into the Australian constitution many of the principles worked out by American courts in regard to the relation between the states and the national government. Among these was the principle of dual federalism, by which the High Court held that the powers of both states and Commonwealth were limited by the lodgement of different powers in the other government. The questions involved turned primarily upon the extent of Commonwealth power over the regulation of industrial

---

[27] In the author's judgment the best examination of the history of dual federalism is to be found in Edward S. Corwin, *The Twilight of the Supreme Court* (New Haven: Yale University Press, 1934), or in his brief lectures, *Constitutional Revolution Ltd.* (Claremont, Calif.: Claremont Colleges, 1941).

[28] *National Labor Relations Board* v. *Jones & Laughlin Steel Corp.*, 301 U.S. 1 (1937), to which should be added *United States* v. *Darby Lumber Co.*, 312 U.S. 100 (1941).

disputes extending beyond a single state and the power of each government to tax the income of employees of the other government. The limitations which the court perceived and enforced were not expressly stated in the constitution; in consequence the Judicial Committee refused to enforce them, adhering instead to its traditionally strict and verbal interpretation of British statutes.[29] For the Judicial Committee dual federalism was not an operative principle, since it rested upon inferences from such intangible criteria as the character of federalism. The Australians responded to the Judicial Committee's decisions by a 1907 statute transferring ultimate control over the Australian constitution out of the hands of the Judicial Committee and into the hands of the High Court itself.[30] From that time until 1920 the High Court continued to employ the principle of dual federalism in its interpretation of the distribution of powers. But a great change came in Australian constitutional development in 1920, when, in the famous Engineer's Case,[31] the High Court reversed its position, adopted the stricter interpretation of the Judicial Committee, and expunged the dual federalist interpretation from the Australian constitution. The United States Supreme Court did not reach this position until 1937.

The Canadian story has been quite different. There has never been the kind of controversy between the Judicial Committee and the Supreme Court of Canada that took place in Australia between the Judicial Committee and the High Court. Dual federalism entered the Canadian constitution, however, about the same time it entered those of the United States and Australia, but by a very different route. The principle was no more explicit in the Canadian constitution than in the Australian, but the wording of the distribution of powers in Sections 91 and 92 was quite different from that in the Australian constitution. Moreover the Brit-

---

[29] See principally *Webb* v. *Outrim* (1907) A.C. 81.

[30] Judiciary Act, 1907. See the account of its enactment and consequences in Geoffrey Sawer, *Australian Federal Politics and Law, 1901-1929* (Melbourne: Melbourne University Press, 1956), pp. 82–83.

[31] *Amalgamated Society of Engineers* v. *Adelaide Steamship Co.*, 28 C.L.R. 129 (1920).

ish North America Act contained two lists of power that were expressly said to be mutually exclusive, whereas most of the powers of the Commonwealth were concurrent. What made the problem worse in Canada was that among the exclusive provincial powers was the power to legislate on "property and civil rights," an unintentionally broad and comprehensive grant of authority. The courts soon came to hold that if a matter dealt in any way with property or civil rights it was exclusively within the jurisdiction of the province, and the Dominion was excluded from acting on it. In consequence of this interpretation the reserve powers ostensibly granted to the Dominion by Section 91 came ultimately to reside in Section 92.13, "property and civil rights," and the general reserve power of the Dominion, of which Sir John Macdonald had been so proud, was restricted to use only in extreme national emergencies.[32] The abandonment of appeals to the Judicial Committee in 1949 has not had any serious effect upon this interpretation. There were very few disagreements between the Judicial Committee and the Supreme Court, and the latter, bound by a long line of precedents and decisions, has held closely to the line of interpretation laid down early in the century. Consequently dual federalism is still an operative principle in the Canadian system so far as the interpretation of Sections 91 and 92 is concerned.[33]

A companion principle to dual federalism is that of "implied reciprocal immunity of instrumentalities," which originated in John Marshall's opinion in *McCulloch* v. *Maryland* (1819). Marshall argued that the United States Bank, as an instrumentality of the national government, was immune from State taxation on

---

[32] The leading cases are *A.G. Canada* v. *A.G. Alberta,* A.C. 588 (1916); *Toronto Electricity Commissioners* v. *Snider,* A.C. 396 (1925); and *A.G. Canada* v. *A.G. Ontario,* A.C. 236 (1937) (one of the "New Deal" cases). Useful summaries of the whole development may be found in W. I. Jennings, "Constitutional Interpretation—The Experience of Canada," *Harvard Law Review,* LI (1937), 1–39, and in Dawson, *op. cit.,* chaps. v and vii.

[33] A lucid and concise comparison of the operation of dual federalism in all three federations may be found in Wallace Mendelson, "Dual Federalism in Canada, Australia, and the United States," in *The Study of Comparative Government,* ed. Jasper B. Shannon (New York: Appleton-Century-Crofts, 1949), pp. 127–46.

the ground that "the power to tax is the power to destroy." The immunity of the Federal instrumentality from State taxation or interference was nowhere expressly provided for in the Constitution. Hence the immunity was held to be "implied" by the principles of a federal system. In subsequent decisions the Court also held that governmental functions of the States were immune from Federal taxation and regulation; hence the implied immunity was also "reciprocally" operative between the two governments. This principle has been weakened but not wholly abandoned in the American federation. State functions held to be governmental in character are immune from Federal regulation or taxation, but functions held to be "proprietary" (for example, public amusements, liquor sales, commercial ventures) are subject to nondiscriminatory taxation and regulation by the national government. Since the national government may exercise only assigned powers, all of its activities are governmental and therefore immune from State taxation.

The Australian history of the doctrine of implied immunities was coterminous with that of dual federalism, of which it is logically a part. Indeed the question of dual federalism often turned on the question of reciprocal immunities, most particularly in the form of one government's ability to tax the salary of the other's employees. So long as the American "liberal" interpretation was employed by the High Court, it was easy to infer from the constitution that each government was limited by the separate existence of the other, and to deduce from that existence that the instrumentalities of the one were immune from interference by the other. But after 1920 and the resort by the High Court to the strict, literal, interpretation preferred by the Judicial Committee, the implied prohibitions and immunities virtually disappeared. Consequently the doctrine has had very little place in the Australian federal system since the Engineer's Case in 1920.[34]

In Canada there is no story to tell. Both the Supreme Court

---

[34] Australian law appears to be somewhat uncertain on this point, for there have recently been several renewed suggestions of implied immunities. See the discussion by Geoffrey Sawer in Paton, *op. cit.*, pp. 63–67.

and the Judicial Committee adhered from the beginning to a strict verbal interpretation of the British North America Act, and since that act contained no express limitations barring either government from impinging upon the instrumentalities of the other, no such limitations could be inferred from any external criterion, even though dual federalism has been consistently employed since the 1890's.

The most significant impact of judicial interpretation, however, has been in the expansion of the powers of the national government, for it has been through the judicial reinterpretation of the distribution of powers that the "balance" of federalism has been decisively shifted to the general government—at least in two of the federations. Judicial review has been most significant in this regard in the United States, next most significant in Australia and least of all in Canada. Indeed in Canada the impact of judicial interpretation has been to strengthen the provincial rather than the national powers.

In the United States the effect of judicial review in strengthening national power may be seen most clearly in the commerce power and in the power to tax and spend. In the early decades of the republic the Supreme Court took a broad view of the powers of the national government, especially in the period of John Marshall's tenure on the Court. One of the more notable of the decisions was *Gibbons* v. *Ogden* (1824), in which the majority defined "commerce" as intercourse among the States. By the end of the century a much narrower interpretation had been adopted, so that the powers of the Congress were considerably straitened. The reversal of this trend was given a very considerable boost after 1937 with the abandonment of dual federalism and in several decisions in which the power of Congress over interstate commerce was broadened to include power over almost the entire economy. The development has now reached the point where one can say that there is no commerce in the United States that is so exclusively intrastate as to be beyond the power of Congress to regulate.[35]

---

[35] For illustration of its use to regulate noneconomic matters: standards of pure foods and drugs (*Hipolite Egg Co.* v. *U.S.*, 220 U.S. 45 [1911]);

Much the same thing has taken place with regard to the taxing power. There has been a gradual expansion of the uses of the taxing power by Congress and a reduction of the limitations on the exercise of that power. Congress can use the taxing power to regulate or prohibit activities as well as to produce revenue; the only limitations seem to be that the tax must be for the purpose of paying the debts of the United States or for providing for the common defense or general welfare. In consequence Congress can *tax* and *spend* for the general welfare, even though it has no constitutional power to *regulate* for the general welfare.[36]

The kind of expansion that has taken place with regard to the commerce and taxing powers can also be found with regard to other powers in the Constitution, principally that mixture of grants of authority collectively called "the war powers."

The expansion of national power is often misrepresented, however, by both its critics and its supporters. What has really happened is not that the constitutional authority itself has grown but that the subject (for example, interstate commerce) over which that authority is to be exercised has grown. In the early nineteenth century there was very little commerce that could be called interstate; in the middle of the twentieth century practically all commerce is interstate in one way or another. The change that has taken place is in the commerce rather than in the power. Congress has always had the authority to regulate the subject, but with the growth of the economy the subject has become national or interstate in character. The same kind of argument can be made with regard to the war powers. So long as the United States maintained an isolationist and neutralist attitude, the war powers meant little. But in the twentieth century,

---

regulation of prostitution (*Effie Hoke* v. *U.S.*, 227 U.S. 308 [1913]); stolen automobiles (*Brooks* v. *U.S.*, 267 U.S. 432 [1925]). The extension to virtually total power to control the economy can be seen in *National Labor Relations Board* v. *Jones & Laughlin Steel Corp.*, 301 U.S. 1 (1937); *Wickard* v. *Filburn*, 317 U.S. 111 (1942); and *Katzenbach* v. *McClung*, 379 U.S. 294 (1964).

[36] The taxing power and these "limitations" on it are found in Article I, Section 8, of the Constitution. The basic judicial analysis of the taxing power is found in *U.S.* v. *Butler*, 297 U.S. 1 (1936).

after two world wars, a "police action," an "advisory" role in Southeast Asia and a continuing threat of nuclear holocaust, the subject of defense or "war" has come to mean a great deal more than it once did, and the power of Congress has expanded accordingly.

In both the United States and Australia the commerce power is limited to interstate and foreign commerce. In Canada the power appears to be much broader, for the Dominion Parliament is authorized to regulate all trade and commerce.[37] But the ability of the Dominion to make use of this power has been strictly circumscribed by court decisions that have held it to be in conflict with the provincial power over property and civil rights. The result is that the Dominion power over trade and commerce has been whittled down to little more than the power to charter corporations. In Australia, although the wording of the clause is very similar to that in the United States Constitution, the power has meant very little and has been but little used. The explanation appears to lie in a judicial and legislative reluctance to use the commerce power owing to the uncertainty and apprehension about Section 92, which prescribes that trade and commerce among the states shall be absolutely free.[38]

The corresponding judicial broadening of national power in Australia took place around a different authority. Section 51.35 confers on the Commonwealth government the power to legislate for "the conciliation and arbitration of industrial disputes extending beyond the limits of any one state." The High Court has dealt with this clause in much the same way that the Supreme Court in America has dealt with the commerce clause: each of the words and ideas contained in the statement of authority has been argued and expanded. For example, the American Court

---

[37] The national power in the United States extends to "commerce with foreign nations, and among the several states, and with the Indian tribes" (Article I, Section 8); in Australia to "trade and commerce with other countries, and among the states" (Section 51.1); and in Canada to "the regulation of trade and commerce" (Section 91.2).

[38] On Section 92 see note 9 above. For a comparison of the three commerce powers, see Wheare, *op. cit.*, pp. 129–41.

spent long years trying to define the difference between interstate and intrastate commerce and has now arrived at a very broad definition of national power through these decisions. So in Australia there have been many decisions seeking to distinguish between those industrial disputes that do, and those that do not, extend beyond the limits of any one state. Other Commonwealth powers (for example, the war powers) have been treated in the same way and have been similarly broadened, but so far as judicial interpretation is concerned, it is the industrial-dispute power that has provided the major vehicle for national expansion.[39]

In Canada the trend of judicial interpretation has been markedly different. Since the late nineteenth century the Canadian Supreme Court and the Judicial Committee of the Privy Council have regularly given a higher priority to provincial power than to Dominion power. This may be attributed to the strict technique of interpretation employed by the Judicial Committee, to the fact that the framers of the constitution made an egregious mistake in listing the powers reserved to the Dominion in Section 91, to the very broadly stated provincial power over property and civil rights and to the adoption and persistence of the doctrine of dual federalism, which has principally operated to restrict the Dominion government. In effect the broad general power reserved to the Dominion at the head of Section 91 has been almost entirely dissipated, and the reserved powers in the constitution may be said to lie in the property and civil rights clause of Section 92.13. The consequence is that, while the Dominion may legislate for the purposes mentioned in Section 91 (the "illustrations" of the general power), the validity of its legislation is tested against the more broadly stated exclusive powers of the provinces, and it may not use its general or reserved power unless there exists an extreme national emergency. If the act in question can be held to come under Section 92, then

---

[39] See the discussion by G. Sawer in Paton, *op. cit.*, pp. 306–9; also his *Australian Constitutional Cases* (Melbourne: Law Book Co. of Australasia, 1948), chap. v.

the Dominion cannot act; almost anything can be found in Section 92 if the court is willing to look for it diligently.

Should we then conclude that the national power is more severely circumscribed in Canada and in Australia than it is in the United States? Yes, on the basis of judicial interpretation. The difficulty is that judicial interpretation does not tell the whole story of the expansion of national powers. In both Canada and Australia (and in the United States too, though differently and to a lesser extent) the power of the national government has been broadened through the exigencies and devices of public finance in such a way as to produce about the same result in expanding national powers that judicial interpretation has produced by itself in the United States.

2. Public Finance

In any federation two distributions of authority are necessary to make the federal system work. One of these, called the distribution of powers, is the obvious distribution of legislative or regulatory authority. In addition, however, there must also be, whether explicitly or by implication, a distribution of fiscal resources. The two distributions must somehow be in equilibrium, for the government that performs a function must have sufficient tax resources to pay the costs of performing the function. The difficulty is that the distribution of powers and the distribution of tax resources are very difficult to keep in balance, for the forces that alter the one do not necessarily alter the other in the same way. In all three federal unions the fiscal resources of the national government have expanded more rapidly than its legislative functions. The result has invariably been that the national government has more tax resources than it needs, and the states are left with more functions to perform than tax resources with which to perform them.

The growing problem, therefore, is to bring these two distributions back into equilibrium. There appear to be three ways in which this can be done. The first is to transfer functions outright from the states to the national government. Efforts have been made in every federation to do just this. The Australians have considered a whole series of constitutional amendments by which legislative powers would be transferred to the national government, but with one exception [40] they have invariably been turned down by the electorate. In Canada there have been two instances [41] in which functions have been transferred to the Dominion, but it is very difficult to amend the Canadian constitution, since no one knows yet exactly how it can be done. In the United States efforts to accomplish this have seldom gotten beyond the preliminary stages, owing to the extreme sensitivity of States-rights groups about the autonomy and authority of the States. It is fair to conclude, therefore, that this solution to the problem is not politically feasible.

The second device would be to transfer tax resources from the national government to the states, but this encounters a different sort of difficulty, fiscal rather than political, for the fact is that there is no correlation between the tax resources that might be transferred and the functions to be performed in the several states. President Dwight Eisenhower's Joint Federal-State Action Committee spent two years to find a way by which certain Federal taxes and certain grant-aided programs might both be transferred to the States, but the effort resulted in almost complete failure. The transfer of tax resources merely exaggerates the differentials among the States. Thus it is fair to conclude that this second device is as fiscally difficult as the first one is politically difficult.

The third alternative is to transfer, not tax resources, but cash from the national government to the states, in the form of grants-in-aid. Every federation has resorted to this device in one form or another, and in each of the three countries here considered the national grants to the states have been developing

---

[40] In 1946 an amendment authorized the Commonwealth to provide several social services.

[41] The British North America Act of 1940 transferred unemployment insurance to the Dominion and that of 1951 authorized it to provide old-age pensions.

through virtually the whole life of the federation to the point where they now constitute a major source of revenue to the states and provinces.

The fiscal resources of the national government have in each case tended to grow, although in quite different ways. In the United States, adoption of the Sixteenth Amendment made it possible for the national government to levy taxes on personal and corporate incomes without apportioning those taxes among the States in accordance with population. The income tax has made it possible for the United States to draw uniformly upon a tremendous body of nationwide revenues from which it would otherwise be barred and which would not be readily accessible to State income taxation.

In Australia the principal strengthening of the national revenues came from the uniform-tax scheme, adopted during and after the Second World War, in which the Commonwealth government adopted a uniform income tax throughout the country and forced the states out of the income-tax field in return for compensatory grants. Theretofore the states had levied income taxes at widely varying levels, which meant that any Commonwealth tax had to be very limited and that in many states there were large blocks of income not taxed by either state or national government. The establishment of a national monopoly on the income tax has given to the central government the same sort of significant increase in fiscal strength that the Sixteenth Amendment gave in the United States.

In Canada a somewhat different system has been necessary, inasmuch as the British North America Act assigns exclusively to the provinces all direct taxes, presumably including the income tax. After a long series of consultations between the Dominion and the provinces, an arrangement was reached by which the provinces voluntarily turn over to the Dominion the power to levy personal and corporate income taxes. The provinces then, like the states in Australia, receive compensatory grants to replace their lost revenues. Although not all provinces have regularly "rented" all their taxing power to the Dominion, the arrangement has nonetheless enabled the Dominion to levy taxes on a broad national basis so that, as far as the practical operation of the system is concerned, the income tax has become a device and resource of the national government.

In each federation the enlargement of the fiscal power of the central government has been accompanied by an elaborate system of grants-in-aid to the states. The grants themselves differ in purpose and character and are calculated on different bases. Some of them are unconditional, some are conditional; some are based on a per capita distribution, some are based on state needs; some require systematic conformity to national standards and purposes, some are general grants that the states may use as they will. But in each country the component units have come to be more and more dependent upon the central government for the revenues that enable them to perform their functions. This not only has altered the character of the federal relationship but has given rise, particularly in Australia and Canada, to a whole new set of institutions designed to manage the distribution of federal funds and control the fiscal activities of the two governments. In Canada these matters are handled through regular Dominion-Provincial Conferences; in Australia the Premiers' Conference decides on the compensatory grants under the uniform-tax scheme, and the Commonwealth Grants Commission decides on all other grants-in-aid. In addition the Australian Loan Council regulates public borrowings by both Commonwealth and states.[42]

In each case what has happened is that the society has become more and more highly industrialized, the population more highly urbanized and trade and commerce more obviously national in character. The economy is no longer rural and agricultural but industrialized, interdependent and specialized, each part supplying the needs of other parts. The old doctrines of laissez faire have been abandoned, being replaced by elaborate regulatory and social-welfare policies which enhance the activities of government and the costs of administration. Moreover in all three

---

[42] The best recent study of the fiscal problems and relations of a federal state is A. H. Birch, *Federalism, Finance, and Social Legislation* (Oxford: Clarendon Press, 1955).

federations the costs of defense have risen sharply in the years since the Second World War. The consequence of all these changes has been that the central government has had to undertake and accept a vastly enlarged responsibility. But the industrialization of the country, coupled with the national control of the income tax, has meant that the fiscal powers of the central government have been even more greatly enhanced.

In each of the three nations the traditional conception of federalism, based, as Dicey said, on legalism, has been fundamentally altered. Traditionally federalism was conceived as a balance of power between the national government and the states, two equal and coordinate spheres, each possessing sovereignty. The distribution of powers was viewed as an area for legal battles, as indeed it was; a court was the arbiter of the system, and the delineation of powers and functions was a task for the courts to perform. But the reality has been fundamentally altered. The changed interpretation of powers, together with the growth of fiscal resources, has lodged an authority in the national government that is unlike anything contained in the traditional conception. The power of the purse has given to the national government a control over activities at both state and national level that was unknown in earlier years. In effect the court has abandoned its role as arbiter of the system—almost wholly in the United States, nearly as much in Australia and to a very considerable extent in Canada. The consequence of these two developments, judicial and fiscal, is that federalism in all three federations has come to be more and more a political matter and less and less a legal matter.[43]

3. The Accommodation of Law and Practice

To what extent then have the three federations been able to accommodate the constitutional law of federalism to the new realities of federal government? The answer is not quite the same

---

[43] See the writer's "The Legal and Political Determinants of American Federalism," *Southwestern Social Science Quarterly,* XXXIV (1953), 40–56; also the shrewd comparative analyses by J. A. Corry, "Constitutional Trends and Federalism," in Lower, Scott *et al., op. cit.,* pp. 92–125.

in each country. In the United States the accommodation has gone pretty far: the old argument about the two sovereignties competing with and balancing each other has been firmly settled in favor of the general government. The United States, by virtue of its fiscal control, its income tax, its power to regulate commerce, its ability to tax and spend, and its commitment to the demands of national defense, can do virtually anything it wishes to do. It is safe to say that the federal system now places almost no limitations at all upon it.[44]

In Australia much the same argument can be made, although the development has seemingly not gone quite so far. Much more of the accommodation is found in the quasi-legal field of public finance and less of it in the judicial expansion of the powers of the government themselves.

In Canada the accommodation has scarcely taken place at all so far as the law is concerned. There have been only the two amendments mentioned above that have enhanced federal power, and the pattern of judicial interpretation has changed but little. In Canada even more than in Australia the accommodation has been almost entirely in terms of financial relations between the Dominion and the provinces.

Even so much the same result has been achieved, although the techniques and the extent of the accommodation of law and practice are quite different in the three. The basic issues are no longer phrased as legal issues but as political questions. In the United States the distribution of "powers" and the assignment of functions as between the national government and the States are now matters for the policy decision of the general government. In Canada the central control of finance, plus the all-important political fact that very few people care to raise constitutional challenges to the benefits that come from present fiscal relations, have meant that a practical kind of federalism has emerged which overrides or ignores the legal difficulties that arise from the dual federalist interpretation of the constitution. In Australia the

---

[44] It is also true that it places very few limitations on the States. See the discussion that follows.

uniform-tax system, plus the distribution of compensatory grants through the Premiers' Conference, has given a tremendous control to the central government, but a control that assigns both considerable revenue and extensive functions to the states. The point is, however, that these are all political values, political processes and political decisions. Federalism has become a political rather than a legal phenomenon.

VI

THE CHANGED CHARACTER OF FEDERALISM

These far-reaching changes in the character of federal government, together with the transformation of the society that subtends it, have clearly produced a significant alteration in the nature of modern federalism—significant, indeed, that many people have suggested that federalism is either obsolescent or dead.[45] A closer examination, however, suggests that such a conclusion is at least premature, and more likely just plain wrong, for it rests upon a faulty assessment of what has actually happened. In the old sense of a balance of powers and a struggle between competing sovereignties, federalism may well be dead, but it displays a continued and indeed increasing vitality if we view it in terms of social and political conduct within a changing pattern of state-national relations. This altered but persistent vitality manifests itself in several different ways.

1. The Decentralization of Functions

First of all one must be careful to distinguish between the centralization of power and the centralization of governmental function, for the two do not necessarily go hand in hand. The centralization of governmental power has not been accompanied by a corresponding centralization of governmental function— even in the United States, where the centralization of legislative

---

[45] The classic statement is that by Harold J. Laski, "The Obsolescence of Federalism," *New Republic*, XCVIII (May 3, 1939), 367–69.

authority has been most pronounced. The period of centralization of governmental authority in the United States—say from 1937 on —has also been the period in which there has developed an elaborate array of devices for what is called cooperative federalism. Cooperative federalism is a system by which state and national governments supplement each other and jointly perform a variety of functions. The point to be made of this is that the national government, with its enlarged powers, has supplemented rather than supplanted the performance of functions by the States, through cooperation between administrative agencies, through the decentralization of Federal administrative functions, through complementary legislation and through other devices.

The ancient Cooley Rule [46] is still operative in the United States and in accordance with it the Supreme Court every year upholds half a dozen State regulations, even in areas where the national government might act if it wished to do so. In various areas the national government and the States exercise a concurrent regulation, the statutes of each being designed to supplement those of the other. The United States has adopted laws of various sorts designed to facilitate and enhance State administration of State laws. For example, in the regulation of gambling and the sale of liquor a national statute has provided that an action in violation of a State law (for example, the importation of liquor) is also a violation of the national law. Finally in several matters (for example, insurance [47]) in which the national government has been clearly declared by the courts to have jurisdiction, the Congress has transferred that jurisdiction to the States. This has been done not by constitutional amendment but by a kind of congressional abdication of function. The point is not that these things are not within the power of the national government but that the

---

[46] From the U.S. Supreme Court decision in *Cooley* v. *Board of Wardens of the Port of Philadelphia,* 12 Howard 299 (1851). The "rule" is that in a sphere in which the United States might legitimately act but has not acted, the States may act so long as there is no need for uniformity of action.

[47] See *U.S.* v. *South-Eastern Underwriters Assn.,* 322 U.S. 533 (1944), for the nationalization of the power, and *Prudential Insurance Co.* v. *Benjamin,* 328 U.S. 408 (1946), for Court approval of the decentralization of function.

national government has exercised its power in such a way as to lodge the function itself in the States rather than at the national level. It is worth noting that the ability of Congress to decentralize the function depended upon a constitutional interpretation that centralized the power.

Something of the same thing can be argued about Canada and Australia. In both countries the important central power arises from the central control over finance (although in Australia there has also been a considerable judicial expansion of national powers), and in both there has also developed a corresponding system of national grants to the states or provinces. In Canada and Australia these grants are mainly unconditional, with the result that the important policy decisions on how to spend the grant money rest with the states to a far greater extent than in the United States. In America all the grants are subject to conditions upon their acceptance and use, for they are clearly designed to achieve national purposes. Hence, the growth of central fiscal power in America has meant a somewhat greater degree of centralization in decision making. In Canada and Australia the use of unconditional grants leaves much of this decision-making power, and hence much of the decision on function, with the states and provinces.

Even in the United States, however, where the conditions on the grants do appear to transfer decision-making authority to the national government, State administrative officers are consulted to a surprising extent in making the decisions on the conditions that go along with the use of the grant funds. Indeed in many instances the decision on the character of the conditions is actually made by State administrative officers rather than by officers of the national government itself.[48]

Another observation should be made about the fiscal and administrative relationships within the United States. The frag-

---

[48] See W. Brooke Graves, *American Intergovernmental Relations* (New York: Charles Scribner's Sons, 1964), p. 809; also Morton Grodzins, "The Federal System," in the Report of the President's Commission on National Goals, *Goals for Americans* (New York: Prentice-Hall, 1960), p. 266.

mentation of power which lies at the heart of the American governmental system can be observed at both State and national levels. There is an increasing specialization and fragmentation of authority in the executive-administrative branch itself, at the State level by constitutional and legal tradition and at the national level by the increasing technological specialization of governmental functions. This means that there are channels of communication and functional decision making that run direct from administrative officers of the State to corresponding administrative officers of the national government, and these channels are to a large extent technologically isolated from the political branches of government. The result is that State and national officials, many of whom are professionally rather than politically oriented, are relatively free to develop administratively satisfactory arrangements concerning joint purposes and programs and the joint use of federal funds—free, that is to say, from political control or sensitivity on the part of governor or President, to say nothing of state legislature and the Congress.

Nothing of this sort can be found in Canada or Australia, because the basic condition of fragmented power is lacking. The character of responsible cabinet government means that political control extends through the administrative system to a considerably greater extent than is true in the United States. Thus political concerns are more completely excluded from these arrangements in the United States than in the other two federations, and State officials are significantly influencing what appears to be a Federal program.

It is no good talking simply about the centralization of power. That can be conceded in all three federations, in the sense of both fiscal power and constitutional power. Crying States rights in the sense of decrying national power is flogging a dead horse; those who would decentralize power would reverse history. Since power has already been centralized, it is impossible to seek a decentralization of power through a conscious decision of the national government, for the very decision to decentralize power could only be made by the government that possesses it. Indeed to seek a decentralization of function is merely to concede that the power to make the decision decentralizing functions is lodged in the place where it is made.[49] The point, however, is that the centralization of power has not been accompanied by a centralization of function; indeed the centralized power of the national government has frequently been employed to make the decision that the functions of government shall be decentralized.

2. Party Systems

Since the exercise of authority is inevitably based upon a political decision, it behooves us to examine the extent to which the political process itself is centralized or decentralized. The focus of such an examination is obviously the party system.

It goes without saying that the American party system is highly decentralized, a proposition requiring no elaborate explanation. One reason for this decentralization, however, is surely the existence of the Federal system. That is to say, the constitutional structure of federalism still compels political parties to organize on a Federal basis, for the State as a site of power and function constitutes a separate and different objective of political party activity. American parties are decentralized in at least three different senses. First, the local parties are discrete units, existing for the pursuit of control over State and local governments. Second, national parties can only intermittently and ineffectively control local parties. Third, local parties do exercise a considerable control over the national parties. In consequence the party system, with its emphasis upon State and local units, helps maintain a decentralization of decision making and thus the Federal System. Legalistic federalism itself, as conceived and contrived by the fathers of the Constitution, is no longer very important; but the fathers' system helped to create weak parties, and thus ironically—as Morton Grodzins has pointed out—what the fathers sought to avoid, namely, parties, has

---

[49] See Morton Grodzins' argument about the fatuity of "decentralization by order" in his article in Goldwin, *op. cit.*, pp. 21–22.

served to achieve what the fathers sought to accomplish, namely, the fragmentation of power.[50] One may say, therefore, that in America the decentralization of power within the political parties operates to strengthen the decentralization of the political decision-making process and in consequence gives a strength to federalism that it would not otherwise have. This is a cyclical argument. The character of the parties sustains federalism, and federalism sustains the decentralized character of the parties; but the argument is no less valid for being cyclical. Politics is often a merry-go-round.

The more interesting concern is with the character and role of party in Canada and Australia. Both possess parliamentary systems in the British tradition, and the British parliamentary system, with its responsible party system, both presumes and encourages a highly disciplined, centralized, party system. Federalism has the opposite influence. The combination of these contrary influences results, as we have seen, in a party system midway between the two extremes. The hypothesis has been that in Canada and Australia, the party system, to the extent that it is decentralized, helps maintain the decentralization of power and hence both sustains and articulates the principle of federalism.

In Canada as in America there are two levels of the party system, Dominion and provincial. But the party systems at the two levels are quite different. At the national level there is a straightforward two-party competition, to which one must add a variety of seldom successful minor parties, whose presence does not seriously vitiate the two-party principle. At the provincial level, however, the two-party system of the Dominion breaks down; in most of the provinces one of the national parties faces a local party that may also compete as a minor party at the national level. Only in Ontario and in the Maritime Provinces is the national party system reproduced at the local level. Recent studies suggest that people vote in quite different ways in provin-

---

[50] "American Political Parties and the American System," *Western Political Quarterly*, XIII (1960), 998.

cial and national elections,[51] and the strength in some provinces of Social Credit, the New Democratic Party, the traditionally French-oriented parties of Quebec or even of the Liberals in Newfoundland displays little correlation to the success of those parties in national elections. The national party cannot exercise a completely effective control over the provincial party, even when the provincial party bears the same label. The provincial party leaders conceive themselves to be agents of their own local party and province, not mere instruments of the national party organization, and they bargain with the national government to secure a fair share of the grant distribution without much regard to the question whether they are members of the political party that controls the national government. Provincial party decision making, therefore, is largely a local affair, and there is a decided disjuncture between the local or provincial party organization and the national party organization.[52]

In Australia there appear to be three parties at the national level, but the Liberal and Country parties have maintained an electoral and governmental alliance against the Labour party for most of the postwar era, so there is actually a two-party system at the national level. At the state level, however, the Liberal-Country coalition has not had the strength or coherence that it has had at the national level. The three parties compete separately in the states,[53] along with a sprinkling of minor groups, but their effectiveness and success vary widely. It happens that in nearly every state there is a two-party competition, but it is

---

[51] See Howard A. Scarrow, "Federal-Provincial Voting Patterns in Canada," *Canadian Journal of Economics and Political Science,* XXVI (1960), 289–98; Dawson, *op. cit.,* pp. 575 ff.; also Robert L. Alford, "The Social Bases of Political Cleavage in 1962," in *Papers on the 1962 Election,* ed. John Meisel (Toronto: University of Toronto Press, 1964), p. 204.

[52] One of the most thoughtful studies of this relationship is contained in an unpublished paper delivered at the 1961 meeting of the American Political Science Association by Steven Muller of Cornell University, "Federalism and the Party System in Canada."

[53] There are exceptions to this, especially as regards the Country party, which has the most decidedly regional orientation of the three. It has a number of completely safe seats, but it has no organization in Tasmania, and in South Australia it has always been merged with the Liberals. Overacker, *op. cit.,* p. 307.

not the same two-party competition that takes place in the national government. The Labour party in particular has had difficulty in holding its state and national parties together. The recurring controversies within the party in New South Wales suggest how difficult it has been for the national party to maintain the sort of discipline over its local organizations that one is accustomed to in Great Britain.[54] Hence although the Labour party has long advocated a much greater centralization of governmental power, it is in fact the least centralized of the three major political parties. The Liberal and Country parties have traditionally favored decentralization of governmental power on principle, and the national leadership of these parties has not made any serious effort to coerce or discipline the state party organizations.

Thus in Australia as in Canada the state party organizations are more or less autonomous and do not conceive themselves to be merely the local arms of the national party organization;[55] federalism has produced a measure of decentralization. But one must guard against overstressing the local autonomy in party organization. In spite of the federal structure and the traditional value assigned to state autonomy in all three parties, each of them is a strong national party with a national program and a national coherence. The system is not so decentralized as that of the United States; neither is it so centralized as that of Great Britain. The federal system helps sustain a relative decentralization, and this fragmentation of political authority within the party system helps to maintain the fragmentation of political authority in the system of government.[56]

3. The Social Values of Federalism

Discussions of federal government frequently miss the point, for they tend to concentrate on powers, jurisdictions, "balances" and other legal questions; but the primary requirements for

---

[54] See *ibid.*, chaps. iii–iv, and especially pp. 84, 100, 318–19.

[55] This is a particular thesis of James Jupp's *Australian Party Politics*, cited above, note 16.

[56] Riker, *op. cit.*, pp. 119–20.

federalism are diversities among the peoples of a nation and diverse values of the people within the society. There is accordingly a psycho-sociological complex of values in any society which determines the shape and character of political and governmental institutions. Federalism, no less than other forms of government, is a response to the values of the society.

This point is most obviously seen in Canada, where federalism has been essentially a French-English relationship and because of that fact essentially unique. Federalism in Canada, although it takes a broader form, is basically a means by which the two "races" live together and pursue certain purposes in common. The Canadian federal system is really a means of accommodation of the French-speaking and the English-speaking Canadians, disguised by a broadly based constitutional structure which assigns to each of the ten provinces an almost equal place in the system. This two-sidedness of Canadian federalism channels and distorts the whole argument about federal government in Canada.

Federalism is a complex and cumbersome system; it has value because people think it has value. In the United States, for example, despite the growth of national power, a great deal of popular thinking about government is still in the more traditional Federal terms; people still talk about States rights, assuming that there continues to be a balance or struggle between the States and the national government. In point of fact the interests about which this controversy turns are more frequently region- than state-oriented, but the constitutional tradition and structure assign to States rather than to regions the legal authority and hence the political value. The States-rights movement in the United States for the past fifty years has been largely a cloak to hide a laissez faire argument about governmental activity in the economy and, despite the obvious irrelevance of much of the argument, it is still used. The point is that those who use it know full well that it constitutes an effective political appeal. Whether States rights means anything or not in terms of law and practice, it unquestionably means a great deal so far as politics is concerned. Many of the States in the American union were created artificially and arbitrarily, in order to fill out a map or add factional seats in the Senate. But federalism endows the component parts with all the attributes of particularity and tends to engender a sense of difference and value where none may theretofore have existed. Ultimately and fundamentally federalism rests not on constitutional or legal bases but on the profound psychological and sociological values of the people whose diversities, real or imagined, it is designed to protect and articulate.

Australia displays rather less regional or state loyalty than does Canada or the United States. Indeed one is sometimes tempted to wonder why the Australians retain their federal system. The Australians often wonder about this also. But Australian states like American States engender and perpetuate their own loyalty systems, and although the Gallup Polls in Australia have sometimes suggested that the Australian people would be prepared to abandon federalism, they also suggest that, so long as federalism is to be retained, the states must be given an important and viable role in its operation.[57] There has been for some years considerable public support for the creation of new states in Australia to be carved out of the large territories of the six existing states. Moreover constitutional proposals to enlarge the legislative powers of the Commonwealth have been regularly repudiated by the Australian electorate. There appears to be considerable public support for the maintenance of federal government, which is not likely to be overborne by legal or fiscal arguments about the practical centralization of governmental authority.

VII

Conclusion

Despite the expansion of national power in all three federations, whether by judicial interpretation, by the growth of fiscal

---

[57] See R. S. Parker, "The People and the Constitution," in *Federalism in Australia,* ed. G. Sawer, pp. 135–89, and Gordon Greenwood, "The Case for Extended Commonwealth Powers," in the same volume, pp. 37–63, esp. p. 62; also the writer's *Federalism and Constitutional Change,* pp. 136–42.

powers or by a combination of both, and despite the consequent politicization of federalism, federalism remains a meaningful, active and viable system of government. It is quite different from what it once was: it no longer represents a meaningful controversy between national and state governments; it turns much more significantly on the policy decision of the central government than upon a judicial battle between the two governments. But it remains significant, even though its character is altered.

In the first place, decentralization of governmental functions is quite as significant as centralization of legal and fiscal powers; in the second place, the working of the party system helps maintain a decentralization of political authority and political decision making; in the third place, the persistence of a complex of psychological and sociological values and predispositions means that the basic forces that called federalism into being seem likely to sustain it in operation, however changed its character. In each case what is emerging is a federalism of functions instead of powers—a federalism of politics instead of law.

In these fundamental aspects the similarities among the three federations appear to be more significant for the long run than the differences among them.

KARL H. CERNY
Georgetown University

FEDERALISM IN THE
WEST GERMAN REPUBLIC

To UNDERSTAND THE DEVELOPMENT of federalism in the West German Republic since its establishment in 1949, it is useful to review previous German efforts to establish federal systems of government. In the aftermath of the collapse of Nazi totalitarianism the development of West German federalism was only partially influenced by the requirements of the Allies. With the exception of the Communist minority the Germans who met in the Bonn Parliamentary Council during the constitutional deliberations of 1948–49 were already in broad agreement on the desirability of establishing a federal government. From their point of view the task was to re-establish a federal system that would improve upon the attempts at federalism in the Hohenzollern Reich and in the Weimar Republic.

They were reacting against both the extreme centralization of the Nazi regime and the presumed shortcomings of their pre-Nazi federal traditions. An examination of this historical record, undertaken in the first section of the essay, helps to underline the differences of origin, structure and environment of German federalism as compared with the English-speaking federations.

In the second section there is consideration of the growth of German federalism since 1949. Like the English-speaking federations the German system has had to cope with a trend toward ever increasing centralization. Admittedly the pattern of German response is thus far the product of a very short period of time. It is nevertheless possible to note the types of institutional problems and adjustments that have occurred. Comparing them with the experience of English-speaking federations may serve to indicate common problems of contemporary federalism in developed industrialized societies, as well as special problems associated with the German variant.

I

FEDERALISM IN THE HOHENZOLLERN REICH AND THE WEIMAR REPUBLIC

The fact that it was Prussian leadership which effected the unification of Germany in 1871 had decisive importance for the molding of the German federal tradition. Throughout the earlier part of the nineteenth century the loose league of thirty-nine German states which emerged from the Congress of Vienna in 1815 had served as a classic example of a confederal form of government (*Staatenbund*). Mounting dissatisfaction with the inadequacies of the German Confederation did not lead to agreement on a satisfactory alternative. As the failure of the Frankfurt Assembly of 1848 made clear, the quest for greater unity among the German states was severely hampered by differences of conception and interest regarding the number of states that were to be included in the new Germany and the degree to which the new government was to be constructed according to conservative or liberal principles. Subsequent unification in 1867 and then finally in 1871 did not imply that these differences had been satisfactorily resolved. Rather, as a result of the wars against Denmark, Austria and France, Prussia imposed her conception of a Germany that would exclude Austria and that would be formed according to conservative principles. And inasmuch as Prussia under Bismarck's leadership opted for a federal arrangement for the new state, it was Prussia that set the terms for the federal bargain.[1]

The terms of the federal bargain were guided by Prussia's twin desires to retain her identity as a separate German state and her hegemony over the newly proclaimed Second Empire or Hohenzollern Reich. Her identity as a separate state would have been threatened in a unitary system. Not only did this solution imply in principle the subordination of purely Prussian interests to the interests of the wider Reich, but also, given the opposition of other German states, the only way that a unitary system could have been achieved was through annexation of these states by Prussia. In the process Prussia would have absorbed political units with different traditions and cultures; the maintenance of her own distinctive culture could conceivably have been undermined.[2] Thus a federal solution offered the possibility of unification, which would be palatable to Prussia as well as the remaining twenty-four states.

But if for these reasons a federal solution appeared desirable, the particular type of solution would have to insure Prussia's hegemony. In terms of population and territory Prussia was overwhelmingly the largest member unit of the proposed new federation.[3] Furthermore it had been her leadership that had finally secured unification. Prussia would hardly be prepared therefore to accept a federal solution in which the member units would participate as equals in the political process.

---

[1] The concept of the federal bargain is developed in William H. Riker, *Federalism: Origin, Operation, Significance* (Boston: Little, Brown & Co., 1964). Professor Riker's approach, including his emphasis on the importance of the military security factor in the federal bargain, is well illustrated by the German example of the Hohenzollern Reich.

[2] In fact, after the Austro-Prussian war of 1866 Prussia did annex Hanover, the Electorate of Hesse, Nassau and Frankfurt. But the purpose was limited to joining the eastern and western provinces of Prussia. See Koppel S. Pinson, *Modern Germany: Its History and Civilization* (2nd ed.; New York: The Macmillan Company, 1966), chap. vii.

[3] Prussia had close to three-fifths of the population and controlled about two-thirds of the territory of the Reich. The next largest state was Bavaria with about one-fifth of the population. A popular reference work containing much useful information on German federalism is the short paperback by Karl Heinz Walper, *Föderalismus* (Berlin: Colloquium Verlag, 1966).

Although the resulting federal structure included some adjustments to the demands of the other member units, it clearly bore the stamp of Prussian goals. The problem of the division of powers was handled rather differently from the method devised by the United States' constitutional Framers. Essentially the German method made a distinction between legislative and executive powers.[4] Since Prussia intended to dominate the political process of the federation, the legislative powers accorded to the national government were extensive, indeed far more extensive than those delegated to the United States Congress. On the other hand the actual administration of national legislation was to remain largely under the jurisdiction of the member units. Apart from the federal postal service and the navy, the national government had no separate independently established field agencies. Thus a unified legislative approach to common problems of the Reich entailed minimal interference in the long-established administrative structures and practices of the member units. For the average German citizen the establishment of the Reich brought about no changes in the government officials with whom he had to deal.

This basic method of dividing powers in the federation was subject to some important qualifications. The member units retained both legislative and executive jurisdiction in areas touching particularly upon their different cultural interests, such as education, religion and local government. Equally important, the member units had predominant power in the field of finance. Not only did they collect the taxes, but they also retained the lion's share of the income. The national government was dependent upon yearly grants (*Matrikularbeiträge*) from the member units

---

[4] Arnold Brecht has suggested that the German method provides for a "horizontal" division of powers in distinction to the "vertical" division of the United States. See Arnold Brecht, *Federalism and Regionalism in Germany: The Division of Prussia* (New York: Oxford University Press, 1945), chap. vi. The book is an excellent introduction to the structure and practice of German federalism in the Hohenzollern Reich and the Weimar Republic.

to supplement its income from such indirect taxes as customs and tolls.[5]

Given this division of powers, the effectiveness of the national government would obviously depend on the kind of national institutions organized to formulate national policy and coordinate its execution among the member units. In form the central organ for this purpose was originally intended to be the Bundesrat or Federal Council. Composed of representatives of the German states, it was different in several respects from an American-style Senate. For one thing representation was not equal. The size of each state's delegation was specified in the constitution. For another thing the representatives were actually plenipotentiaries of the governments of the member states. Patterned after the Diet of the former German Confederation, the Bundesrat was originally regarded as a permanent congress of diplomatic representatives from the federating states. Members were thus not free to vote according to their independent judgment. They were bound by instructions from their individual governments and cast the votes of their states as bloc votes. Finally the Bundesrat possessed considerable powers beyond the equal legislative powers which it shared with the Reichstag, the popularly elected lower house of the national parliament. According to the constitution it was empowered to: advise in first instance on legislation introduced by the Chancellor and his government; give its consent to the dissolution of the Reichstag; formulate administrative rules, supervise state administration and settle disputes among the national government and the member units; and, as a mark of its sovereign powers, declare war, make peace and give its consent to constitutional amendments.

Despite these imposing powers the Bundesrat proved in practice to be much less important than the Reichstag in the affairs of the Hohenzollern federation. In part this was a consequence of

---

[5] Besides the qualifications mentioned in this paragraph, mention should be made of the so-called reserved rights (*Reservatrechte*) of certain states of the federation. For example, Bavaria, Württemberg and Saxony retained their own indirect beer and liquor taxes; Bavaria and Württemberg maintained separate postal administrations and their own armed forces.

Prussian domination of the activities of the chamber. Almost invariably the Prussian Prime Minister was also the Imperial Chancellor. In that capacity he was *ex officio* the Chairman of the Bundesrat and cast the seventeen votes to which Prussia was entitled. Fourteen votes were sufficient to block any constitutional amendments, thus enabling Prussia to protect the prerogatives of the Kaiser (the King of Prussia) in military and foreign affairs and to set the limits within which formal change of the federal system could occur. Conversely, if Prussia wished to move positively, she generally had sufficient influence over some of the smaller weaker members of the federation to secure a majority of the fifty-eight votes of the Bundesrat. A measure of the early decline of the Bundesrat was to be found in Bismarck's tendency to bypass the chamber in his consultations with the member states. The latter in turn had the tendency to send members of their bureaucracy as delegates. Rather than explore the potential powers of the Bundesrat, these members concentrated on protecting the administrative interests of their individual governments.

The development of the Hohenzollern federation was therefore little affected by the role of the Bundesrat. Prussian hegemony and the wishes of national party leaders in the Reichstag played the major role in formulating national policy and securing its coordinated administration. When the interests of Prussian leaders and national party leaders coincided, efforts at further uniform solution of public problems could and did proceed quite far. When the interests did not coincide, the ensuing controversy did not involve the Bundesrat but rather the Kaiser, the Chancellor, his ministers and the party leaders of the Reichstag. The secret sessions of the Bundesrat kept it out of the public view; in any event its preoccupation with administrative matters was not likely to excite public attention. The Bundesrat became associated with bureaucracy, the absence of Reich administrative field agencies and Prussian domination. These came to be the connotations of the term "federalism" in Germany. The possible connection between "federalism" and "freedom," "democracy" or "liberalism" was difficult to establish in the German context.

Indeed the convinced "democrat" or "liberal" in Germany was much more likely to be a firm champion of the unitary state. In view of the origins and structure of the Hohenzollern federal system, the maintenance of the system implied the maintenance not only of the particularistic interests of the many disparate German states but also, if not chiefly, of their forms of government. Although some city-states such as Bremen and Hamburg had republican forms of government, the dominant form was monarchical, and the tone was set by Prussia. Until the defeat of the German armies in the First World War, the Prussian three class electoral franchise for her own parliament remained the symbol of Prussian opposition to liberal constitutional reforms. And since the federal system assured Prussian domination of Reich affairs, the prospects for liberal parliamentary reform at the national level were as bleak as in Prussia proper. Understandably, the cause of liberalism and democracy became linked with opposition to the German version of federalism.

The opportunity for reform came with the sudden collapse of the German war effort in 1918. The abdication of the German Kaiser and other monarchs and princes of the German states, the revolutionary proclamation of the German republic based on the principle of popular sovereignty and the emergence of the so-called Weimar coalition majority of Social Democrats, Democrats and Center party representatives on the national level foreshadowed a much more centralized political system. In the constituent assembly which met in 1919 to draw up the constitution of the Weimar Republic, the dominant goal was to establish a national government whose predominance over the states (now called Länder [6]) could not be questioned. Thus national legislative powers were expanded. More importantly, although the Länder were to continue to play a role in the administration of national legislation, the national government was authorized to

---

[6] The use of the new term itself implied a reduction in status of the member states. Since the term has no clear English equivalent, the German form will be used throughout this chapter. The singular is Land; the plural, Länder.

establish its own administrative field agencies. In the area of finance the national government collected its own taxes; in fact it took over the collection of some former Länder taxes as well, returning part of the proceeds to them.

The formal powers of the Bundesrat, which became the Reichsrat, were sharply reduced. The principles of unequal representation and instructed Länder delegates were retained, although representation was more clearly based on population. With only a suspensive veto the Reichsrat no longer had equal legislative powers with the Reichstag. In many other ways its powers declined. Thus it lost the power to consent to Reichstag dissolution, the power to supervise the coordination of administration and the symbolic sovereign powers to declare war, make peace and prevent the passage of constitutional amendments. Unlike the old Bundesrat the Reichsrat no longer played a role in deciding upon punitive action against a recalcitrant Land. Under Article 48 of the Weimar constitution the President and Chancellor were authorized to deal with emergency situations. Finally, the role of Prussia in the Reichsrat was restricted. Although the loss of territories required by the Versailles peace settlement chiefly affected Prussia, she was still by far the largest of the German Länder in terms of population and territory. To prevent her domination of Reichsrat proceedings, it was specified that no Land would be entitled to more than two-fifths of the sixty-six votes in the Reichrat and that the Prussian vote was to be split between the central Land government and the thirteen administrative provinces into which Prussia was divided. The votes from the provinces were "independent" and could not be instructed by the Land government.

As outlined by the Weimar constitution, the decisive shift in the formal balance of powers was fully confirmed by practice. In the serious social and economic crises of the postwar period successive national governments expanded their financial controls and sponsored a proliferation of national administrative field agencies. As a result German as well as foreign observers debated the question whether the Weimar Republic should properly be characterized as a federal system or as a unitary state with certain decentralizing features.[7] Whatever the merits of the respective sides of the debate it is important here to note that the centralization of the Weimar Republic took place within the structural confines of a system that differed only in degree from the Hohenzollern system. Furthermore the extent of centralization can be easily exaggerated. With but few changes the Länder retained the boundaries of the former German states. For example, the attempt at dividing Prussia into self-governing provinces was defeated at the Weimar constituent assembly. The tremendous disparity in size and population between Prussia, middle-sized states such as Bavaria and dwarf states such as Lippe was retained. Whether large or small these Länder continued to have almost exclusive responsibility for such matters as education and local government and administrative responsibility for such matters as justice and police. If their dominance over finances was gone, they were nevertheless assured by national legislation of a fixed percentage of the taxes collected by the national government. And the Reichsrat, weak as its formal powers were, continued to exert some influence. The administrative expertise of its members played a role in the formulation of legislation. Even the suspensive veto was not an idle threat, since the Reichstag's shifting majorities did not always guarantee the required two-thirds vote for purposes of overriding the veto.

In practice neither "centralizers" nor "federalists" were satisfied with the Weimar Republic. For the former the process of centralization had not gone far enough. The maintenance of traditional Länder boundaries made efficient administration impossible. Prussia was practically a second central government;

---

[7] In his well known book Professor Wheare argues, for example, that the Weimar Republic "does not provide us with an example of federal government." See K. C. Wheare, *Federal Government,* 4th ed. (New York: Oxford University Press, 1964), p. 24. A brief introduction to the debate among Germans can be obtained in Johannes Mattern, *Principles of the Constitutional Jurisprudence of the German National Republic* (Baltimore: The Johns Hopkins Press, 1928), pp. 341–57.

Lippe was entirely too small as an administrative agency.[8] The growing dependence of municipalities on national financial aid was not matched by adequate national supervisory controls, since the Länder retained basic responsibility for local government. And in general the retention of Länder administrations and the multiplication of national administrative agencies in the field led to costly duplication of effort, confusion of administrative responsibilities and a lack of adequate controls. Conversely "federalists" had a somewhat different list of complaints. They pointed to excessive proliferation of national agencies and to the ever decreasing financial independence of the Länder and municipalities. They also criticized the restricted role of the Reichsrat and demanded greater participation by Länder governments in the formulation and execution of policies.

In short the Weimar Republic certainly hastened the process of centralization. Yet "federalism" continued to be a live issue. Equally important the debate among Germans about federalism was structured in terms of a system inherited from the Hohenzollern Reich. Centralizers thought of reorganized Länder boundaries, national administrative agencies in the field, national financial domination and a weakened Reichsrat. Federalists thought of administrative responsibility of the Länder, greater financial independence for the Länder, and a strengthened Reichsrat. It was the Nazi regime that put an end to this debate by the coordination (*Gleichschaltung*) of the Länder with the totalitarian controls of party and state. In the aftermath of the Nazi collapse the new West German political leaders soon indicated that they had not forgotten the legacy of German federal experience or the issues in terms of which federal problems had traditionally been debated.

---

[8] It should be noted, however, that Prussia was no longer the bastion of conservative and reactionary politics. Although the Weimar coalition lost its majority at the national level, it remained in power in Prussia until the demise of the Weimar Republic.

II

THE ESTABLISHMENT OF THE GERMAN FEDERAL REPUBLIC

When the six-power London Conference agreed in 1948 on the re-establishment of a central German government for the occupation zones of France, Great Britain and the United States, the requirement that the new government be federal in character was entirely acceptable to a majority of West German political leaders. After the debacle of Nazism reaction against centralization and extremist nationalism predisposed Germans to accept some form of federal system which could also serve as a most useful means for eventual reunification with Germans in the Soviet zone of occupation. Moreover the rump Germany of the three Western occupation zones included areas such as the Rheinland, Bavaria, Baden, Württemberg and the free cities of Bremen and Hamburg that had traditionally supported federal solutions as means of protecting their distinctive cultures.

This simple listing of German motives does less than justice, however, to the change of values among the political elite and the change of social conditions which had occurred in the immediate postwar years. With respect to the change of values the significant point is that "federalism" came to be associated with such terms as "democracy" and "liberty" and rather less with such terms as "particularism" and "separatism" of the Hohenzollern and Weimar periods.[9] Unquestionably this change was the product of a reaction against Nazism, but the positive implications deserve to be emphasized.

Catholics explored the federal applications of their social principles of subsidiarity and solidarism. Socialists and liberals saw in federalism a useful additional check on majority rule in a parliamentary system. In the process of this re-examination not

---

[9] A good discussion of this point can be found in Peter H. Merkl, *The Origin of the West German Republic* (New York: Oxford University Press, 1963), chap. ii.

only traditional federalists but also their traditional liberal and socialist opponents saw a positive value in federalism no matter how much they might differ about the specific type to be established. Only among communists was federalism automatically suspect as a form of government.

The change in social conditions for a federal solution in postwar Germany deserves to be emphasized as well. In part the change was caused by the radical redrawing of traditional Länder boundaries within a much smaller German state. What the Weimar Republic had proved unable or unwilling to do, the victorious Allies accomplished, for reasons of their war goals or of administrative convenience in establishing zones of occupation. Thus, by decree of the Allied Control Council on February 25, 1947, Prussia as a formal political entity was dissolved. Admittedly the former provinces of Prussia had already been carved up between the Soviet and Western zones of occupation. But the symbolic dissolution of Prussia removed one of the major problem areas of previous German federal systems.

Moreover, in organizing local and Land governments within the Western occupation zones (as in the Soviet zone), no particular effort was made to respect traditional Länder boundaries. Of the eleven Länder which originally formed the German Republic in 1949 (Berlin, the twelfth Land, has always been a special case),[10] only Bavaria, Bremen and Hamburg retained essentially the same boundaries. The other eight Länder were curious mixtures of parts of traditional Länder; some were formed out of predominantly non-Prussian areas; some were new creations of former Prussian provinces. One result was that, compared with the Hohenzollern and Weimar periods, the degree of disparity

---

[10] In 1952 the Land of Baden-Württemberg was formed out of three of the original eleven Länder. In 1957 the Saar became the tenth Land of the federation. The Germans count Berlin as the eleventh Land at the present time, but the Western allies have consistently refused to do so, on the grounds that Greater Berlin is still the responsibility of the four occupying powers, including the Soviet Union. In practice Berlin sends representatives to both houses of the German parliament. Although these representatives can be active in legislative committees, they do not vote in plenary sessions.

among the Länder with respect to size and population was reduced.[11]

But the degree to which the populations of these Länder felt
any sense of identification with their new governments was prob-
lematical. Not only were some of the Länder artificial creations
because of their new boundaries, there had also been massive
internal migration which had begun under the stress of Allied
bombing and military advance and then had reached flood tide
with the millions of postwar refugees and expellees from Eastern
Europe and Soviet-occupied Germany. As they settled throughout Western Germany, these migrants weakened the sense of
local patriotism that had developed over generations, often based
on distinctive cultural traditions.[12]

With the possible exception, therefore, of Bavaria, Bremen and
Hamburg, the social conditions for a federal solution in postwar
Germany were hardly comparable with the conditions of the
Hohenzollern Reich and the Weimar Republic. The federal solution could not very easily be related to deeply felt local loyalties
and cultural differences. To the extent that there was a sense of
separate Länder interests and a desire to retain a measure of
Länder autonomy, the reason was more closely associated with
the fact that at the time of the Bonn constitutional deliberations,
the Länder were already going political concerns, whereas such

---

[11] The German Länder are still far from being equal. In terms of territory
the largest Land is Bavaria, which is somewhat bigger than West Virginia;
the smallest Länder, such as Bremen, Hamburg and the Saar, have less
territory than Rhode Island. In terms of population, North
Rhine–Westphalia has about the same population as California; Bremen,
the smallest Land, has less than one million inhabitants. For a good brief
discussion see Roger Hewes Wells, *The States in West German Federalism:
A Study in Federal-State Relations, 1949–1960* (New York: Bookman
Associates, 1961), chap. 1.

[12] It is frequently observed that the average German citizen has neither a
strong attachment to his Land nor to the federal system of government.
See Gerhard Schmidtchen, *Die befragte Nation: über den Einfluss der
Meinungsforschung auf die Politik* (Frankfurt am Main: Fischer Bücherei,
1965), p. 40. On pp. 116–36 Schmidtchen provides an interesting case study
of the decline of popular support for a movement demanding the establishment of a separate Land of Baden as a means of preserving its distinctive
culture.

central government as existed was still rudimentary and under more direct Allied supervision. For with the United States taking the lead, the Western Allies had rather quickly authorized the holding of elections and the drafting of new democratic constitutions at the local and Land levels. The creation of central government institutions was delayed because this was to be the product of joint Four Power agreement. When Soviet and French opposition prevented immediate progress, the United States took the lead in organizing bizonal institutions with the British for purposes of dealing with the serious economic and social postwar crisis. Yet even after the French zone was included in 1948, the central institutions were at best rudimentary. The Allies sought to maintain close supervision and, apart from German administrative experts, the German political leaders who played a role were delegates or members of the Land governments. In the meantime at the Land level there had already been several years of concentrated political activity. The new constitutions had been put into practice; Land party organizations had been formed; the administrative services had been thoroughly reorganized and progressively freed from direct Allied supervision. Understandably, the Germans who were involved in these activities developed a sense of Land consciousness and could be expected in view of earlier German traditions to demand a measure of Land autonomy. Although not all could point to the traditions of a Bavaria, they could be expected to defend their existing institutions and to argue their case in terms of the changed outlook toward the value of federalism as a form of government.

As has been intimated, general agreement among German political leaders in favor of a federal solution at the constitutional deliberations of the Bonn Parliamentary Council of 1948–49 did not extend to the type of federal system that should be devised. Indeed the establishment of the specific structure of the federal system became one of the most hotly debated issues of the Council.[13] In terms of the major parties represented at the Coun-

---

[13] The best English analysis of the Bonn Parliamentary Council's deliberations on federalism is by John Ford Golay, *The Founding of the Federal*

cil Socialists (SPD) and Liberals (FDP) were at one end of the spectrum of opinion. In general they supported a more centralized federal structure. At the other end were members of the Christian Social Union (CSU), the Bavarian affiliate of the new Christian Democratic Union (CDU). CSU members favored a more decentralized structure in keeping with their greater emphasis on the particularistic interests of their Land. In the broad center of the spectrum were members of the CDU. Although Christians and especially Catholics were traditionally inclined toward a more decentralized federal system, the CDU in 1948–49 did not have a common point of view. Since at that time the CDU was not yet a fully organized national party, much depended on particular CDU Land party organizations. Members of the CDU from the British zone of occupation were more inclined toward centralization; members from the French and American zones were more inclined toward decentralization.

In the end the specific structure of the federal system was necessarily the product of compromise, influenced to some extent by Allied intervention, yet basically resting on agreements among German party representatives. What was significant is that the controversies among them and ultimately the agreements were heavily influenced and structured by past experience with federalism in the Hohenzollern Reich and the Weimar Republic. Both centralizers and decentralizers automatically thought in terms of the traditional German division of federal powers. To rely on Land administrations for the execution of national legislation was a decentralizing solution. To permit the establishment of national administrative field agencies was a centralizing solution. Both centralizers and decentralizers automatically assumed that the establishment of a Bundesrat would be a more federal, that is, decentralizing, solution. To opt for an American-style Senate in which the members are directly elected by popular vote

---

Republic of Germany (Chicago: University of Chicago Press, 1958), Part I. It is to be remembered that the Germans, in order to stress the temporary nature of their government until reunification is achieved, prefer to talk about the Basic Law (*Grundgesetz*), rather than the constitution (*Verfassung*), of the Bonn Council.

(or, as originally provided, by state legislatures) was to opt for a centralizing solution. These assumptions were never seriously debated; the argument was over specific proposals, and these were evaluated in terms of the assumptions.

In fact apart from the issue of taxing and spending, which was treated as a separate and special problem, there was little controversy over the federal division of powers. The national government was delegated extensive legislative powers, its concurrent powers covering such a wide area of social and economic life that the American occupation authorities objected to the undue centralization. To the Germans, however, the proper balance was to be found in the constitutional provisions granting major responsibilities to the Länder for the execution of national legislation. Against the background of Weimar experience, this arrangement was viewed as a decentralizing solution and gave evidence of the extent to which the Socialists and Liberals were prepared to support federalism. In addition it was specified that to the Länder were reserved all powers not specifically delegated to the national government. If a reading of the extensive delegated powers raised questions about which powers might conceivably be reserved to the Länder, it was understood among the Germans that the reserved powers included such areas as local government, education and in a more general way cultural affairs (the so-called *Kulturhoheit* of the Länder).[14]

Although the division of powers in the field of finances became a matter of controversy among the Germans, the cause was Allied interference with compromise arrangements that the Germans had initially accepted by a large majority in the Council. In reaction against Weimar experience German party representatives were in agreement that the Länder should be guaranteed financial independence. But they also were in agreement that the Weimar system of national collection and distribution of tax

---

[14] The scope of these reserved powers is wider than the words "local government" and "cultural affairs" may suggest at first glance. Thus cultural affairs include education in the broadest sense, radio, television, theaters, museums, libraries, the press. Local government includes such matters as police, public health and regional planning.

proceeds had proved to be efficient and should be retained. Accordingly they proposed a national fiscal adminstrative system. The income from certain specified taxes would automatically accrue to either the national government or the Länder, and the income from the three largest revenue-producing taxes (income, corporation and turnover taxes) would be shared between the national government and the Länder. The size of the shares would be decided upon by national legislation, and in the passage of such legislation the Bundesrat, the organ that was to represent the Länder governments, would have an absolute veto. The Allies —particularly the Americans—objected to this arrangement on the grounds that the financial independence of the Länder could not adequately be secured unless they had their own fiscal administrative agencies for the assessment and collection of taxes that were assigned to them by the constitution.

It was at this point that controversy arose among the Germans. Their proposed financial arrangement formed part of a developing series of compromises. Insofar as some Germans were prepared to accede to Allied demands on the financial issue, they were reopening other compromise agreements, including such matters as the structure and powers of the Bundesrat. The entire work of the Bonn Parliamentary Council was threatened with collapse, the SPD taking the lead in urging that either the Allies withdraw their demands or the Germans refuse to proceed with their constitutional deliberations. Ultimately new compromise formulas were agreed upon. Bowing to Allied demands, the Germans provided for joint fiscal administrative agencies. The national government was assigned major indirect taxes, including the turnover tax; the Länder were assigned predominantly direct taxes, including the income and corporation taxes. It was stipulated that the national government could claim a share of the income and corporation taxes; the size of the share would be subject to the absolute veto of the Bundesrat.

As can be noted from the preceding, the Germans regarded the new Bundesrat as an important instrument for the defense of Länder interests. Indeed the structure and powers of the Bundesrat were the issues over which the Germans probably had the greatest controversy. Once again agreement could be reached only by compromise, the final product being a federal council stronger in formal powers than the Reichsrat of the Weimar Republic and weaker than the Bundesrat of the Hohenzollern Reich. In structure the Bundesrat followed earlier German practice, with the exception that the disparity of voting strength among the instructed Länder delegates was sharply reduced. Henceforth no Land was to receive less than three votes or more than five of the forty-one votes of the chamber (Berlin has four nonvoting seats). In part this formula reflected the change of Länder boundaries; in part it gave an advantage to the Länder with smaller populations.

It was, however, with respect to the powers of the Bundesrat that the compromise character of the chamber was most clearly to be seen. As in the past it was to participate in the passage of legislation and in the formulation of rules for the administration of national legislation, but the extent of its power in these areas depended on whether the subject matter involved essentially financial and/or administrative questions. In such instances (*Zustimmungsgestze*) the Bundesrat was to have an absolute veto; in others, it was to have only a suspensive veto.[15] The Bundesrat therefore was not to have full equality with the Bundestag, the proposed lower house of the new parliament. But the Länder were to be assured an equal voice in those matters that particularly affected them under the federal division of powers. In addition the Bundesrat had an equal voice in the approval of constitutional amendments, appointed an equal number of members to the newly established Federal Constitutional Court, and had sole responsibility to approve measures taken by the Chancellor under the restricted emergency procedure of the constitution.

---

[15] There is no one article in the constitution that specifies the subject matter over which the Bundesrat can exercise its absolute veto. Its power is specified in a whole series of articles throughout the constitution. Thus the category of "administrative" questions includes, among other things, attempts by the national government to undertake punitive action against a recalcitrant Land.

The controversy over the Bundesrat and the solution finally achieved symbolize perhaps best of all the type of federal system that was established by the Bonn constitutional framers. Quite clearly the institutional structure was heavily influenced by previous German experience. In terms of that experience the structure was readapted with the purpose of reversing a trend toward centralization which had already begun under the Hohenzollern Reich, had proceeded quite rapidly under the Weimar Republic, and had then been pushed to extremes under the aegis of the Nazi party. The Bonn framers, however, did not react solely against the Nazis; they reacted against the Weimar and Hohenzollern experiences as well. And they did so amidst conditions that seemingly called for a Weimar type of solution. After all the territory of the new German Federal Republic was only one part of the former Weimar Republic; the new Länder were themselves largely artificial creations; the staggering problems of reconstruction seemingly demanded common nationwide solutions. Despite these changed conditions the Germans opted for a federal system that in German terms was more decentralized that the one they had known under Weimar. The role of the Länder was to be strengthened, not only by relying on them more extensively as administrative organs of the nation-state, but also by guaranteeing their governments greater participation in the decision-making process of the federation.

III
THE GROWTH OF FEDERALISM
IN THE GERMAN FEDERAL REPUBLIC

Against the background of past German experience the efforts of the Bonn constitution framers have thus far proved to be surprisingly effective. To be sure, like the English-speaking federations, the federal system of the Bonn Republic has undergone considerable change, which at times has belied original assumptions. If the change has prompted the familiar charge that federalism has become obsolescent, the record nevertheless suggests that the interaction among institutions, social conditions and social values can sustain the vitality of the federal solution as a method of decentralizing the modern nation-state. In the following survey of particular aspects of Germany's pattern of development, students of English-speaking federations will note both the persistence of certain common problems of modern federalism as well as the differential impact of the German variant of federalism.

1. Judicial Interpretation

German experience with judicial interpretation in the federal system has been to some extent unexpected and surprising.[16] Given the German method of dividing federal powers the national government has always been granted extensive authority to legislate on matters requiring uniform national treatment. Unlike the United States and Canada, for example, there has never been any question that the national government may deal with economic and social welfare problems. In the Hohenzollern Reich there was no provision for judicial interpretation of contested jurisdiction, resolution of such disputes being entrusted to the Bundesrat. In the Weimar Republic recourse to judicial settlement of federal disputes was possible, but led to no significant developments. Since the Bonn Republic followed the previous practice of dividing federal powers, there was no particular reason, therefore, to expect that the newly established Federal Constitutional Court would play a significant role.[17]

[16] A good introduction to the problem can be found in two short books by Edward McWhinney: *Constitutionalism in Germany and the Federal Constitutional Court* (Leyden: A. W. Sythoff, 1962); and *Comparative Federalism: States' Rights and National Power* (2nd ed.; Toronto: University of Toronto Press, 1965). An excellent commentary on Court decisions, organized according to the relevant articles of the constitution, is available in G. Leibholz and H. J. Rinck, *Grundgesetz für die Bundesrepublik Deutschland: Kommentar an Hand der Rechtsprechung des Bundesverfassungsgerichts* (Köln-Marienburg: Verlag Dr. Otto Schmidt KG, 1966).

[17] According to the legislation of 1951 the court was to be composed of twenty-four members divided into two senates, some members to be appointed for life, others for terms of eight years. The Bundestag and the

In two leading cases, however, the court has clearly affected the growth of the German federal system. The first case, the so-called Concordat decision of 1957, involved a conflict between the treaty power of the national government and the reserved power of the Länder over education. More specifically the Land of Lower Saxony had passed legislation establishing a common nondenominational school system for all children. The national government challenged the constitutionality of this legislation on the grounds that it conflicted with the German-Vatican treaty or Concordat of 1933, whereby Catholic students were guaranteed separate schools. Conceivably the court might have decided that the Concordat was no longer in effect or alternatively that it could not be regarded as having the full status of a treaty in international law. Instead the court accepted the Concordat as a fully valid treaty, yet at the same time, unlike American and Canadian precedents, upheld the constitutionality of the Lower Saxony legislation. According to the decision the treaty power of the national government could not extend to an infringement of the reserved power of the Länder in the field of education.

The second case, the so-called TV case of 1961, involved a conflict between the exclusive power of the national government to legislate on postal services and telecommunications and the broad reserved powers of the Länder over cultural affairs. After various efforts to secure general agreement among the national government and the Länder, the Adenauer government had sought on its own authority to establish a second television station, claiming that the national government's exclusive power over postal services and telecommunications necessarily included television. This time several Länder challenged the constitutionality of the action on the grounds that the national government was infringing on their power in the field of cultural affairs to super-

Bundesrat each choose half the members of the court. The legislation of 1956 provides for an ultimate reduction of the two senates to sixteen members, as judges retire or signify that they do not wish to stand for re-election. Unlike the United States Supreme Court the German court does not deliver majority and minority opinions; there is only one published joint opinion on a given case.

vise the organization and content of TV programs. In its decision the court granted that the national government's power extended to such technical matters as determining the frequency for a proposed new TV station, but on the essential question whether such power could extend to the actual organization of the station and the type of programs to be transmitted, the court upheld the reserved power of the Länder. In effect such implied powers as the national government may have in the field of television could not be construed so broadly as to infringe on the power of the Länder over cultural affairs.

Quite apart from the actual points of constitutional law the wider effect of the court's decisions in these two cases has been twofold. First, it has introduced an element of rigidity in the German method of dividing federal powers where none had been expected. Second, it has encouraged a type of legalistic states-rights thinking about the federal system that Bavarians had generally been the first to champion but that had not heretofore been widely shared.

The potential extent of the court's influence, however, must not be exaggerated. Even on the assumption that the court does not change its pattern of interpretation, it is unlikely that it will assume the role of the United States Supreme Court in the 1930's or of the Judicial Committee of the Privy Council in Canada before 1949.

For one thing the reserved powers of the Länder are hardly an uncharted terrain which would permit liberal judicial construction. Länder powers such as those over education and cultural affairs include fairly definite areas in the German legal tradition. Moreover the extensive and explicitly enumerated exclusive and concurrent legislative powers of the national government must be taken into account. As previously noted, the American occupation authorities objected to the excessive scope of national powers in the initial version of the constitution. At their insistence the Germans finally introduced three criteria in Article 72, any one of which had to be satisfied before the national government could resort to the use of its concurrent powers. If the purpose of these criteria was to provide a check on the national government, they have failed. Certainly, the Constitutional Court has not chosen to interfere with the judgment of the national political authorities as to when the criteria are satisfied. It would be wrong, therefore, to view the Concordat and TV cases as examples of a tendency on the part of the court to rewrite the constitution in favor of the Länder. There are limits on how far it can go. It has not seized every occasion to strike down national government activity. Furthermore cases can be cited where the court has been quite prepared to declare Länder actions unconstitutional.[18] In fact the court would apparently prefer to avoid the concept of a competitive federalism. Thus in the Concordat case it denied neither the validity of the treaty nor the power of the Länder to establish educational systems contrary to the treaty. If the result appeared paradoxical, the court suggested that the solution was to be found in an application of its principle of federal comity (*Bundestreue*). As it has elaborated this principle in a number of cases, there is not only the negative injunction that the national government and the Länder must faithfully respect the constitutional boundaries of their spheres of power, but also the positive injunction that the successful operation of the German federal system requires joint cooperation for the solution of common problems.

Perhaps the most important long-term significance of the Concordat and TV decisions is that they have demonstrated once again the difficulty of dividing federal legislative powers so as to take account of changing conditions. Even the German method of granting the national government extensive legislative powers to deal with foreseeable national problems has been overtaken by events. The apparently minor reserved powers of the Länder

---

[18] The most frequently cited case is the Referenda on Atomic Weapons decision of 1958. Here the court decided that a Land could not authorize the holding of local referenda on the issue of arming the Bundeswehr with atomic weapons. Such an issue belongs to the jurisdiction of the national legislature. Even if the referenda are purely advisory, they can place pressure on the national legislature and interfere with the normal legislative process.

have turned out to be important after all, and they are likely to remain so. New developments comparable with the phenomenal growth of television after 1949 cannot be ruled out. But more important is the ever expanding conception of the proper functions of government in modern society. As governments are increasingly expected to improve educational opportunities both in terms of quantity and quality, as they are increasingly expected to establish proper standards for urban living, the reserved powers of the Länder are bound to raise controversy. To the extent that present court decisions remain unchanged and cooperative arrangements are not worked out, the federal system will be increasingly criticized for its rigidity and its failure to adjust to modern society.

2. The Bundesrat

Compared with the conciliar chambers of the Hohenzollern Reich and the Weimar Republic, the Bundesrat of the German Federal Republic has thus far proved the most effective instrument for the Länder governments to influence the policy-making process of the federation.[19] Although this result was clearly the intention of the Bonn constitution framers, the structure and powers of the Bundesrat, as these emerged from the constitutional deliberations, were no guarantee that the institution would in fact play a significant role. With a quite similar structure and considerably greater powers, the Bundesrat of the Hohenzollern Reich had proved to be relatively unimportant. But the old Bundesrat had been dominated by Prussia; the present Bundesrat faces no such problem. Furthermore, despite the efforts of

---

[19] Two excellent discussions of the present Bundesrat are: Edward L. Pinney, *Federalism, Bureaucracy, and Party Politics in Western Germany: The Role of the Bundesrat* (Chapel Hill: University of North Carolina Press, 1963); and Karlheinz Neunreither, *Der Bundesrat zwischen Politik und Verwaltung* (Heidelberg: Quelle & Meyer, 1959). An earlier but still useful work is by Hans Schäfer, *Der Bundesrat* (Köln: Carl Heymanns Verlag, 1955). A recent and more popular paperback reference work is by Gebhard Ziller, *Der Bundesrat* (Frankfurt am Main: Athenäum Verlag, 1966).

national political party leaders to influence the political complexion of the present Bundesrat, they have not been completely successful. Party strength in the Bundestag is not automatically reproduced in the Bundesrat. Depending on the issue the requirements of coalition politics in the Länder can often lead Bundesrat members to adopt rather different policy positions from those of their colleagues in the Bundestag.

To these factors must be added the early willingness of the Bundesrat members to explore the potential powers of their institution. The most important developments in this respect have been based on the Bundesrat's absolute veto power. In distinguishing between subject matter over which the Bundesrat was to have an absolute or a suspensive veto, the Bonn constitution framers had assumed that the scope of legislative activity affected by the absolute veto would be relatively small. Subsequent practice has not supported this assumption. Of the approximately 1,900 bills that have been passed between 1949 and 1965, almost half (937) were potentially subject to the absolute veto power of the Bundesrat. Not only has there been continuing controversy over which bills fall into this category, but the Bundesrat has successfully insisted that if a legislative bill contains provisions that are subject to its absolute veto, then the entire bill, not just the particular provisions, is subject to the veto.

The result has been to strengthen the role of the Bundesrat throughout the entire legislative process. It must in first instance advise on cabinet-initiated proposals, and these comprise a goodly majority of legislative proposals. After the bill has passed the Bundestag, it must come back to the Bundesrat for its consent. If there are differences between the two houses, an attempt can be made to secure agreement through the mediation committee (*Vermittlungsausschuss*), a procedure somewhat similar to the conference-committee procedure of the United States Congress.[20] At each of these stages, the Bundesrat has been able to

---

[20] One important difference is that the German membership is constant and does not change according to the nature of the bill. Moreover the terms of reference of the committee are in each instance strictly defined. Each house of the German parliament is represented by eleven members. In

increase its influence insofar as a particular bill is subject to its absolute veto. Indeed one commentator suggests that, at the stage of the mediation committee, the Bundesrat has so successfully exerted its influence that the distinction between bills subject to an absolute or suspensive veto has become somewhat blurred.[21]

The much greater influence of the Bundesrat on the legislative process should not be taken to mean, however, that it exerts its influence in the manner of an American-style Senate. The factors that help account for the greater effectiveness of the Bundesrat, as compared with its predecessors in the Hohenzollern Reich and the Weimar Republic, have not led to any major changes in the character of its role as a second chamber in the German political process. Like its predecessors the present Bundesrat has not played an openly political role. Although its formal membership is composed of instructed delegates who are members of their respective Länder cabinets, these political leaders have not used the Bundesrat as a political forum for public debate or adjustment of policy differences. To a large extent the plenary sessions of the Bundesrat merely formalize decisions that have been taken elsewhere.

It is in the standing committees of the Bundesrat, where proposals are examined with a view to recommending Bundesrat action, and in the Länder cabinets that real influence is exercised. Technically the members of committees should be the instructed delegates of the Länder cabinets. The standing orders of the Bundesrat, however, permit the delegates to send alternates, who may be and usually are ranking civil servants from the Länder administrations. Although there is to be sure give-and-take discussion and adjustment of policy differences in committee, the focus of interest tends to be on the administrative implications of a proposal and not so much on the broader policy implications. After the committees have formulated their recommendations, these are then sent to the various Länder cabinets for considera-

---

the case of the Bundesrat members (one for each Land including Berlin) they are not subject to instructions from their governments.

[21] Neunreither, *op. cit.*, p. 85.

tion. Once again there is discussion and adjustment of policy differences. But the discussion is among the members of individual Länder cabinets, and the adjustment more often than not is among different party members of coalition cabinets. The delegates from these cabinets who form the membership of the plenary sessions of the Bundesrat are thus bound by the compromise decisions of their cabinets, as these decisions in turn have been structured by the recommendations of the Bundesrat standing committees.

Accordingly, there is very little room for maneuver in Bundesrat sessions. Debate is not likely to change any votes. The sessions are largely a means of officially registering earlier Länder cabinet decisions, a point reinforced by the fact that there are relatively few plenary sessions of the Bundesrat. On the average delegates meet on a Friday every two to three weeks.

In part this practice reflects the dual responsibilities of the delegates. As members of the Länder cabinets they are in charge of executive departments in their Länder and are responsible to Länder parliaments. These duties necessarily restrict the amount of time available for their duties as Bundesrat members. Furthermore, according to the constitution, the Bundesrat must fulfill its legislative duties within rigid time limits. It has three weeks within which to give its advice on cabinet-initiated proposals, two weeks to decide on bills that have passed the Bundestag, and one week for bills that have come out of the mediation committee and been accepted by the Bundestag. The tendency is to permit the maximum amount of time for deliberation by the Bundesrat committees and then by the Länder cabinets. Many of the agenda items for a Friday plenary session of the Bundesrat have reached the end of their prescribed time limits and cannot possibly be dealt with at any great length during the course of a heavy agenda. The assumption underlying the infrequent sessions is that the deliberative process has taken place elsewhere.[22]

---

[22] In addition to the references cited in note 19 two useful journal articles on the decision-making process of the Bundesrat are: Peter H. Merkl, "Executive-Legislative Federalism in West Germany," *American Political*

In addition to this rather unusual decision-making process, the role of the Bundesrat has been affected by the efforts of national party leaderships. Recognizing the potential power of the Bundesrat to obstruct the passage of major legislative policies, Adenauer and his CDU advisers at the national level sought soon after the establishment of the German Federal Republic to influence the composition of Länder cabinets and thereby the political complexion of the instructed delegates to the Bundesrat. Land CDU party leaders were urged to form coalitions only with those parties represented in the coalition government at the national level. A natural further step was to participate actively in Land parliamentary elections with the aim of insuring CDU-led cabinets or at least preventing victory by the SPD, the major national opposition party.[23] Although these efforts were never completely successful, Adenauer and subsequent German chancellors have largely managed to avoid a hostile majority of national opposition parties in the Bundesrat. This has not meant automatic acceptance of their specific proposals. It has rather meant that the Bundesrat as an institution has not become the instrument of the recognized opposition parties to the national cabinet and its supporting majority in the Bundestag. With the exception of the European Defense Community treaty German chancellors have not faced defeat on those broad principles of policy where party lines have been sharply drawn.

Of course the Bundesrat may suggest amendments to specific

Science Review, LIII (1959), 732–41; and Karlheinz Neunreither, "Politics and Bureaucracy in the West German Bundesrat," *ibid.,* pp. 713–31. Apart from deliberations during the rigid time limits prescribed by the constitution, there can be considerable informal discussion between political leaders of the national government and the Länder as well as between their civil servants before the cabinet formally introduces its measure for an advisory opinion of the Bundesrat. Bundesrat members can also follow proceedings in the Bundestag and participate in the deliberations. The time limits of the Bundesrat do not therefore necessarily set the time limits of the entire deliberative process. But of course the Bundesrat as an institution is still not involved in these more informal consultations.

[23] These early efforts of the Adenauer government have been analyzed by Arnold J. Heidenheimer, "Federalism and the Party System: The Case of West Germany," *American Political Science Review,* LII (1958), 809–28.

proposals. And where party lines are not sharply drawn, the amendments can be quite far-reaching. But such activities do not lead the Bundesrat to assume a stance of open political confrontation with the national cabinet and its majority in the Bundestag.

If the role of the Bundesrat is therefore rather different from that of the United States Senate, it is also rather different from that of the second chambers in Australia and Canada. Admittedly like the latter chambers it does not serve as a political check on the national cabinet and the popularly elected lower house. But its potential significance is not thereby exhausted. The deliberative process prior to a Bundesrat plenary session can and does mean that government proposals are examined and tested by a source independent from the Bundestag in which the government can generally rely on a safe majority. Given the composition of Bundesrat committees, this independent supervisory function tends to focus on the administrative implications of government proposals. The resulting recommendations gain strength because of the expertise of Länder administrations, the support of Länder cabinets and the willingness of delegates and alternates to explore the constitutional powers of the Bundesrat. Thus the Bundesrat can become the vehicle whereby the Länder are in a position to protect precisely those administrative interests that are their major responsibility under the German division of federal powers.

The Bundesrat can and does perform more than a merely protective function for Länder administrative interests. The legislative record until 1965 demonstrates that the Bundesrat has rarely resorted to the use of its absolute veto. Instead the members prefer to call upon the procedure of the mediation committee. This preference undoubtedly supports the presumption that the Bundesrat members are fairly successful in the bargaining process with the Bundestag members. Even so they are forgoing the negative role of rejecting unsuitable proposals in order to play the more positive role of determining the actual content of legislation.

The development of the Bundesrat since 1949 has received a goodly amount of criticism. There has been a continuing expression of concern over the potentially excessive role of Land civil servants in the policy-making process. Suggestions that the instructed delegates of the Bundesrat play a more active political role have been motivated by a desire not only to control civil servants but also to secure wider consideration of *policy* alternatives. It would appear, however, that such suggestions point to a radical transformation of the structure and powers of the Bundesrat as well as of the German method of dividing federal powers. The present role of the Bundesrat cannot easily be divorced from other aspects of the German variant of federalism or from traditions and customs developed since the days of the Bundesrat in the Hohenzollern Reich. Whatever its limitations the Bundesrat provides students of English-speaking federations with an example of a quite different type of second chamber. Within its institutionalized framework there is an interesting attempt to gear the administrative experience of Länder governments into the central policy-making process.

In German terms the Bundesrat represents thus far the most effective effort to reconcile the continuing trend toward centralization with a continuing meaningful role for the Länder governments.

3. *Public Finance*

In keeping with the experience of the English-speaking federations the development of the German Federal Republic illustrates the persistent problem of modern federal systems in maintaining a proper balance between functions to be performed and ability to pay. In West Germany the problem has not taken the form of the national government's fiscal resources expanding more rapidly than its legislative functions, as is the case in Canada, Australia and the United States.[24] The problem is somewhat more

---

[24] See above, p. 125-128.

complicated; so, too, are present efforts to find a new balance between functions and resources.

Under the terms of the Bonn constitution, the fiscal resources of both the national government and the Länder have been subject to limits which both levels play a role in determining. For one thing, apart from certain specified taxes whose proceeds revert either to the national government or to the Länder, the proceeds from income and corporation taxes are shared according to a legislative formula over which the Bundesrat has an absolute veto. Secondly, the Bonn Republic has carried over from the Weimar Republic the practice of insuring that the Länder with markedly lower tax yields receive additional income in one of two ways: either the wealthier Länder make contributions to the poorer, or the national government provides special financial help out of its own revenues.[25] In either case the requisite national legislation is once again subject to the absolute veto of the Bundesrat.

Given the above arrangements, it might be tempting to assume that the problem of public finance in the German federal system has been that the national government with its extensive legislative powers under the German division of federal powers has inadequate resources, and that the Länder with their largely administrative functions have more resources than they need. Neither part of the assumption would be correct. To be sure the national government has regularly demanded a greater share of the income and corporation tax proceeds. But the revenue which the national government has thus far received has made possible not only programs in such areas as reconstruction, economic recovery and social welfare where it clearly has jurisdiction, but also mounting subsidies and loans in areas where its jurisdiction is questionable. Minister presidents of the Länder and finance ministers of the national government have on occasion noted that

---

[25] This process is known as horizontal finance equalization. The sharing of the income and corporation taxes is known as vertical finance equalization. For a useful brief survey of the problem of public finance, see Wells, *op. cit.*, pp. 59–65.

the system of subsidies threatens to undermine the sphere of competence reserved to the Länder, warnings similar to those that are often expressed in the United States and Canada. Conversely the Länder governments have found themselves increasingly hard pressed to provide sufficient revenue for improved educational systems, specialized help for segments of industry and agriculture, and contributions to the local governments under their jurisdiction. The plight of local governments is perhaps worst of all. Their own tax yield is inadequate and highly uneven; their share of the Länder portion of income and corporation taxes is insufficient. As a result their indebtedness has mounted to alarming proportions.

To a degree, therefore, the problem of public finance in the German Federal Republic has aspects similar to the experience of the English-speaking federations. The significant difference, however, is that the national government does not independently control the type of expanding fiscal resources which make possible systematic programs of financial aid as a means of influencing the performance of an ever larger number of Länder functions.

At some point the national government will have to request a larger share of the high-yield income and corporation taxes. For this the Länder governments must give their consent in the Bundesrat. Since the Länder share of these taxes forms an extremely important part of their total income, the Länder governments are not likely to accept the national government's request unless they also agree to the purposes for which the larger income is to be used. Moreover, although the device of the grant-in-aid is not unknown in Germany, its use as a means of redistributing income from wealthier to poorer Länder is limited by the more accepted arrangement of the wealthier Länder making direct general contributions to the poorer Länder. Once again, the use of national fiscal resources cannot so easily skirt the question whether it is the national government or the Länder which should be performing particular functions. Accordingly an imbalance between functions and ability to pay in the German federal system is difficult to solve unless there is fairly general agreement

among both the national government and the Länder governments on the role each level is to play in the system. Such
agreement can provide the basis for bargaining when the Bundesrat must give its consent to the proportionate shares of income
and corporation taxes and the contributions of the wealthier to
the poorer Länder.

The logic of this conclusion has thus far been supported by the
pattern of controversy over the sharing of income and corporation taxes. Before 1955 the shares were determined on an annual
basis, the national government receiving at first only 17 per cent
of the proceeds, then at times as much as 38 per cent. In an effort
to avoid the annual haggling and with the hope of placing the
entire system on a more stable basis, the 1955 financial amendments to the constitution provided among other things that until
1958 the national government was to receive $33\frac{1}{3}$ per cent of the
tax proceeds and thereafter 35 per cent. Despite the serious
controversy and the eleventh-hour compromises that preceded
this agreement, there was recognition that a constitutional arrangement could not insure stability on this issue. Thus it was
stipulated that the shares could be renegotiated every two years
with the consent of the Bundesrat. The expectation that further
change would be needed was amply borne out. By 1964 and after
a mammoth controversy the proportion had changed to the point
where the national government was to receive 39 per cent of the
tax proceeds for a two-year period.

At this stage the certain prospect of further controversy and
the general dissatisfaction with the entire process of reaching
agreement led to an important breakthrough. Shortly after the
passage of the 1964 legislation the Chancellor and the minister
presidents of the Länder agreed to the establishment of a commission of experts charged with preparing a report on needed
financial reforms. It was also stipulated that the so-called Troeger Commission was to re-examine the division of functions as
these had developed among the national government, the Länder
and the local governments. In terms of this re-examination the

commission was then to suggest whatever redistribution of tax proceeds seemed appropriate.

The report of the Troeger Commission was published early in 1966 and has since formed the basis for negotiations between the Erhard and Kiesinger cabinets on the one hand and the Länder governments on the other.[26] Although it is hazardous to predict whether or how far the report will be implemented, a brief consideration of some of its key features is valuable as a guide to the current German approach to the problem of public finance in the federal system.

Probably the central feature of the report is to be found in its concept of *Gemeinschaftsaufgaben* ("joint" or more properly "community responsibilities," that is, responsibilities that are to be shared by the national government and the Länder). According to the Troeger Commission the impact of continuing industrialization and urbanization of German society, coupled with the desire to achieve such publicly proclaimed goals as full employment, sound economic growth and monetary stability, have led to increasing recognition of the principle that the national government must play a more active role in planning and regulating the development of German society from a nationwide point of view. Full implementation of this principle, however, would unquestionably undermine the jurisdiction of the Länder in the federal system. Consequently the commission proposed a new category in the division of federal powers of the constitution. This category would define as joint responsibilities of the national government and Länder functions heretofore under the jurisdiction of the Länder but having come to require national consideration, long-term planning and sizable public expenditures. For such problem areas as the establishment and expansion of universities, the promotion of research institutions, the construction of local

---

[26] See Kommission für die Finanzreform, *Gutachten über die Finanzreform in der Bundesrepublik Deutschland* (Stuttgart: Verlag W. Kohlhammer, 1966). The report contains a mine of information not only on the problem of public finance but also on developing patterns of federal cooperation.

transportation facilities and the economic improvement of regions, the national government and the Bundesrat should henceforth formulate common plans and determine guiding directives. The execution of these decisions would remain under the exclusive jurisdiction of the Länder, and the costs would be shared on a fifty-fifty basis between the national government and the Länder. In addition the poorer Länder would receive special contributions from the wealthier Länder.

Quite clearly the assumption of the Troeger Commission was that if agreement can be secured on a division of functions such as the *Gemeinschaftsaufgaben,* then the problem of tax reform not only can be seen in better perspective but should also be easier to solve. Despite its many far-reaching proposals for reorganizing the division of exclusive taxes among the national government, the Länder and the local governments, it is interesting to note that the commission suggested no change in the procedure of sharing the revenue from income and corporation taxes. What it did suggest was that the income from the national government's turnover tax should be added to the common fund subject to sharing. It refrained from stipulating percentages and proposed continued reliance on the bargaining process between the national government and the Länder governments.

Whether or not the assumption of the Troeger Commission proves to be well founded, the report clearly indicates that the solution of the problem of public finance in the German federal system lies in a serious examination of a possible redistribution of functions between the national government and the Länder. In the English-speaking federations, as Professor Livingston has noted, such examination is politically unfeasible.[27] In the German federal system the same conclusion does not automatically apply. Given the existence of the Bundesrat, it is possible to propose an expansion of the functions of the national government that does not immediately imply the loss of functions among the Länder. The concept of *Gemeinschaftsaufgaben* provides an interesting

---

[27] See above, p. 125, 126.

example. Of course agreement is not thereby guaranteed because, as is shown below, there is a price that individual Länder will have to pay if they accept such an arrangement. Still the Troeger Commission was not merely engaged in wishful thinking when it advanced its concept of *Gemeinschaftsaufgaben* as a new form of cooperative federalism.

4. Patterns of Federal Cooperation

The German Federal Republic has witnessed an extensive growth of informal and formal methods of cooperation between the national government and Länder on the one hand and among the Länder on the other. Although not called for in the Bonn constitution, this development has in large measure been welcomed as a useful addition to the pattern of cooperation in the decision-making process of the Bundesrat. In terms of past German experience it has demonstrated both the continued decline of particularistic interests among the Länder and their recognition of the need to coordinate policy in a highly interdependent society. The sheer scope of the development, however, has raised some interesting constitutional and political issues. If at present the constitutional debate has largely subsided, the political debate is likely to continue, since it involves conflicting interests and values.

The types of cooperation between the national government and the Länder are quite varied. An early effort to provide a formal institutional channel for consultation was the establishment in 1949 of the National Ministry for Bundesrat and Länder Affairs (*Bundesministerium für Angelegenheiten des Bundesrats und der Länder*); it was matched by the Länder sending plenipotentiaries to head separate Länder offices in Bonn. Chiefly useful in maintaining contacts on national legislation, this channel has been supplemented by conferences between the Chancellor and the minister presidents of the Länder or between the national minister of a particular executive department and his counterparts of the Länder. In addition to the exchange of information and the coordination of policy and its execution in their separate jurisdictions these contacts between the national government and the Länder have led to the establishment of common institutions such as the Council on Higher Learning (*Wissenschaftsrat*) in 1957 and the German Council on Education (*Deutscher Bildungsrat*) in 1965. Both councils have had the task of developing common plans and goals and of suggesting ways in which the national government and the Länder can best coordinate future policies.

Cooperation among the Länder has been even more extensive. There are fairly regular conferences among minister presidents and among the heads of various executive departments. In the case of the ministers of culture and education the conference technique has been replaced by a permanent institution with subject committees, a separate secretariat and its own headquarters in Bonn: the Permanent Conference of the Ministers of Culture and Education of the Länder in the German Federal Republic (*Ständige Konferenz der Kultusminister der Länder in der Bundesrepublik Deutschland*). Via treaties, executive agreements and resolutions, the Länder have not only coordinated their policies but also agreed to joint use of institutions of a particular Land (such as the school for public administration in Speyer) or to the establishment of common institutions (such as the second TV station at Mainz which followed upon the Federal Constitutional Court decision of 1961). A rough measure of the scope of this cooperative activity among the Länder is provided by the more than three hundred treaties and executive agreements between 1949 and 1960 and the more than five hundred resolutions of the Permanent Conference of Ministers of Culture and Education during the same period of time.

It was the establishment of the second TV station that perhaps played the major role in sparking the constitutional and political controversy over the growing pattern of federal cooperation in the German Federal Republic. Critics have not questioned cooperation involving the coordination of policies among the various members of the federation, with the individual governments obligated to give effect to whatever agreements have been reached. There has likewise been no criticism of a treaty which deals with the solution of a problem affecting some but not all Länder, insofar as the individual Länder governments continue to control how it is given effect. All such instances involve examples of a cooperative federalism that are not only acceptable but also highly desirable.

Criticism has arisen at the point where the coordination of policies or the acceptance of treaties leads to the establishment of institutions whose decisions are self-executing. In the case of the second TV station the Federal Constitutional Court declared that the national government has no authority to establish such an instrumentality. On the other hand an individual Land government also lacks authority. In consequence all the Länder jointly established by treaty an independent public corporation to transmit programs throughout the entire country. This independent corporation appears to some to be a "third level" (*eine dritte Ebene*) in the federal system. Constitutionally minded critics have questioned whether this third level of governmental activity is legally valid. Politically minded critics have questioned whether the development of such activity does not imply inadequacy in the division of federal powers, requiring an explicit redistribution of functions.

The constitutional controversy, although by no means exhausted, has largely given way to a growing consensus on the legal competence of the Länder jointly to establish common institutions. For many critics the problem is no longer so much whether the Länder can establish a second TV station, but rather whether the specific type of corporation that was established has unconstitutional features.[28] Thus the potential impact of the constitutional controversy on the growing pattern of cooperation in

---

[28] An interesting example of this point of view is provided by Klaus Obermayer, "Krise und Bewährung des Föderalismus," *Die neue Ordnung in Kirche, Staat, Gesellschaft, Kultur*, I (1965), 20–32. An exhaustive and favorable discussion of the constitutional issues can be found in Franzjosef Krapp, *Die verfassungsrechtliche Zulässigkeit gemeinsamer Ländereinrichtungen* (Bonn, 1962).

the German Federal Republic is somewhat limited. The political
controversy, however, has not subsided, and its potential impact
remains quite broad. Political critics can and still do raise the
question of principle. If joint action of all the Länder made
possible the establishment of a second TV station, then perhaps
the matter is national in scope. If the Länder have found it
necessary to establish a well articulated Permanent Conference
of the Ministers of Culture and Education with headquarters in
Bonn, then perhaps the educational system requires action from a
national point of view. Indeed, by agreeing to the establishment
of the Council on Higher Learning in 1957 and the German
Council on Education in 1965, the Länder have tacitly admitted
the need of the national government to play a role in the field of
education. To be sure it is better to have this pattern of federal
cooperation than to have none at all. But as the pattern widens in
scope and becomes more intensified in particular subject areas,
the logic of this development in a federal system points to granting jurisdiction to the national government. And in the German
federal system granting jurisdiction to the national government
does not exclude the Länder. Through the Bundesrat their governments will continue to play a role in formulating policy. The
administration of the policy will continue to remain under their
jurisdiction and be subject to the absolute veto power of the
Bundesrat.

If the above argument seems to have a compelling logic, it
must be recognized that the opposing view has its strong points as
well. For one thing, given the pattern of growing cooperation, the
issue is (or can be) between two kinds of national solution to a
particular problem and not so much between a national solution
on the one hand and limited Länder solutions on the other.
Secondly there is an important difference between the role of the
Länder governments in the Bundesrat and their role in organizations such as the Permanent Conference of the Ministers of
Culture and Education. In the Bundesrat an individual Land can
be outvoted by either an absolute or a two-thirds majority. In the
Permanent Conference the individual Land is bound only to the

extent that the Land government agrees to be bound. The argument thus turns to an examination of those interests and values that are considered to be so important that they warrant the continued power of individual Land governments to play, if they so wish, a completely independent role. Not surprisingly it is above all the field of education which is most often mentioned as an example for discussion. Historically, even during the period of Weimar centralization, this was a field reserved to Länder jurisdiction. To this day the place of religious instruction in the primary schools, the extent to which schools should be organized to permit selectivity according to ability, even the month when the school year should begin—all these are issues which are hotly debated and differentially determined by the individual Länder. Until such time as there is broader agreement on these issues among the different population groups of the Länder, the possibility of an independent role by an individual Land, coupled with cooperation through the Permanent Conference of the Ministers of Culture and Education, permits the maximum of common policy consistent with respect for divergent interests and values.

It is not likely that the opposing arguments which have been sketched above will subside in contemporary Western Germany. Currently, for example, they are very much alive in the negotiations that are taking place to give effect to the Troeger Commission's report. Apart from the merits of the respective arguments what is interesting about them for the student of modern federalism is that they are so thoroughly political in nature. At the root of the controversy is the very real political question of how best to adjust conflicting interests and values. And despite the dire predictions by polemicists that the German federal system is on the verge of becoming a unitary state, or conversely that there is risk of the resurgence of German particularism, it would seem that both sides are talking in terms of an evolving pattern of federal relationships. Those who are advocating a greater sphere of national-government jurisdiction are fully prepared to concede the importance of maintaining Länder participation through such institutions as the Bundesrat. Those who resist expansion of

national-government responsibilities are actively at work in promoting patterns of cooperation that go far beyond a narrow
preoccupation with individual Land interests.

IV

CONCLUSION

Against the background of German historical experience with
federalism the Bonn constitution framers sought to establish a
federal system that in German terms was to be more decentralized than the one they had known in the Weimar Republic. In the
context of Germany after the Second World War, this effort
represented in many ways the use of federalism as a device for
decentralizing a unitary state. Thus far, the effort has proved to
be surprisingly viable, much more so than previous federal efforts
of the Hohenzollern Reich and the Weimar Republic.

Unquestionably some of the contributing factors have been the
dissolution of Prussia, the reorganization of the Länder, the
establishment of active constitutional governments in the Länder
in the years prior to the reestablishment of a central government
and the rise of a political party system that has had its roots at
the Länder level. Equally important have been the change in
views among the political elite as to the values of federalism as a
system of government and the effective adaptation of traditional
institutions such as the Bundesrat to the new constitutional
structure.

Compared with English-speaking federations the German Federal Republic provides an interesting example of alternative
ways to establish a federal structure. The method of dividing
federal powers avoids the duplication of administrative agencies
at both the national and member-unit levels. The Bundesrat is an
unusual second chamber which offers the Länder governments
opportunity for direct participation in the formulation of policy
and in the defense of Länder interests. Understandably these
differences have affected the political process of the German
federation.

Like the English-speaking federations the German model has had to adjust to the increasing trend toward centralization and has undergone considerable growth since its establishment in 1949. Judicial interpretation, although of some importance, has not yet played a major role in the development. Despite the discussions among constitutional lawyers German federalism in practice has been much more a "political" than "legal" federalism. And the "political" nature of German federalism manifests two interesting facets. As demonstrated by the decision-making process of the Bundesrat, much of the tension inherent in the federal process is between the rival bureaucracies of the national government and the Länder. Secondly, as again demonstrated by the role of the Bundesrat, but also by developments on the issue of public finance and the pattern of federal cooperation, controversy over federal questions involves much more immediately the political leaders of the two levels of government. Ultimately solutions for these controversies depend on the leaders' ability and willingness to compromise; they cannot easily be bypassed in the political process. In this respect developments in the German system resemble more closely developments in Canada (for example, Dominion-Provincial Conferences) and in Australia (for example, the Federal Loan Council).[29]

Predictions about the future of federalism in Western Germany are especially hazardous in view of past constitutional instability and the apparent indifference of the present German public (as distinguished from the political elite) to the values of the federal system. Certainly the nature of present-day controversy over federalism does not suggest that the German system will radically change its present course of evolution. A good case can be made, moreover, that the federal system has played an important role in the strengthening of constitutional and democratic practices in the fledgling German republic. German observers are wont to emphasize the value of the system as a device for checking undue centralization of power and for providing additional op-

---

[29] See above, p. 128.

portunities for democratic participation. The outside observer
might add to these the value of the system in placing a premium
on the ability and willingness of political leaders at different
levels of the system to compromise.

Born out of a series of practical compromises in the Bonn
Parliamentary Council, the German Federal Republic has continued to develop in the same spirit. Contemporary German
federalism provides another index of the increasingly pragmatic
quality of German politics. In helping to foster this quality
German federalism has improved the prospects for its own continued evolution.

HARRY KANTOR
University of Florida

LATIN AMERICAN FEDERALISM:
ASPIRATION AND FUTILITY

THREE HUNDRED YEARS of imperial rule by Spain and Portugal did little to prepare the people of Latin America to govern themselves. Governmental power was centralized, especially under the Spanish crown; unification of Church and State and the character of government of the Catholic Church reinforced this centralization. All important positions in the colonies were held by officials sent from Spain, who generally returned to Spain after completing their term. Thus when independence came, the leadership of the new governments had little experience upon which to draw.

Many of them turned to France, England and the United States for guidance. They had read the leading political thinkers of the eighteenth century and had observed the development of the United States with keen interest. Since the United States had been organized as a federal state, many Latin American leaders thought federalism an essential part of republican government and an important contributor to the success of the United States.

Unfortunately, Latin American leaders who favored federalism did not understand what this form of union involved, nor did they comprehend the vast differences between the United States and Latin America. They did not understand that at Philadelphia federalism was created to unite thirteen states which had stable governments and longstanding traditions. They did not perceive that unification was a different process from creating autonomous subdivisions in a country traditionally centralized. Thus in no Latin American country which adopted federalism were lines delimiting the subdivisions drawn with any real understanding of the requisites for creating viable units. In most cases the states or provinces were based on subdivisions created for administrative purposes by the centralized colonial government, and these in many cases had reflected the semifeudal division of land among the conquerors.

Sometimes a province was a city completely surrounded by empty territory. Sometimes the state or province was large in area but had little population. In the few cases where a province or state was large enough and had enough population to function, it completely overshadowed other states. In the United States federalism worked because the central government began with limited powers and grew through the years. In Latin America it did not work because the central government in all the federal states simply never relinquished enough power to the states or provinces to allow them to become true self-governing units.

Some leaders of Latin American independence aspired to a federal system uniting all of the former Spanish colonies. This proved impossible, because while the Spanish crown had united all the disparate areas and peoples from what is now the southwestern part of the United States to Tierra del Fuego, with the crown gone there was no commonly accepted symbol of authority. At the time of the breakup of the Spanish Empire, the colonies were being administered under the Vice-Royalties of Mexico, Nueva Granada, Peru and La Plata. Each of these encompassed a vast area but none remained intact after independence.

During the Empire of Iturbide, Mexico included everything from the southwestern United States to Costa Rica. This soon fell apart, with one province of Central America remaining with Mexico. The Central American states then tried to remain united, but in a short time Central America became five independent states. Nueva Granada began independence as the federal state of Gran Colombia but by 1830 had divided into three independent states, which by the twentieth century had again divided to become four. Chile became independent of Peru and continued as an independent state. In the Vice-Royalty of La Plata the revolutionary government based on Buenos Aires claimed control over all the area of the former Vice-Royalty, but Uruguay, Bolivia and Paraguay refused to accept the hegemony of Buenos Aires and separated to become independent states.

There were compelling reasons to adopt some decentralized form of government in the former Spanish colonies. In the first place in nearly every new state there was no national cultural cohesion, most being conglomerations of people thrown together by territorial lines drawn by the conquerors. Unity achieved during the independence movement was not unity *for* but rather unity *against*. With the enemy gone the various groups returned to regional and local loyalties centering on the self-sufficient economic unit, the latifundia. In addition the difficulty of transportation and communication because of mountains, jungles and rivers tended to separate the various nuclei of population. Local feeling was strengthened by the tradition of municipal autonomy which helped to center attention upon the city closest to where one lived. Thus federalism, which permits regional diversity, was in a way a natural system for the Latin American countries.

There were, however, strong forces in the new states for unitary government. The tradition of Spanish authoritarianism was strong, bred by centuries of colonial rule. Uniformity was stimulated by the system of Roman law and by the unifying influence of the Roman Catholic Church, the dominant religious institution.

Federalism was introduced in the early years of independence into Mexico, Central America, Gran Colombia and Argentina. Even in some of the smallest states attempts were made to introduce federalism. Chile tried federalism in its constitution of 1826 by dividing the country into eight provinces, each with substantial authority, but this lasted only two years. Honduras tried federalism in the 1824 constitution, and it lasted until 1831. Colombia tried federalism in the constitution of 1853 but abolished it in 1886. In the twentieth century, of the twenty republics in Latin America, four are organized as federal systems.

Unitary government prevailed in most of Latin America because only strong governments could hope to cope with problems of mass illiteracy, poor communications and transportation and the sharp cleavage between the small Europeanized urban upper class and the mass of illiterate rural people. When two governments have jurisdiction over the same persons, disputes inevitably arise in the exercise of powers. The new republics could not endure such disputes, for there was neither a politically sophisticated citizen body nor a sufficient supply of trained public officials.

The experience of the Latin American republics with federalism has been discouraging. Yet the fact that a country tries to be federal means something. Against a long tradition of strongly centralized government, and in the face of most difficult and persistent social, economic and political problems, some Latin American countries continue to struggle for a genuine division of power between the center and the local units. They continue to aspire to effective union without uniformity. And in the twentieth century Latin American states have undertaken a number of ventures into international cooperation to resolve common economic problems, ventures which it was thought would not alter significantly national sovereignty.

1

ARGENTINA

As a Spanish colony Argentina developed in such a way that it was almost inevitable federalism would be the logical form of organization when independence came. The country was settled by people coming from three different directions. Some came east from Chile, some came south from Upper Peru and some came by sea to the Rio Plata area. The first permanent settlements were Santiago del Estero, founded in 1553; Tucumán, in 1565; Cordoba, in 1573; Mendoza, in 1561; and San Juan, in 1562. Buenos Aires, which has dominated the country in the twentieth century, although the scene of a short-lived settlement in 1536, was permanently established only in 1580.

Argentina contained little gold or silver and no large population of docile Indians who could be forced to work large latifundias. Thus settlements of hardworking farmers and cattlemen developed. Although the colonial government was all-powerful and highly centralized, it never developed close supervision over the various nuclei of population. The local *cabildos* in each city developed into governments and with the passing of the decades came a feeling of loyalty to the locality. Eventually the *cabildos* became provincial governments.

Isolated from the mainstream of Spanish life in America, Argentinians developed a feeling of self-sufficiency which was strengthened when, during 1806 and 1807, the people of Buenos Aires, through their own resources and courage, succeeded in expelling English invaders. At an early time antagonism between the people of Buenos Aires, known as the *Porteños* (the people of the port), and the inhabitants of the interior, based in part on economics and in part on geographic isolation of the various colonies, became a significant factor in national life. There was a great cultural difference between the two groups. The *Porteños* in Buenos Aires were richer, had many Negro slaves, were more cosmopolitan and were always in closer contact with Europe. The people of the interior had few Negro slaves, were more religious, more tradition-minded and much poorer.

When independence came to the Viceroyalty of La Plata, it soon disintegrated, and four countries emerged: Argentina, Uruguay, Paraguay and Bolivia. Argentina required many decades before the area could be organized under a government acceptable to most of the population. For more than fifty years a struggle went on between Buenos Aires and the rest of the area, a struggle marked by wars, even anarchy. The first fairly stable era came after 1829, when Juan Manuel de Rosas, Governor of Buenos Aires, succeeded in dominating the other provinces militarily and setting up a dictatorship.

Rosas called himself a federalist, but there was nothing resembling federalism in Argentina during his regime. He centralized all power in Buenos Aires, governing through terror, a secret police and frequent assassinations. But the spirit of localism persisted, for the cultural differences between Buenos Aires and the rest of the country continued. Thus Rosas was overthrown in 1852 by armies from the interior. Eventually the city of Buenos Aires was separated from the province of Buenos Aires to become the national capital of the new federal republic. This arrangement was confirmed in the constitution of 1853, although the fighting continued until about 1880.

Argentina is now described as a federal state, which in 1966 consisted of twenty-two provinces, a federal capital district and the federal territories.

The basic weakness of Argentina federalism is that it was intended to unite Buenos Aires and the other provinces which are strikingly disproportionate in population and resources. It is estimated that in the 1850's Buenos Aires province contained about two-thirds of the country's population and about three-fourths of the country's wealth. Since the city of Buenos Aires contained the only port in the country at that time, and export and import taxes were the chief source of government income, it was inevitable that Buenos Aires would dominate the country, no matter what kind of government was set up. Even with the transformation of the city of Buenos Aires, the province remains the country's largest in size and population and by far the richest.

Under the constitution of 1853 the grant of power to the national government was so broad that little was left to the provinces, even though they were given all residual powers. To complicate matters the provinces never fully used the powers they possessed. Instead they turned to the national government because they lacked the resources to finance necessary activities. Subventions from the national government made possible provincial action, but with the money came national regulations for its use.

In addition the Argentine constitution gave the national government power to "intervene in the territory of a Province in order to guarantee the republican form of government or to repel foreign invasions, and at the request of the constituted authorities, to support or re-establish them, should they have been deposed by sedition or invasion from another province." This provision has been used to negate Argentine federalism.

Soon after it was organized, the national government began to intervene whenever anyone who disagreed with the president of the republic was in control of a province. There have been hundreds of interventions, and they have been as frequent in the twentieth century as in the nineteenth.

Intervention has come to be accepted by the Argentine people. The president is supposed to get the consent of the Senate for intervention, when that body is in session; but there have been cases in which the Senate refused to agree to intervention, and the president intervened nevertheless. Generally the president sends troops to the province to eject the elected governor, legislature and courts. A representative of the president, the intervenor, then takes over all executive, legislative and judicial powers. He eventually arranges an election, which generally results in persons favorable to the president receiving the most votes.

Intervention has many serious consequences in addition to negating federalism. Most important it prevents the development of effective provincial government. In addition a political party cannot build up a base of power in one or more provinces while preparing to enter the national electoral struggle. Anything like a competitive party system has great difficulty in coming into being.

The problem of making federalism work in Argentina continues in the 1960's to be what it was in the 1860's: How can a balance be set up between provinces so different in size, population and resources? In 1963 four electoral districts, three provinces and the Federal District, contained 69 per cent of the country's registered voters and accounted for 71.5 per cent of all votes cast in the July, 1963, election. The four districts received 123 of the 192 seats in the Chamber of Deputies, leaving 69 seats for 19 provinces, or an average of 3.6 deputies per province, with 10 provinces (of 22) receiving the minimum of 2. Contrast this with the United States, where only 5 states of 50 received the minimum representation in the House of Representatives and the largest state, New York, had 10 per cent of the seats in the House. Buenos Aires, the largest province in Argentina, had 26 per cent of the seats in the Chamber of Deputies (see Table I).

TABLE I

ARGENTINA The Population and Area of the Component Parts of the Argentine Federal System

Unit	Population in 1960	%	Area in (Sq. Miles)	%
Federal Capital	2,959,746	14.82	76	0.01
States:				
1. Buenos Aires	6,707,498	33.58	118,722	11.07
2. Catamarca	167,859	0.84	38,530	3.59
3. Cordoba	1,762,803	8.83	65,178	6.08
4. Corrientes	537,284	2.69	34,491	3.22
5. Chaco	549,462	2.75	38,458	3.59
6. Chubut	140,951	0.71	86,729	8.09
7. Entre Rios	808,465	4.05	29,419	2.74
8. Formosa	180,449	0.90	27,818	2.59
9. Jujuy	245,926	1.23	20,543	1.92
10. La Pampa	158,436	0.79	55,368	5.16
11. La Rioja	126,950	0.64	35,640	3.32
12. Mendoza	812,970	4.07	58,224	5.43
13. Misiones	379,378	1.90	11,503	1.07
14. Neuquen	109,021	0.55	36,314	3.39
15. Rio Negro	193,848	0.97	78,363	7.31
16. Salta	408,987	2.05	59,743	5.57
17. San Juan	355,131	1.78	33,249	3.10
18. San Luis	171,230	0.86	29,625	2.76
19. Santa Cruz	52,648	0.26	94,162	8.78
20. Santa Fe	1,879,310	9.41	51,341	4.78
21. Santiago del Estero	479,265	2.40	52,208	4.87
22. Tucumán	775,770	3.88	8,694	0.81
Territorio Nacional de la Tierra del Fuego	7,955	0.04	8,072	0.75
Total:	19,971,342	100.00	1,072,470	100.00

Figures taken from *Censo Nacional 1960. Población. Características Principales de la Población Obtenidas por Muestreo* and *Resultados Provisionales* (Buenes Aires, 1960, 1961). Square kilometers transposed to square miles by author.

Argentina will probably never develop a functioning federal system until the provincial boundaries are reorganized, and especially until the Province of Buenos Aires is broken into two, three or four provinces. The crisis in Argentina which has persisted since 1930 is due in large part to her now antiquated economic system, but it is complicated by the country's failure to develop a functioning constitutional political system.

II

BRAZIL

In colonial Brazil large landowners had a great deal of power over local activities. This localism was so strong that separatist movements developed at an early date and were strengthened by the centralized government established by the empire founded in 1822. Thus on the creation of the republic in 1889 Brazil adopted federalism as a part of the constitutional system. Because of wide variations in its economy, people, climate and physical geography, Brazil seemed particularly fitted to be a federal state. Even in the middle of the twentieth century many Brazilians still look upon themselves as Gauchos, Paulistas, Mineiros, Cariocas and Sertanejos living together in a country called Brazil.

Although the country had made a great deal of progress under the emperor, Dom Pedro II, there was much dissatisfaction with his rule. Local landowners who had always dominated local affairs resented the authority of the state governors appointed by the emperor and continuously pressed for self-government for the municipalities and the provinces. In 1873 the emperor alienated devout Catholics when he jailed some priests in a constitutional dispute. When the imperial government freed the slaves in 1888, it alienated most of the landowners. The empire was destroyed in 1889.

Thus the Republic of Brazil was organized in large part by those seeking to preserve an antiquated social structure, rather than by Brazilians interested in liberal and progressive social, economic and political institutions.

Brazilian federalism from 1889 to 1930 was of an unusual nature. Although presumably implemented to give the states greater power, it was dominated by São Paulo and Minas Gerais, the two richest and most powerful states. The presidency rotated between politicians from the two states during most of the years from 1894 to 1930. In each state there developed a strong political machine controlled by the state governor. The governors controlled the election of the state's representatives to the national congress. These representatives functioned more like ambassadors than as legislators in a national government. They were in the capital to give their support to the national president, who in turn gave his support to the governors of the states. No national political parties were active, and all elections were controlled.

During the 1920's there was a series of revolts against the national government. The incumbent president in 1930, who was the former governor of São Paulo, tried to impose another governor of São Paulo as the new president, thereby breaking one of the rules of the game. A coalition of leaders of the small states and those from Minas Gerais started an armed revolt which succeeded in capturing the government. A new era began for Brazil under the leadership of Getulio Vargas.

Vargas abrogated the republican constitution and governed as a dictator during most of the time from 1930 to 1945. São Paulo leaders revolted in 1932, but after heavy fighting Vargas' troops were victorious. Vargas helped to strengthen Brazilian nationalism and destroyed the dominant position of São Paulo in the national government. Otherwise he changed very little. The Vargas government continued to serve an oligarchy of landowning aristocrats. Although industrialization increased and the country became more prosperous, no changes in the system took place until the enthusiasm for democracy which swept the world in 1945 affected Brazil, and Vargas was overthrown by the armed forces.

A new constitution was adopted in 1946 which again provided for a federal republic. In 1966 Brazil consisted of twenty-two states, three territories and a federal district in which the national capital is located.

Federalism is weak in Brazil, primarily because only three or four of the states have ever had sufficient resources to finance necessary activities. In recognition of this disequilibrium the 1946 constitution allotted to the most populous states under-representation in the national Chamber of Deputies. It also provided that a fixed percentage of national revenue must be given to the states and the municipalities. Since 1946 there has been an attempt to give special status to regional planning organizations such as the Northeast Development Agency (SUDENE), the Amazon Valley Authority and others.

The constitutional division of powers between the national and state governments gives the national government control over national security, foreign and interstate commerce, the currency and the postal service. In addition the national government has the sole right to legislate in the fields of civil, commercial, penal, electoral, aviation and labor law. It also regulates the practice of the technical and liberal professions, operates the ports and has the power to expropriate property. Finally the national government has the right to intervene in the establishing of governments in the states.

In 1964 the armed forces took control of the country, expelled the president and began to reorganize the country's political machinery.

The basic problem in Brazil has always been that only a few of the states were viable political units. The attempt to give the smaller and weaker states over-representation in the Chamber of Deputies solved no problems. In the larger and richer states with comparatively high literacy rates, as mass movements developed after the Second World War, politics became more responsive to the population. In the backward and poorer states with high

illiteracy, the old conservative, traditional landowning aristoc-
racy controlled elections. As a result the Chamber of Deputies
became increasingly responsive to conservative political ma-
chines in the small states, while at the same time the president
was being elected by popular vote. This could only lead to
conflict between the legislature and the executive.

From 1945 to the present Brazil has lived through a series of
crises. The junta in 1966 was trying to reorganize the government
and the political party system but had not faced the problem of
what to do about the constitutional but unworkable federal system.

There is real doubt as to whether there ever has been federalism in Brazil. Under the 1946 constitution the national Congress
has the power to amend the constitution by itself. When, to this
power in the national government, is added the power to intervene in the states, there is little of formal federalism left.

The basic problem remains in the imbalance between the states
(see Table II). In 1951, for example, the State of São Paulo and
the Federal District (now the State of Guanabara) paid to the
federal government over 65 per cent of all the revenues collected
by the national government, and at the same time these two units
collected 56 per cent of the revenues collected by all twenty
states and the federal district. The state of São Paulo, with 18.28
per cent of the country's population in 1960 and 2.91 per cent of
the country's area, was paying 41 per cent of the nation's income
tax and casting 25 per cent of the total national vote. Whoever
pays the piper usually calls the tune.

In the last decade the capital of Brazil was transferred to
Brasilia, a new city built about five hundred miles from the coast
in the state of Goiás. Brasilia was built at a fantastic cost in
money and effort in an attempt to turn the country's energy
toward her unexploited interior. Unfortunately this could not
transform the country overnight, and the money spent helped to
increase the country's inflation. In October, 1966, the conflict in
the country became so acute that the military government dis-
banded the legislature and began to rule without it.

TABLE II. BRAZIL The Population, Area, and Budgets of the Component Parts of the Brazilian Federal System

Unit	Population in 1960	%	Area (Sq. Miles)	%	1964 Income (000 Cruzeiros)	1964 Expenditures (000 Cruzeiros)
Federal District	143,131	.20	2,244	.07	47,058,993	47,058,993
States:						
1. Acre	160,208	.23	58,889	1.79	181,104	. . .
2. Alagoas	1,271,062	1.80	10,704	.33	8,032,100	9,190,642
3. Amazonas	721,215	1.02	604,393	18.38	4,529,794	5,283,776
4. Bahia	5,990,605	8.44	216,556	6.59	54,051,752	46,815,372
5. Ceará	3,337,856	4.70	57,134	1.74	28,098,616	24,845,925
6. Espírito Santo	1,188,665	1.67	17,600	.53	16,431,064	18,316,630
7. Goiás	1,954,862	2.76	247,848	7.54	24,385,758	25,651,752
8. Guanabara	3,307,163	4.66	523	.02	200,555,000	217,395,539
9. Maranhão	2,492,139	3.51	126,864	3.86	5,150,498	5,162,874
10. Mato Grosso	910,262	1.28	475,378	14.47	4,498,426	5,355,292
11. Minas Gerais	9,798,880	13.81	226,648	6.90	168,350,485	172,447,730
12. Pará	1,550,935	2.18	482,261	14.66	3,303,187	3,524,329
13. Paraíba	2,018,023	2.84	21,760	.66	18,343,842	10,885,325
14. Paraná	4,277,763	6.03	77,028	2.34	77,633,129	78,725,634
15. Pernambuco	4,136,900	5.83	37,937	1.16	47,592,042	48,386,497
16. Piauí	1,263,368	1.78	96,861	2.95	1,753,435	2,112,631
17. Rio de Janeiro	3,402,728	4.81	16,564	.50	79,547,964	76,294,084
18. Rio Grande do Norte	1,157,258	1.63	20,464	.62	6,455,000	6,452,082
19. Rio Grande do Sul	5,448,823	7.67	108,923	3.32	163,698,850	162,832,093
20. Santa Catarina	2,146,909	3.03	37,050	1.13	42,613,142	35,118,068
21. São Paulo	12,974,699	18.28	95,689	2.91	627,224,400	529,501,040
22. Sergipe	760,273	1.07	8,490	.26	2,725,821	3,518,794
Disputed District Territories:	384,297	0.54	2,043	0.06		
1. Amapá	68,889	.10	54,147	1.65		
2. Roraima	29,489	.04	88,820	2.70		
3. Rondônia	70,783	.10	93,815	2.86		
Total	70,967,185	100.00	3,286,633	100.00	1,632,214,402	1,534,875,102

Figures taken from *Anuário Estatístico do Brazil—1965* (Rio de Janeiro, 1965), pp. 32–33, 473–74.

III
MEXICO

Federalism has never functioned well in Mexico, although it has been incorporated into the country's constitutional structure during most of its history.[1] When independence came, politically active Mexicans, reacting against the centralized tyranny of the colonial government and attracted by the success of the United States, thought the adoption of federalism would help to create a strong republic. Although this point of view was not unanimously accepted by the founders of the republic, and struggles between federalists and advocates of a unitary system continued for more than fifty years, federalism was introduced into Mexico's political system by the Congress in 1824. Abandoned in 1835, reintroduced in 1847, abandoned briefly again in 1853, federalism was reconfirmed in the revolutionary constitution of 1857 and included in the 1917 constitution. By 1917 federalism was so universally accepted in Mexico that the members of the constitutional assembly did not even debate the issue. Despite such longstanding agreement it is doubtful that true federal government has ever functioned in Mexico.

Several forces have tended to negate federalism in the country. Geographic and human diversities have always promoted localism and regionalism, but localism and regionalism tended to separate the various groups so much that an integrated state could not function. It was this in large part that led to the loss of half of the country (Texas, New Mexico, Arizona and California) to the United States. Thus since pre-Colombian times the problem of knitting the population into an integrated society has existed. Federalism, by accentuating local power, helped to prevent integration. Although federalism has been a part of the formal structure of the political system, the practical necessity of

---

[1] A recent book, *The Mexican Political System*, by L. Vincent Padgett (Boston: Houghton Mifflin, 1966), does not even list Federalism in its index, nor is the subject dealt with in the book.

keeping the country under control has resulted in bypassing federalism.

In the second place the Mexican states vary greatly in size, population and resources (see Table III). They were created by

TABLE III

MEXICO The Population and Area of the Component Parts of the Mexican Federal System

Unit	Population in 1960	%	Area (Sq. Miles)	%
Federal District	4,870,876	14.0	579	1.0
States:				
1. Aguascalientes	243,363	.7	2,157	0.3
2. Baja California	520,165	1.5	27,064	3.6
3. Campeche	168,219	.5	21,660	2.9
4. Coahuila	907,734	2.6	58,506	7.7
5. Colima	164,450	.5	2,106	0.3
6. Chiapas	1,210,870	3.5	28,520	3.8
7. Chihuahua	1,226,793	3.5	95,376	12.6
8. Durango	760,836	2.2	46,184	6.1
9. Guanajato	1,735,490	5.0	11,807	1.6
10. Guerrero	1,186,716	3.4	24,625	3.2
11. Hidalgo	994,598	2.8	8,101	1.1
12. Jalisco	2,443,261	7.0	30,933	4.1
13. México	1,897,851	5.4	8,284	1.1
14. Michoacan	1,851,876	5.3	23,108	3.0
15. Morelas	386,264	1.1	1,907	0.2
16. Nayarit	389,929	1.1	10,662	1.4
17. Nuevo León	1,078,848	3.1	24,918	3.3
18. Oaxaca	1,727,266	5.0	36,811	4.8
19. Puebla	1,973,837	5.7	13,093	1.7
20. Querétaro	355,045	1.0	4,543	0.6
21. Quintana Roo	50,169	.1	16,224	2.1
22. San Luis Potosi	1,048,297	3.0	24,259	3.2
23. Sinaloa	838,404	2.4	22,424	2.9
24. Sonora	783,378	2.2	71,385	9.4
25. Tabasco	496,340	1.4	9,519	1.2
26. Tamaulipas	1,024,182	2.9	30,814	4.1
27. Tlaxcala	346,699	1.0	1,511	0.2
28. Veracruz	2,727,899	7.8	28,107	3.7
29. Yucatán	614,049	1.8	16,744	2.2
30. Zacatecas	817,831	2.3	28,965	3.8
Territorio Sur de Baja California	81,594	.2	28,439	3.7
Total	34,923,129	100.0	759,335	100.0

Figures taken from *Compendio Estadistico de los Estados Unidos Mexicanos, 1962* (Mexico City, 1962), p. 17; and from *VIII Censo General de Población— 1960. Resumen General* (Mexico City, 1962), p. v.

the Constituent Congress of 1824 from divisions of the land made by its conquerors, and they were never viable political units either before or after becoming states. In area the range is from 1,554 square miles to 94,806 square miles, with an arithmetic average of less than 25,000 square miles, about two-fifths the size of the average state in the continental United States. The population of the states varied in 1960 from a low of 112,321 in Colima to a high of 2,040,231 in Vera Cruz. Only seven of the twenty-nine states had a population of more than one million. The Federal District had a population of about five million, far more than any of the twenty-nine states. Thus the self-governing units of the Mexican federal system proved to be too small to function effectively, especially since the national capital, not a member of the federal system, was the most important unit in the country.

In the third place Mexico was made into a federal state from the top, whereas the successful federal countries of the world became federal through the fusion of previously existing organized self-governing political units. The component parts of Mexico's federal system never grew together or came together by agreement, but rather were unified by the force of Aztec, Spanish or republican armies, and have throughout their history been kept united by force.

Further, the character of Mexico's party system prevents the functioning of federalism. The one-party setup was created as a mechanism to knit the country together. To do this, the party keeps control of all elections at all levels of government and enforces a centralized policy.

Last, but by no means of least importance, the Mexican constitution contains articles giving the central government the power to intervene legally in the functioning of the States. Article 76, Clause V, states that the Senate of Mexico has the power:

to declare, wherever the constitutional powers of a state have disappeared, that the condition has arisen for appointing a provisional governor, who shall call elections in accordance with the constitutional laws of the said State. The appointment of a governor shall be made by the Senate from a list of three proposed by the President of the Republic, with the approval of two-thirds of

the members present, and during adjournments, by the Permanent Committee, according to the rules. The official thus appointed cannot be elected constitutional governor in the elections
held pursuant to the call which he issues. This provision shall
govern wherever the Constitution of a State does not make provision for such cases.

In addition Clause VI states that the Senate shall have the
power:

to settle political questions which may arise between the powers
of a State, whenever any of them shall apply to the Senate for
that purpose, or whenever, by reason of such questions the Constitutional order shall be interrupted through a conflict of arms.
In this event the Senate shall declare its decision, subjecting itself
to the General Constitution of the Republic and to that of the
State.

Utilizing these clauses and his power over the dominant party,
the Institutional Revolutionary Party (PRI), the president of
the republic, acting through the secretary of the interior, sees
that no one who is not acceptable to him is elected in any state.
The question of who is governor of a state usually comes before
the federal government, because two or sometimes three candi-
dates, each with a legislature, claims to have been elected. All
election results must be accepted by the federal government;
each candidate therefore sends telegrams to the president, the
secretary of the interior and the Senate to announce his victory.
The office of the secretary of the interior, acting through the
Senate or the Senate's Permanent Committee, decides which candidate is to be recognized and tells the local military commander
to see that the winning candidate and his legislature are installed
in office. Nor is this all. The constitution also authorizes the
central government to see that democratic governments prevail in
the states, that the constitution and the federal laws are published and executed by the state officers, that constitutional guarantees are not denied and that peace is maintained between the
different branches of the state government. As a result the central
government can intervene in the states for any of the above
reasons and has continued to do so throughout Mexico's history.

In recent decades the federal government has not exercised its power to intervene in the states as much as it did previously, but this does not mean that the states are more independent. Rather through the years the PRI has become so strong that it can obtain the resignation of any governor who has lost the confidence of the national government.

Despite all this, the growth in population and the improvement of transportation and communication systems are resulting in the states becoming more viable. The size of Mexico makes it essential that some problems be handled at the state level.

The future of federalism is intimately related to the ever changing role of the PRI and efforts to democratize governmental machinery. In recent years, to strengthen the opposition, special seats have been set aside in the national legislature for minority parties which are unable to win seats in the single-member districts used in the Mexican elections. From this it is only another step to allow a minority party to get control of one or more states. Should a minority party ever win control of a state and be permitted to govern it, a long step will have been taken to make federalism a reality. More important, however, is the need to reorganize the states so that they will be powerful enough to take upon themselves the tasks a local government should perform. There is no movement in this direction, and until the PRI relaxes its control and the states are reorganized, the Mexican states will continue to play a very minor role in the Mexican federal system.

IV

VENEZUELA

Venezuela's constitution of 1961 created a federal republic divided into twenty states, a federal district, two federal territories and federal dependencies consisting of seventy-two offshore islands. Federalism has traditionally been a part of Venezuela's constitutional system, and a long and bloody war fought from 1859 to 1863 is known as the Federal War. Yet Venezuela has never actually had a true federal system; through the years the states have lost their powers. In 1925 the states lost the power to elect their executive, the governor. In the 1940's justice was nationalized, and the states lost their judicial systems.

By the time the 1961 constitution was written, most political leaders in the parties had come to the conclusion that real federalism with true autonomy for the states was impossible. Since 1953 the name of the country no longer is the United States of Venezuela, but rather the Republic of Venezuela. The constitution gives the national Congress power to grant to the states or municipalities control of specific matters within the competence of the national government "in order to promote administrative decentralization." Yet the states remain weak, in large part because of great variations in area and population.

The State of Bolivar contains within its area 26.09 per cent of the country's total area but only 2.84 per cent of the population. Zulia on the other hand had 12.23 per cent of the population in 1961 and only 6.91 per cent of the area (see Table IV).

Venezuelan states have the power to merge, alter their boundaries or cede part of their territory to other states or to the federal government with the consent of the national Senate. Each state is autonomous and equal to every other state. The states have the power to organize rural and urban police, to establish governments as they see fit and to legislate on all matters not reserved to the national government or to the municipal governments. Each state is headed by a governor appointed by the president of the republic, although the constitution gives the national Congress the power to set up a system of elections for governors. This has never been done, and the governor is both the executive head of the state and an agent of the national government. He can be removed from office by a two-thirds vote of the state legislature.

The states have limited taxing power and receive most of their income from the national government through a grant-in-aid system, by which the national government distributes to the states between 12.5 and 15 per cent of the regular budget. Under the formula used, 30 per cent of the money is divided among the states in equal parts and 70 per cent in accordance with

TABLE IV. Venezuela Population, Area, and Budgets of the Component Parts of the Venezuelan Federal System

Unit	Population in 1961	%	Area (Sq. Miles)	%	(1963 Bolívares) Income	(1963 Bolívares) Expenses
Federal District	1,257,515	16.71	745	.21	298,156,999	319,023,560
States:						
1. Anzoátegui	382,002	5.08	16,714	4.75	13,119,794	12,821,086
2. Apure	117,577	1.56	29,529	8.39	3,339,192	3,224,087
3. Aragua	313,274	4.16	2,707	0.77	14,701,629	14,739,098
4. Barinas	139,271	1.85	13,587	3.86	3,036,078	2,989,320
5. Bolívar	213,543	2.84	91,868	26.09	7,040,109	5,906,719
6. Carabobo	381,636	5.07	1,795	0.51	20,802,384	20,898,908
7. Cojedes	72,652	0.97	5,813	1.62	2,475,511	2,423,114
8. Falcón	340,450	4.52	9,573	2.72	6,984,747	6,436,359
9. Guárico	244,966	3.26	25,085	7.12	6,920,159	7,048,568
10. Lara	489,140	6.50	7,643	2.17	16,567,813	16,637,768
11. Mérida	270,668	3.60	4,362	1.24	5,183,152	5,123,455
12. Miranda	492,349	6.54	3,069	0.87	57,248,352	56,290,886
13. Monagas	246,217	3.27	11,155	3.17	3,063,965	3,199,044
14. Nueva Esparta	89,492	1.19	444	0.13	2,628,807	2,573,870
15. Portuguesa	203,707	2.71	5,867	1.67	9,046,257	6,979,237
16. Sucre	401,992	5.34	4,554	1.29	6,548,717	6,544,596
17. Táchira	399,163	5.31	4,285	1.22	13,788,747	13,117,253
18. Trujillo	326,634	4.34	2,856	0.81	5,111,856	5,042,125
19. Yaracuy	175,291	2.33	2,741	0.78	5,375,384	5,157,861
20. Zulia	919,863	12.23	24,357	6.92	59,028,482	56,972,738
Federal Territories:						
Amazonas	11,757	0.16	67,840	19.27	958,565	960,095
Delta Amacuro	33,979	0.45	15,517	4.41	1,130,481	1,141,202
Federal Dependencies	861	0.01	46	0.01	none	none
Total	7,523,999	100.00	352,152	100.00	562,257,180	575,250,949

Figures taken from *IX Censo Nacional de Población. Resultados Preliminares de Crecimiento de los Centros Poblados y su Distribución por Tamaño* (Caracas, 1962), pp. 9–10; and from *Anuario Estadístico de Venezuela: 1965* (Caracas, 1967), pp. 15, 296.

the distribution of population. These funds do not strengthen the states much, for the governor draws up the state's budget and submits it to the legislature. Although the states have limited taxing power, there is little left to tax after the national government is through taxing.

In recent years conventions of governors have been held to improve the functioning of the state governments, but little has been accomplished. At the third convention of governors in February, 1960, the minister of internal relations explained how governors should function in the view of the national government.

We believe that the governors should act as agents of the national power and not limit themselves to questions of an exclusively local character. Therefore, we have asked you to assume fully functions in the administrative as well as in the political order and to coordinate the activities of all the functionaries of the Ministries in every one of the branches of the administration. This has fundamental importance because of the necessity to coordinate national planning with regional.[2]

If the governors act in harmony with the minister's wishes, their role resembles that of a French prefect much more than that of a governor of a state in a federal system.

Venezuela, therefore, is not really a federal state but one in which the national government dominates the "autonomous and equal" states. This is an inevitable result of the way the states are organized. The Federal District, with 16.71 per cent of the country's population in 1961, is the nation's most populous subunit, and its income in 1963 was almost five times as great as that of the most populous state. To make federalism work, Venezuela will have to reorganize her states to make them viable.

V

THE FUTURE OF FEDERALISM IN LATIN AMERICA

The experience of four Latin American states with federalism cannot be considered a very hopeful one. In all the federal states

---

[2] Dr. Luis Augusto Dubuc, Minister of Internal Relations, in *III Convencion de Gobernadores. Febrero de 1960* (Caracas: Imprenta Nacional, 1960), pp. 30–31.

in the world there is a tendency toward centralization, but what is most striking in Latin America is that none of the federal states ever divided its territories so that the component parts could develop into strong self-governing units. Latin America has been an unintegrated area throughout its history, and federalism simply does not fit into the cultural pattern, the settlement pattern or the political habits of the people.

At the same time there is manifest a great desire to continue federalism in all four of the states. If ever stable constitutional government is established in these countries, a type of federalism peculiar to Latin America may be developed. This hypothesis is supported by events in Mexico and Venezuela, which have been the most stable of the four in the 1960's. Regional or local loyalties have strengthened through the years. As Mexico and Venezuela become more democratic, the wishes of the people in the various states may be more respected, and a true federalism may be developed.

Some students assert that Mexico is developing a form of functional federalism based on the peculiar character of the one-party system. The author rejects this hypothesis. As of 1966 the PRI remained a tool useful to the central government and used by it to help to knit the country together. The various sectors of the PRI are no more federal units than the states, because they can be abolished, reorganized and transformed overnight by the central government.

In Brazil and Argentina it is impossible to forecast what will happen. Their military governments are trying to reorganize the party systems and the governmental machinery, but in neither country has anything been done to reorganize the states and provinces into viable units.

A notable and continuing phenomenon in Latin America is the desire to unite some of the smaller states in a federal organization. In Central America this movement has been particularly strong, and since the United Provinces of Central America dissolved in 1838, many attempts have been made to reunite the five republics. The latest attempt to foster cooperation between the Central American republics has been the creation in the 1950's of the Organization of Central American States (OCAS) to coordinate the efforts of the five republics to improve their educational and economic systems and to sponsor activities which would lead to the economic and political unification of the area. The Central American states have succeeded in cooperating best in the economic and educational fields. A Central American Common Market is now close to reality. A Central American Bank for Economic Integration is functioning to stimulate economic growth and cooperation. A Central American Clearing House has created a Central American peso to simplify the settling of commercial debts. Other Central American cooperative organizations are the Central American Research Institute for Industry and Technology, the Nutrition Institute, the Higher University Council and the Graduate School of Public Administration for Central America and Panama. The leaders of the OCAS envision the economic knitting together of the area as helping to bring about the future political unification of the area.

Other attempts to foster cooperation among the Latin American states are the Latin American Free Trade Association and the Latin American Parliament. Many of the area's political parties favor such cooperation, particularly the Peruvian Aprista Party, which has advocated the political unification of Latin America for more than forty years.

Yet the future of Latin American federalism, either within the four federal republics or in an international organization of all or part of the twenty republics, depends mostly upon the political development of the area. The republics must discover how to control their military, expand their economies, educate their illiterate populations and maintain stable constitutional governments. If they cannot achieve these goals, Latin America will be what it has been throughout most of its history, the victim of the exploiting forces of native oligarchies, foreign business enterprises, adventurous military officers, true believers in the Communist utopia. One cannot be too optimistic when, of the twenty republics, nine were in 1966 governed by military juntas or "constitutional" governments created by military dictatorships.

Yet the spirit of freedom which the American soil seems to

breed makes one hopeful that Latin America will in the future
look more like Uruguay, Costa Rica and Chile than like Haiti,
Nicaragua or Argentina. Just as the Vargases, Perez Jimenez, the
Batistas, the Trujillos, the Rosases, the Diaz and the other dicta-
tors of the past were finally eliminated, so the "Papa Docs," the
Fidel Castros, the military juntas, the Somozas and the General
Stroesners of today will be destroyed. Then in a freer atmosphere
federalism may have a chance to function.

SELECTED BIBLIOGRAPHY

General
James, Herman G. "Federalism in Latin America." *Bulletin of the Pan
    American Union*, LV (Sept., 1922), 229–40.
Argentina
Rowe, Leo Stanton. *The Federal System of the Argentine Republic.*
    Washington, D.C.: Carnegie Institution of Washington, 1921.
Zorraquín Becú, Ricardo. *El Federalismo Argentino.* 2nd ed. Buenos
    Aires: La Facultad S.A. Librería y Editorial, 1953.
Brazil
Dell, Edmund. "Brazil's Partly United States." *The Political Quarterly*,
    XXXIII (July–Sept., 1962), 282–93.
Machado Horta, Raul, *et al. Perspectivas do federalismo brasileiro.* Belo
    Horizonte: Universidade de Minas Gerais, 1958.
Martin, Percy Alvin. "Federalism in Brazil." *Hispanic American Histor-
    ical Review* (May, 1938), 143–63.
Walker, Harvey. "Federalism in Brazil." *State Government*, XVIII
    (March, 1945), 43–44.
Mexico
Mecham, J. Lloyd. "Mexican Federalism—Fact or Fiction?" *Annals of
    the American Academy of Political and Social Science*, CCVIII
    (March, 1940), 23–38.
———. "The Origins of Federalism in Mexico." In *The Constitution
    Reconsidered.* Ed. Conyers Read. New York: Columbia University
    Press, 1938, 349–65.
Spain, A. O. "Mexican Federalism Revisited." *The Western Political
    Quarterly*, IX (Sept., 1956), 620–32.

PART III

THE FUTURE
OF FEDERALISM

The "FUTURE OF FEDERALISM" may be, as Professor Henry Teune writes, a "fuzzy phrase." If what is meant is whether federalism will survive in those countries where it now exists, the answer is probably affirmative. Beyond this, Professor Teune believes, a future for federalism lies in its being useful in the underdeveloped and emerging nations as a means of effecting political integration, that is, of awakening political consciousness of, identification with and commitment to a political community and a government.

If viable statehood and essential economic development depend upon the establishment of a reasonably strong national government, then federalism may be useful in transferring in some degree the loyalty now attaching to localities, to a central government. Latin America and India may be cases in point. Where political integration is extremely limited—where there is no real political community in the consciousness of a large number of the inhabitants of a "state"—federalism, because it assigns significance to local governments as well as to the center, may help in forming attachment to local governments which in time can carry over to the center. Some African and Asian countries may be cases in point.

Thoughtful readers of the preceding essays must certainly

entertain some doubts about these hypotheses. Despite the variations in form and practice in countries where federalism is a vital
part of an ongoing enterprise, the similarities among the United
States, Canada, Australia and West Germany are more notable:
a genuine desire for union without unity among a relatively
sophisticated people who are experienced in self-government and
have a more nearly adequate supply of persons with the political,
administrative and legal skills required to run a government.

For those countries where political community scarcely exists,
where statehood in any but the most formal or legalistic sense
scarcely exists, a discussion of federalism seems highly irrelevant,
and a federal system a venture far beyond the reach of leaders
who must struggle to stay in power and to begin to feed their
people. For those for whom statehood is truly viable, it seems
that a federal system may founder either on the rock of inequality
of the member states in resources and population or on the rock
of an insufficient number of politicians and statesmen.

Something called "federal" may be attempted and may persist
in the new states. In time it may take on the characteristics of
what is now called a federal system. Alternatively the definition
of "federal" may be altered to encompass new systems.

HENRY TEUNE
University of Pennsylvania

THE FUTURE OF FEDERALISM:
FEDERALISM AND
POLITICAL INTEGRATION

F EDERALISM CONTINUES TO BE a major concept in political science, an important part of both normative and empirical political theory. The concept of federalism may have a long future in social science research, if its place in empirical theory and research is recognized. It is my purpose to suggest some of the directions that systematic research on federalism may take.

Two modes of analysis can be distinguished in the discourse about federalism as an empirical phenomenon. In the language of research design one mode concerns federalism as a dependent variable; the other, federalism as an independent variable. One mode of analysis explains or accounts for the phenomenon of federalism; the other uses federalism in the explanation of political behavior.

The central argument of this essay is that research on federalism as an explanatory factor, a factor that has consequences for political behavior, will be more productive than direct attempts to explain federalism. Knowledge about the consequences of federalism for political behavior may play a critical role in explaining and predicting adaptations of federal forms of government.

The argument will be developed first by illustrating certain methodological difficulties characteristic of attempts to explain federalism; second by a presentation of three structures of explanation for federalism, labeled explanatory sketches; and finally by suggesting a few strategies for study of the consequences of federalism, particularly as those consequences are relevant to what is happening within the governmental systems of underdeveloped societies. The proposition that federal or decentralized governments will generate political integration more rapidly and more easily than decentralized governmental arrangements will be examined.

I

METHODOLOGICAL DIFFICULTIES
IN EXPLAINING FEDERALISM

The first methodological difficulty, perhaps more psychological than methodological, concerns definitions of federalism. Because federalism is often the characteristic to be explained, the dependent variable, the dichotomous scale is often satisfactory for this purpose. A country is either federal or it is not. Whatever the implicit or explicit factors making up the definition of federalism, the definition functions as a simple means for dividing governmental systems into two groups. Further, since the total number of countries is limited, the definition of federalism often turns out to be denotive, that is, all of the instances of federalism can be specified by listing. Of course there are ambiguities, but with denotive definitions it is not difficult to be clear about ambiguities by specifying the doubtful cases.

The literature on federalism provides some categories for distinguishing between federal systems. There are "middle" categories such as K. C. Wheare's quasi-federalism.[1] Or it is possible to distinguish between effective and formal federal systems. The

---

[1] K. C. Wheare, *Federal Government* (New York: Oxford University Press, 1964), pp. 19, 24. According to Wheare both Canada and the USSR are quasi-federal systems.

latter categories keep the United States and the USSR distinct from each other in the analysis of federalism.

If explanation is the goal of research, then explanations of only federal and nonfederal political systems are not so satisfactory as explanations of the *degrees* of federalism, however defined.[2] Increased knowledge about federal governments will be dependent on the development of scales.

The second difficulty in explanations of federalism results from the complexity of characteristics to which the term conventionally refers. Although a scale of federalism may provide a simple sorting of countries, the factors on which the scale is based are complex. The subtle and sometimes substantial differences between federal systems are obscured in the decision to put certain countries into a federal category. Aggregating characteristics into a single configuration will possibly reduce the scope of characteristics to be explained.

Whether federalism is explained as a dichotomous or as a quantified concept, whether it is refined with distinctions such as on the differences in the locus of delegated and residual powers there remains the difficulty arising from the small number of instances or cases of federal systems. The number of nation-states that are "federal" or have the combination of characteristics that have been used to designate a federal political system in whatever degree or kind is a statistically unstable number; even a very simple distinction between federal forms such as "effective" or "formal" results in so few cases that it is difficult to generalize.

The small number of cases flows directly from the use of the concept of federalism as a characteristic of government. Thus each government in the world can have only one place on a scale. The many elements used to characterize a government as federal produce one instance of federalism, often expressed in gross terms of federal or nonfederal.

---

[2] William Riker discusses the problem of measuring federalism. See *Federalism: Origin, Operation, Significance* (Boston: Little, Brown & Co., 1964), pp. 125–35.

The fourth difficulty with explanations of federalism concerns the ex post facto nature of the data. In efforts to explain why the United States is a federal system research is confined to information that happened to be recorded. Even when an explicit statement about motives for establishing a federal government is given by the decision-makers themselves, as in *The Federalist,* there are seemingly unlimited possibilities for speculation about what the decision-makers meant. Historical research can to some extent increase the number of cases by inclusion into the universe of federal governments those that have failed.[3]

These difficulties, if they have been properly interpreted, point to the research possibilities of (1) redefining federalism in terms of the decentralization of units within political systems, (2) developing scales of decentralization and (3) using federalism as an explanatory factor. If this were done, it would be possible not only to examine many kinds of consequences but also to have available for inquiry hundreds of thousands of observable cases of those consequences.

II

Some Explanatory Structures of Federalism

Without presenting a survey of all kinds or types of explanations of federal systems, it is possible to distinguish a few major explanatory sketches to be found in political science literature. Evidence for the connection between the variables in these is still largely a matter of plausibility rather than of systematic research. It is perhaps important to note that a good deal of the evidence is based on the experiences of the United States, Canada and Australia.

The first and perhaps the most pervasive explanatory sketch consists of attributing a set of goals or motives to some segment of political leaders and then inferring that a federal form of government was the most viable means for achieving those goals.

---

[3] For an example of the "success-failure" approach to the study of nation-states see Karl W. Deutsch *et al., Political Community and the North Atlantic Area* (Princeton: Princeton University Press, 1957).

To cite one of the standard works on federalism, by K. C. Wheare, "So far then, it would seem that federal government is appropriate for a group of states or communities, if, at one and the same time, they desire to be united under a single independent general government for some purposes and to be organized under independent regional governments for others. Or, to put it shortly, they must desire to be united, but not to be unitary." [4] This of course is a very general expression of the motive explanation. Professor Wheare goes on to specify some of these motives:

Communities have been led to desire union from a variety of reasons. But in the modern federations some factors seem always to have been present. A sense of military insecurity and of the consequent need for common defence; a desire to be independent of foreign powers, and a realization that only through union could independence be secured; a hope of economic advantage from union; some political association of the communities concerned prior to their federal union either in a loose confederation, as with the American states and the Swiss cantons, or as parts of the same Empire, as with the Canadian and Australian colonies, geographical neighbourhood; and similarity of political institutions. . . .[5]

Of course these motives are not enough to explain federalism. Something about perception of means must be added. Once the motives and the perceived means of achieving them are appraised, then one of the most frequently used laws or propositions concerning human behavior must be employed: that human beings act to secure their goals.

What is often lacking is a statement about motives for maintaining relatively autonomous constituent governments. These goals, although perhaps obvious, may be more complicated than goals attainable through union. Determining only *critical* motives is not simple. For example, Charles Beard spent a good deal of effort arguing over an economic motive for a federal form of government. Beard's argument centers on the problem of quantifying and weighting motives rather than on whether or not any

[4] Wheare, *op. cit.*, p. 36.
[5] *Ibid.*, p. 37.

economic motive was present at all. Attributing motives and then weighting them is a complicated task, as demonstrated by psychological research.

Even if motives are clearly defined, there is the problem of what combination of them produces the action necessary to institute a federal system. Professor Wheare asserts that all or most of the motives he suggests must be present. Further, even if motives are clearly defined, there is the problem of who has them. The people who have "federating" motives must have certain leadership positions to institutionalize the means to their goals.

William Riker has written that motives for federalism are not widely shared.[6] His interpretation of federalism is that it is a bargain or negotiated working agreement between people with conflicting goals. It is not clear, however, whether Riker means that one of the preconditions of federalism is a bargaining activity, or whether the federal compact in whatever form is in itself a bargain or the result of negotiation. In other words is the bargain a precondition of federalism, a characteristic of federal constitutional arrangements or part of the definition of federalism? Whatever the case it seems that an important part of any motive explanation of federalism must take into account the fact that motives are not broadly shared. Most students of federalism are aware of this, although it might not be made explicit in their statements about what constitutional designers want.

A second but perhaps more perplexing explanatory sketch is one which attempts to explain the motives themselves. This form of explanation would be more satisfactory than a simple presentation of motives, but it is correspondingly more difficult. Why were motives present in 1787 and not before? Why did they occur? Why do some Nigerian people want independent military security, economic gain and the like? These are tough questions but nonetheless important ones. R. L. Merritt, for example, notes some changes in the perception of "America" before the Revolu-

---

[6] Riker, *op. cit.*, pp. 11–16.

tion, but it is still an intriguing possibility that one may system-
atically explain these changes.[7]

A third and perhaps somewhat productive explanatory sketch
is the attempt to explain federal systems, not by statements
about the motives of leaders, but rather by searching for correla-
tions between environmental characteristics and adaptations of a
federal political system. The characteristics are the common
kinds of social, economic and political data. Professor Wheare
discusses, for example, similarity in language, race, religion and
nationality.[8] He believes the facts do not support the claim that
these are important factors. All of these variables, however,
involve questions of distribution. There are more precise ways of
expressing distributions of language, race and religion than have
been used.

Some hypotheses about relationships between gross characteristics of the political or social system and gross characteristics of
federalism or the absence of federalism include the following: (1)
The greater the heterogeneity of social systems the greater the
probabilities that the political system will be federal rather than
unitary; (2) the greater the area (or the less dense the population) the greater the probability that the political system will be
federal rather than unitary; (3) federal systems will tend to be
"democratic." [9]

This explanatory sketch or scheme has some possibilities. It is
the kind of explanatory scheme which William Riker attributes
to Karl Deutsch and criticizes.[10] Banks and Textor in their *Cross-
Polity Survey* include federalism or the vertical distribution of
power, as they call it, as one of more than fifty variables of

---

[7] See Richard L. Merritt, "Public Opinion in Colonial America: Content
Analyzing the Colonial Press," *Public Opinion Quarterly,* XXVII (1963),
356–71.

[8] Wheare, *op. cit.,* p. 38.

[9] These are "traditional" arguments. For a statement of the third, see
Russell Kirk, "The Prospects for Territorial Democracy in America," in *A
Nation of States,* ed. Robert A. Goldwin (Chicago: Rand McNally & Co.,
1963), pp. 42–64.

[10] Riker, *op. cit.,* p. 15.

political systems.[11] Bruce Russett in the recent *World Handbook of Political and Social Indicators* does not include federalism.[12]

The number of cases of federal governments is too small. Five of the federal systems—the United States, Canada, Australia, West Germany and Austria, all wealthy industrialized nations—account for a substantial part of the relationships between such variables as per capita income and federalism. It may turn out that the most significant feature of federal systems in the world is that over one-third of them were former British colonies.[13]

The foregoing suggests some of the problems that must be faced when explaining federalism. The explanatory sketches are perhaps too crude and the number of cases on which there is reliable knowledge too small. Of course these difficulties should not in any way inhibit careful analysis and research in the effort to explain federalism; but they should prompt a look elsewhere for possibilities of saying something theoretically relevant about federalism. The following will be devoted to what may be an alternative course for research.

III

Federalism as an Explanatory Factor

Among the many predictions about consequences of federalism, two seem to stand out. One concerns the relationship between federal or decentralized government and political freedom; the other is the asserted relationship between federalism and political or social unity. The first, although an important empirical question, also involves moral or ethical questions in the definition of freedom. The second may provoke questions of importance for empirical theory.

---

[11] Arthur S. Banks and Robert Textor, *A Cross-Polity Survey* (Cambridge: M.I.T. Press, 1963).

[12] Bruce M. Russett *et al.*, *World Handbook of Political and Social Indicators* (New Haven: Yale University Press, 1964).

[13] Riker, *op. cit.*, p. 25. Riker notes that the following federalisms were constructed by uniting British colonies: Canada, Australia, India, Pakistan, Malaysia and Nigeria. He also notes that three British-inspired federal systems failed: New Zealand, British West Indies and Rhodesia.

Both questions received attention in *The Federalist*. In order to sell the new government, the proponents made these predictions: (1) that federalism would result in more freedom or at least in no diminution of freedom for those being governed within the new federal structure and (2) that the federal government would be able to enlist enough support or engender enough social and political cohesion that national policies could be implemented and specific goals obtained such as increased commerce and a governmental structure that would endure.[14]

It is because of the asserted correlation between federalism and political and social unity that leaders in underdeveloped countries are interested in knowing about the consequences of a federal or decentralized form of government, as these terms are understood in the United States. An added attraction may be that the manipulation of governmental machinery appears to be more feasible and less costly than the manipulation of economic programs which have been experimented with over the years with less success than expected. If it is possible, in short, to show a connection between decentralized or federal political systems and levels of political cohesion, then federalism will have a very lively future in most countries of the world.

Further consideration of the relationship between divided political power and freedom will be omitted.[15] Even if there were a clearly defined relationship between federalism, divided political power, decentralization and political freedom, it is unlikely that very many political leaders around the world would be interested in federalism. The possibility of federalism as a device for creating national political cohesion is something in which most of the leaders in new nations are keenly interested. It is this relationship that offers great opportunities for political research.

In order to suggest how federalism can be made an increasingly

---

[14] The question of what factors maintain federalism is treated in Riker, *op. cit.*

[15] For an analysis of federalism and freedom see the careful statement by Franz L. Neuman, "Federalism and Freedom: A Critique," in *Federalism: Mature and Emergent*, ed. A. W. MacMahon (Garden City, N.Y.: Doubleday & Co., 1955), pp. 44–57.

viable area for research, it is necessary to take one of the many connotive meanings of federalism and make it precise. Then the dependent variable, political integration, must be defined and indicators of it offered. This is followed by a statement of the sets of hypotheses which are relevant to the connections between federalism and political integration. Some suggestions for experimentation and survey research to test the relationships follow.

IV

DEFINING FEDERALISM AND POLITICAL INTEGRATION

Both federalism and decentralization are relational terms, having reference to characteristics of subunits or governments, each of which is related to a general government. Although there is difficulty in defining governments or constituent governments, a minimum requirement is that each have some specified quantity of autonomy. Without this the unit is treated as an administrative subdivision of some other government.

Local- or constituent-government autonomy is the variable proposed for examination. Given the fact that there are several kinds and often hundreds of instances of more or less autonomous governments, it is possible to research this variable both within and between countries.

As a beginning, autonomy can be defined in two ways: legal autonomy and actual autonomy. It is relatively less difficult to rank kinds of governmental units on criteria of legal autonomy than it is to rank them on criteria of actual autonomy. It would perhaps be worth while to obtain both ranks. These two ranks would permit a somewhat precise statement about the effectiveness of decentralization in a particular country, in addition to providing opportunities for explaining legal formalism as a political phenomenon.

A traditional criterion of autonomy is the capability to raise and spend money independent of the decisions of other governmental units. This criterion both in the legal and factual sense could be one of the components of a scale of autonomy within a country. Other criteria for measuring actual decentralization might be: (1) removal of local officers without prior consultation, (2) the number and intensity of inspections, (3) the number of exhortative messages sent by other units, (4) control over compensation and (5) the number of requests for aid made to other governmental units. A measure of perceived autonomy could be obtained by interviewing local officials. The perceived autonomy of the officials of various governmental units could serve as the definition of autonomy, and the other criteria mentioned above would be indicators of this perceived autonomy.

In a similar sense political integration is a psychological notion. It would be possible to define political integration at every governmental level. If a certain amount of integration were present in a governmental unit, it could be called a political community. For purposes of this discussion the definition of political integration will be restricted to the national or the single most inclusive governmental unit.

Political integration could be defined in terms of the following psychological dimensions: (1) the degree to which the national government is a relevant set of stimuli for the individual, that is, whether there is some minimal level of knowledge about the national government, (2) the degree to which the individual considers the national government capable of influencing his welfare or important in his everyday activities, (3) the degree to which the individual responds favorably to the national government and (4) the degree of the individual's concern for people living within the same country but outside of his immediate environment.[16] These definitional terms require survey research. The little survey research that has been conducted in certain underdeveloped societies such as India and Turkey indicates a low level of political integration in the terms offered above.[17]

---

[16] For an elaboration of these definitions see Philip E. Jacob and Henry Teune, "The Integrative Process: Guidelines for Analysis of the Bases of Political Community," in *The Integration of Political Communities,* ed. P. E. Jacob and J. V. Toscano (Philadelphia: J. B. Lippincott & Co., 1964), pp. 1–45.

[17] For example, see Daniel Lerner, *The Passing of Traditional Society* (Glencoe, Ill.: The Free Press, 1958).

Gross indicators of political integration could be gathered at the constituent governmental level. Some of these indicators could include: (1) actual national governmental taxes as a proportion of income, (2) per capita contributions to the national army and rates of desertion, (3) the performance in meeting national planning goals of economic development, (4) consumption per capita of national political stimuli from the mass media and (5) success in recruiting and in performance of voluntary labor forces on national programs.

At a minimum it should be possible to have ranking of both autonomy and national political integration within local units. Ranking restricts the testing of hypotheses to those units ranked.

V

THE THEORY OF AUTONOMY AND POLITICAL INTEGRATION

The relationship between local governmental autonomy and political integration is built upon an hypothesis of process: the greater the autonomy, the greater the political integration in the long run or after some specified period of time. The connection is an evolving one, and there is therefore an added difficulty in testing it. The process asserts a chain of events. If there are empirical connections between the chain of variables or events, then countries such as Yugoslavia have invested wisely in decentralization. At present, knowledge about these political variables is too meager to arouse any great confidence in the predictions made about the consequences of decentralization.

One way of describing a chain of events is the following: (1) Decentralization engenders a political awakening among the population at the local level; (2) political awakening generalizes from the local governments to the national government; (3) as a result of the generalization from local governments to the national government some level of political integration is achieved; (4) political integration leads to the capacity of the national government to institute widespread change; (5) one of these changes is the economic modernization or growth of the country; and (6) economic modernization provides the resources by which the national government can instill respect for itself and thus obtain some form of political stability. This statement of the connection between levels of autonomy or decentralization and economic growth and political stability is perhaps overcomplicated, but process statements about human behavior are usually complicated.[18]

The complications and uncertainties surrounding these propositions can be illustrated by an examination of the first two, neither of which has been carefully defined. In underdeveloped countries national administrative machinery, designed often according to Western models, does not fit well with the habits and attitudes of village populations. As a matter of fact the population in many cases does not perceive any kind of government as relevant.[19] The term "relevant" should be refined to include both the intensity of the orientation to government as well as the scope or number of things for which governmental activities are considered important. It is not enough that the people vaguely perceive governmental officials as relevant for one or two things, such as minimal police functions or educational films. They must perceive relevance for a large range of activities covering the individual's general welfare.

The first proposition about why local governments are more likely to secure the affections of the population than a national or more remote government involves the traditional argument for decentralization that local governments are more responsive to the particular needs of the population. The hope is that this greater responsiveness conditions the people more rapidly to accept government as a significant factor in their lives.

The second proposition, that newly grown habits with respect to local governments generalize to the national government, in-

---

[18] For an exploration of these factors see U. K. Hicks, *et al.*, *Federalism and Economic Growth in Underdeveloped Countries: A Symposium* (London: George Allen & Unwin, 1961).

[19] See H. Teune, "The Learning of Integrative Habits," in Jacob and Toscano, *op. cit.*, pp. 247–82.

volves the belief that local governmental machinery is more similar to modern national machinery than anything else in the people's environment.[20] This may or may not be the case. It may be that local government is so similar to the traditional patterns in the villages that any contact with local governmental officials reinforces older habits, including that of treating local officials as an alien force.

The question of whether or not favorable attitudes toward local government would in fact generalize to governments in general, including the national government, was a matter on which Alexander Hamilton reflected in *The Federalist* Number 17:

It is a known fact in human nature, that its affections are commonly weak in proportion to the distance or diffusiveness of the object. Upon the same principle that a man is more attached to his family than his neighborhood, to his neighborhood than to the community at large, the people of each State would be apt to feel a stronger bias toward their local governments than toward the government of the Union: unless the force of that principle should be destroyed by a much better administration of the latter.[21]

Hamilton's "principle" is the principle of stimulus saliency. To restate this, salient stimuli are more favorably responded to than less salient stimuli, unless those salient stimuli are negative or punishing. Hamilton was convinced that the national government was at a serious disadvantage with respect to both the frequency and saliency of the stimuli. Not only would the local or state governments be more frequently in touch with the people, but they would also be more "visible." Hamilton elaborated this point:

The operations of the national government, on the other hand, falling less immediately under the observations of the mass of the citizens, the benefits derived from it will chiefly be perceived and attended to by speculative men. Relating to more general inter-

---

[20] Some aspects of this are explored in Edward Banfield, *The Moral Basis of a Backward Society* (Glencoe, Ill.: The Free Press, 1958).

[21] *The Federalist*, ed. Benjamin Fletcher Wright (Cambridge: The Belknap Press of Harvard University Press, 1961), p. 168.

ests, they will be less apt to come home to the feelings of the people; and, in proportion, less likely to inspire a habitual sense of obligation, and an active sentiment of attachment.[22]

If Hamilton's "active sentiment of attachment" is interpreted to mean something like political integration, then his quantitative law or hypothesis about the effect of decentralization on political integration has serious implications for the expectation that decentralization will result in greater political integration. Perhaps one may counter that there are a greater number of speculative men in underdeveloped societies than in eighteenth-century America and that the technology of communications gives an increased salience to national governments. The first argument is highly unlikely, and the force of the second is questioned by the fact that even in the United States, where the technology of mass communications is highly developed, newspapers still devote more space to local than to national news.[23]

It is important to note that not only may there be no connection between decentralization or autonomy of local governments and political integration, but also that there is some possibility that the opposite of the predictions may be true. There is a distinct possibility that societies committed to increases in local autonomy may experience two quite unexpected results: (1) not only may generalization never occur, but certain forms of localism may be reinforced or new forms created where they do not presently exist, and (2) in addition to conditioning the population to respond to local government, certain other habits may form which would directly inhibit one of the important anticipated results of political integration, such as industrialization.

William Riker, as noted earlier, describes or explains federalism as a bargain. Perhaps this is not an accurate explanation for

---

[22] *Ibid.*, p. 169.

[23] A survey of 51 American newspapers in 1953 showed that 42.8 per cent of the domestic news space was devoted to local and state news and 23.4 per cent to national events or happenings in Washington. See The International Press Institute, *The Flow of News* (Zurich, 1953). This is cited by R. L. Merritt in "Perceptions of Unity and Diversity in Colonial America, 1735–1775," Paper Prepared for Delivery before the Sixth World Congress of the International Political Science Association, Sept., 1964.

countries where decentralization was a national or party decision, as in Yugoslavia. But if it is a bargain, the bargain in some way divides up whatever loyalties, sentiments or psychological orientations exist in the society. The pertinent question about the relationship between decentralization and political integration is whether the national or the most general level of government, commanding less loyalty or possessing little in the way of relevance for the population, will in the long run get more than it bargained for initially, and conversely whether the constituent governments will in fact be losing the loyalties of the population.

Perhaps this is not the issue. The issue may be whether there will be a substantial increase in the total amount of sentiment for government so that all levels of government will gain.

1. Testing the Hypothesis: Exploring Relationships

It may be possible to demonstrate that what happened in the United States from the eighteenth to the twentieth centuries supports the contention of a process relationship between decentralization and political integration. William Riker's scale of centralization, a five-point scale of the degree of state and national exclusiveness of action in seventeen governmental functional areas, estimates a 70 per cent increase (according to my calculations) in the amount of centralization in the United States from 1790 to the present.[24] Riker attributes this increase to the decline of state military organizations and the rise in national military forces. Local governmental military forces in underdeveloped societies are generally not allowed although often present. Further if the cost of the Civil War in terms of casualties alone is calculated as part of the price for national unity, then perhaps the cost of national unity in the American experience is not one that many national leaders would be willing to pay.

Social science knowledge at present permits only estimates about what the crude variables are that flow from different

---

[24] For a suggestion of centralization scale see Riker, *op. cit.*, pp. 81–84.

structures of decision making. In order to discover what the dimensions of the problem are, a few laboratory or quasi-laboratory experiments on the consequences of different forms of organization may be useful.

As a rough first suggestion it would perhaps be interesting to try to observe differences in outcomes of decisions, which would be made in three differently contrived experimental situations. Each situation would require a set of experiments with some slight variation in the conditions of the decision.

The first set would simulate the unitary form of decision structure.[25] A group of thirty people would be given the task of dividing a conflictive quantity of money among themselves, for example, forty-five dollars, which could not be broken down into less than dollar units. The process by which the decision was made, such as by an experimentally appointed committee or by majority vote, could be varied.

A second set of experiments would simulate a federal structure. Here, a group of thirty would be divided into groups of ten. Each subgroup could divide nine or ten dollars among themselves, then select a representative to negotiate with the representatives of the other two groups for a certain sum.

The third set would substantially alter the stakes. Only a few dollars would be reserved for negotiation among the representatives of the three groups, and the representatives could be required to secure approval from their constituencies before concluding an agreement. This set with a number of variations would hopefully simulate a confederative structure.

There are many kinds of possible experimental variations with respect to the size of the allocation and how it is divided. The amount to be allocated by negotiation or decision between groups could represent varying degrees of centralization. It might also be interesting to observe these groups in the performance of some task, such as writing an essay that best represents their collective

---

[25] For a statement on the concept of simulation see Harold Guetzkow, *et al.*, *Simulation in International Relations* (Englewood Cliffs, N.J.: Prentice-Hall, 1963).

political views. The groups could be further varied according to personality types, size and means of selecting the decision-makers.

In addition to noting the actual results of the decisions, it would be valuable to try to get some indicators of the social cohesion within the decision-making groups. The following indicators are suggested as related to the political integration variable mentioned earlier: (1) the over-all or mean satisfaction with the outcome of the decisions for both the whole group and the subgroups, (2) the amount of dislike or friendship developed among and between the decisional groups and (3) a general evaluation of the decisional process, according to the yardsticks by which individuals respond to the experimental experiences, such as fairness, worthwhileness and willingness to recommend this kind of decisional structure for other reasons. All of these outcomes would of course be measured by questionnaire. Other outcomes such as the time it takes to make decisions or the hostility expressed during negotiations could be directly observed.

These experiments are only suggestive of what could be done. One of the possible consequences might be added research rigor for political science. The results of these experiments would have to be treated with extreme caution. It may be that all of the results would describe little more than the attitudes of Americans in small groups. The hope is that hypotheses about the consequences of concentrating or dividing the decision-making powers would be discovered.

No one would maintain that what is observed in the laboratory situation, even if governmental officials were the subjects, is what actually occurs in the political world. Depending on the number of interacting elements or individuals the variables may interact in quite different ways. This fact involves laws or propositions about how variables interact. It is quite likely, for example, that if thirty-one rather than thirty individuals were involved in the experiments suggested above, the results would be quite different. The same may be true for thirty-two, thirty-three or forty individuals. This is the problem of composition laws or factors, perhaps a much more serious problem in social science experimentation than the often mentioned one of controlling for all the variables. These composition laws are the laws about which political scientists guess when they suggest the "ideal size" for a representative body; the prediction is that adding one or two or more members to the decision-making body will produce different and less desirable decisions.

2. Testing the Hypothesis: Field Observation

The final test of the relationships between decentralization or local governmental autonomy and political integration would be in real political situations.

With a sample of governmental units scaled according to the degree of actual autonomy, it would be possible to test directly the following hypotheses related to political integration: (1) The greater the autonomy of the political unit the more closely governmental officials will reflect the attitudes of their constituents; (2) the greater the autonomy of the unit the greater the concern of governmental officials and their constituents with national policies and programs; (3) the greater the autonomy of the political unit the greater the awareness of the local population and governmental officials of the place or importance of government in their daily activities.

Although the language of these hypotheses requires something better than simple rank or ordinal scales, it is nevertheless possible to use simple rankings of autonomy and other variables for testing them. The hypotheses further require interviews with both governmental officials as well as local populations. Certain familiar scales such as political alienation and political cynicism could be used. The prediction would be that the greater the autonomy the less the alienation and cynicism. Care must be taken to make sure that the populations tested for or observed for alienation and cynicism have been politicized sufficiently to be alienated or cynical.

VI

Conclusion

Some of the dimensions of the relationships between decentralized government and political integration have been suggested in the foregoing pages. The questions which this relationship raises extend beyond concern as to whether present federal systems will remain; even countries such as Yugoslavia and India are probably capable of maintaining the status quo. The important concern is whether decentralized forms of government will contribute to the development of effective national or large-scale political communities capable of promoting necessary social change and economic development. For India as for other countries it is a question of growth to maintain present levels of economic consumption.

That an effective national government is a requisite for economic growth is a matter on which there is substantial academic agreement; hard evidence does not as yet abound. If it *is* true that political development in the form of effective political community at the national level is a necessary condition for rapid economic growth, then knowledge about what contributes to political integration is of critical importance. E. E. Hagen expressed this in the statement that "economic growth is hardly possible unless there has been some expansion of the sense of social unity beyond the local community." [26]

The question discussed in this essay has been whether decentralization in federal forms of government will contribute to a sense of social unity beyond the local community or whether federal forms will reinforce the sense of attachment to local communities. It may even be important to ask a prior question, whether or not there is any sense of attachment to anything, let alone governmental activities or institutions.

The "future of federalism" is a fuzzy phrase. If what is being questioned is whether federal forms of government will continue,

---

[26] Everett E. Hagen, *On the Theory of Social Change* (Homewood: Ill.: Dorsey Press, 1962), p. 252.

the answer is "Very likely." If the phrase raises the question of whether federal forms of government will increase in number, then the future of federalism depends on how confident political leaders in underdeveloped societies can be that federalism will aid in the development of a national political community and will not be a force in dismantling whatever little national cohesion now exists.

THE BOOK MANUFACTURE

Federalism: Infinite Variety in Theory and Practice was composed, offset printed and bound by Kingsport Press, Inc., Kingsport, Tennessee. The paper is Perkins & Squire Company's Glatfelter Old Forge, Laid Finish. Internal and cover design was by John Goetz. The type in this book is Modern #21.

DATE DUE